THE LOVE

C000129566

Edited by S. T. Joshi   ...23)

Contents

Abbreviations used in the text and notes:

AT   *The Ancient Track* (Hippocampus Press, 2013)
CE   *Collected Essays* (Hippocampus Press, 2004–06; 5 vols.)
CF   *Collected Fiction* (Hippocampus Press, 2015–17; 4 vols.)
IAP   S. T. Joshi, *I Am Providence: The Life and Times of H. P. Love-craft* (Hippocampus Press, 2010; 2013 [paper])
LL   *Lovecraft's Library: A Catalogue,* 4th rev. ed. (Hippocampus Press, 2017)
SL   *Selected Letters* (Arkham House, 1965–76; 5 vols.)

Copyright © 2023 by Hippocampus Press
Published by Hippocampus Press, P.O. Box 641, New York, NY 10156
www.hippocampuspress.com

Cover illustration by Allen Koszowski. Hippocampus Press logo designed by Anastasia Damianakos. Cover design by Barbara Briggs Silbert.

Lovecraft material is used by permission of The Estate of H. P. Lovecraft; Lovecraft Holdings, LLC.

Lovecraft Annual is published once a year, in Fall. Articles and letters should be sent to the editor, S. T. Joshi, % Hippocampus Press, and must be accompanied by a self-addressed stamped envelope if return is desired. All reviews are assigned. Literary rights for articles and reviews will reside with *Lovecraft Annual* for one year after publication, whereupon they will revert to their respective authors. Payment is in contributor's copies.

ISSN 1935-6102
ISBN 978-1-61498-415-3

Falco Ossifracus

Edith Miniter

It pleasures us exceedingly to offer our readers a condensed novel by the renowned Mr. Goodguile. Why pursue the works of this author through Tryouts, Vagrants *and* National Amateurs, *as yet in press, when here is the quintessence? Similar attention is promised later to such of our eminent fictionists as merit it.*

FALCO OSSIFRACUS
By Mr. Goodguile

Any form of inquisition into the meaning of this will be fruitless. Favour me, an' you will, with eternal confinement in a gaol, and everything that I now relate will be repeated with perfect candour.

Again I say I do not know anything at all about it, which is probably why I am making it the subject of this narrative. It is true that I have been for 18 years his closest friend and we have been seen by reputable witnesses near Greenwood, N. Y., Sleepy Hollow by the Hudson, Mt. Auburn, Cambridge, Mass., and Grant's Tomb, Manhattan, but that we possessed tastes mutually morbid or a predilection for graveyards I must strenuously deny.

I seem to remember a weird evening in November. The place was, of course, a cemetery; over the fence peered an inquisitive, waning, crescent moon, and on the fence a vulture and his vulturine a raven and a couple of cormorants remained couchant. Behind the wall I discerned the loud moan of several man-eating sharks, from which I augured that the sea was not above a league distant. A few skulls and cross-bones lay in the foreground, while coffin plates, shreds of shrouds, and mattocks which I instinctively knew appertained to gravediggers, scattered around loosely, completed the remarkable scene.

I had, for some time, missed my companion, but as he was most frequently absent when we were together I thought little of the occurrence. Indeed, the next moment, my attention was arrested by the hurried passing of a completely articulated skeleton, holding its nose, from whence the bright blue blood of a Colonial governor streamed. And this was rather unique, because it had no nose!

Meaning to employ a phraseology which my readers will at once recognize as the common and natural expression of frequenters of tombs, "How's his nibs?" I inquired. Unfortunately a slight nervousness changed the "n" to "r," and the offended object disappeared without replying. I succeeded better, however, with the next bag o' bones, which came forth applying a skeleton hand to the base of a spinal column and groaning frightfully, which was the more peculiar, as it has neither lungs nor windpipe.

"Your pal," came the response, "Iacchus Smithsonia," the name was originally John Smith, but it is always my will that my friends bear a name of my choosing and as cumbersome a one as possible, "is cleaning out Tomb 268."

It was indeed so. In the exact centre of the abode of corruption stood the self-elected subsidiary of Perpetual Care. His shrunken eye sockets, his dropped jaw, as well as practically hairless cranium, proclaimed at one sight a youth who at 15 dwelt far from normalcy, and the impression gained rather than lost by the pennies which, in accordance with a characteristic freak, he invariably wore over his flashing organs of sight. Alone he stood, brandishing the thigh bone of a remote ancestor. I say alone, for the pile of unassorted bones in the corner could hardly be called company, nor yet the half dozen grinning wraiths that floated about in the noisome atmosphere of the sepulchre.

"I am really sorry to have to ask you to absquatulate," he said, employing the choice diction which is so peculiar to we of the educated aristocracy, "but this ain't no place for a feller with cold feet."

As he spoke he pleasantly indicated a ladder dripping with ichor, whatever that is, and bordered by encrustations of nitre. I most wish now I'd made this a poem. As I was unable, through horror, to start at the moment, he went on, "Make yourself scarce, cut sticks, fly the coop, go way back and sit down, 23 for you, advance to the rear, vamoose!" All of which, uttered in the mellifluous tones of unperturbation for which my friend was famed, having no effect on my shattering nerves, he added, politely,

"Good God, Goodguile, get out or I will kick you out!"

At the same time he employed a gesture which in a flash made plain to my understanding the cause for the flight of the second fleeing skeleton.

After that ensued comparative silence. Indeed, I know not how many interminable aeons I wandered stupified through cenotaphs, slabs, mausoleums, urns, icy hands and marble hearts. I do know that I narrowly escaped being bilked of breakfast at my boarding house. The hours are 7 to 8:45 weekdays, and this was of a Tuesday, but not the one the man died of—I strongly desire to obviate any monotony of analogy in this tale.

To my absolute amazement Iacchus was at once discernible as not present. His glass was turned down, as Omar Khayyam recommended, and his Sunday-clean napkin remained folded in its ring as he had placed it the previous evening, cranberry sauce stain outward.

Probably I showed trepidation. I know a few knives and spoons clattered to the floor, a plate shattered the window as it passed en route to the area-way, and my once full cup of coffee flooded the table cloth. My nerves are generally well in hand, I am able to remain calm in the face of any number of ghosts, nor is the miasmal gas of disinterment in the least displeasing to my olfactory organs, but I must admit that seeing my friend's absence, with the odor of Ancient Greece, possibly from frying potatoes, was too much.

Just as I lapsed into unconsciousness the landlady's raucous voice issued as from a necrophagus shadow. And this is what it said:

"You fool, he's got indigestion from a supper of Grilled Bones!"

(*The Muffin Man*, April 1921)

Edith Miniter's "Falco Ossifracus"

Ken Faig, Jr.

Edith Miniter published her parody of H. P. Lovecraft's writing in her one-shot amateur magazine, the *Muffin Man* in April 1921. It ends: "You fool, he's got indigestion from a supper of Grilled Bones!"[1] which mimics the concluding sentence of Lovecraft's own "The Statement of Randolph Carter": "YOU FOOL! WARREN[2] IS DEAD!" (*CF* 1.139). Lovecraft had dreamed most of this story in December 1919 (letter to Gallomo, 11 December 1919, *Miscellaneous Letters* 76–78) and the story originally appeared in W. Paul Cook's *Vagrant* for May 1920. (It only appeared in *Weird Tales* for the first time in February 1925.) Lovecraft had begun to attend meetings of the Hub Club in Boston in 1920, and Miniter could easily have heard the story read aloud there as well as reading it in the *Vagrant*.

The title of the parody references a bird of prey. The precise identification of *Falco ossifragus* is debated. The sea-eagle or ossifrage was painted by Audubon. The biblical ossifrage is also identified with the bearded vulture (*Gypaetus barbatus*) or lammergeier (lamb-slayer) depicted in the following 1885 print. This powerful raptor has the learned behavior of dropping prey onto rocks from high elevations to break bones (hence, the name ossifrage or bone-breaker).

Some sources identify *Falco ossifragus* with Linnaeus' *Falco albacilla* (white-tailed eagle) (1758). Some ornithologists now regard Audubon's famous *Falco washingtoniensis* as a fraudulent compound of several prior-identified species (see Halley).

---

1. All quotations from "Falco Ossifracus" derive from the text found at *Dead Houses* 117–19, reprinted herein.

2. The cemetery explorers in Lovecraft's story were his alter ego Randolph Carter and Harley Warren (standing in for Samuel Loveman).

Above: The Lammergeier, or Ossifrage of Scripture (1885). "These are they of which ye shall not eat: the eagle and the ossifrage, and the osprey." —Deut. 14:12

Below: James Audubon's original painting of *Falco ossifragus* / Sea Eagle, 1863. Credit: New-York Historical Society.

Falx (falcis) was a scythe or sickle and the uncommon word falco (falconis) (*OLD* 672) was constructed from falx + -o to mean a person with toes curved inward like a scythe.[3] Os (ossis) means bone and frango (fregi, fractum) means to break. *OLD* 1274 defines ossifragus as (1) bone-breaker and (2) a bird of prey (especially vulture). Thus, we might interpret the Latin name *Falco ossifragus* as scythe-winged bird of prey. Note that a vulture and his vulturine are among the creatures couchant on the wall of the cemetery visited by Goodguile and Smith

The likeliest supposition is that Miniter saw a nineteenth-century painting or print of the *Falco ossifragus* and recalled it when titling her parody. Perhaps the bearded vulture seemed an apt symbol for Lovecraft's dark fictional subjects and his sometimes mordant personality. "Fric-frac" is French for break-in so Miniter may have chosen to substitute "-fracus" for "-fragus" to add another twist to her title. The protagonists of Miniter's parody are after all tomb-raiders. Or she may have simply misremembered *ossifragus* as *ossifracus*. The past participle of *frango* is after all *fractum*.

The avian title of Miniter's parody was undoubtedly meant to compare bone-crunching habits of its tomb-raiding protagonists with the various raptor species identified with *Falco ossifragus*. The protagonists share with the vulture a preference for dead prey, although the protagonists prefer the bones of fabled ancestors to carrion. On the other hand, eagles or *lammergeiers* dropping prey from high aloft to expose marrow have nothing on the protagonists' predatory predilection for ancestral bones recovered from raided ossuaries.

The purported author of "Falco Ossifracus" was "Mr. Goodguile." The Cambridge Dictionary defines guile as "smart but sometimes dishonest behavior that you use to deceive someone." In some of its shades of meaning "craft,"[4] in addition to referencing a skill, can also involve deceit. Of course, it's meant to parody the surname "Lovecraft": guile certainly implies craft-

---

3. The raptor genus *Falco* received its name from the scythe-like shape of the member species' wings.

4. "Croft," on the other hand, usually refers to an enclosed field or a small farm.

iness and love (at least in its non-sexual context) is good. Both surnames, Lovecraft and Goodguile are bisyllabic with roughly the same accentuation on first and second syllable. In both cases, the first syllable is of four letters and the second of five. On several levels, Goodguile seems like an inspired pseudonym for Lovecraft.

Goodguile commences his narration by informing his readers: "Any form of inquisition into the meaning of this will be fruitless." He cites multiple sightings of himself and his friend John Smith (*Iacchus Smithsonia*[5]) in graveyards over an eighteen-year period but insists: "that we possessed tastes mutually morbid or a predilection for graveyards I must strenuously deny." As narrator, Goodguile assumes an aggressive posture vis-à-vis his readers. Earlier, he had asserted: "Favour me, an' you will, with eternal confinement in a gaol, and everything that I now relate will be repeated with perfect candour."[6] Like Lovecraft, Mr. Goodguile favors British spellings and quasi-archaisms.[7]

Goodguile recalls a weird evening in a cemetery (of course!) in November. The setting as described has elements of surrealism:

> ... over the fence peered an inquisitive, waning, crescent moon, and on the fence a vulture and his vulturine[,] a raven and a couple of cormorants remained couchant. Behind the wall I discerned the loud moan of several man-eating sharks, from which I augured that the sea was not above a league distant. A

---

5. Iacchus was a minor Greek deity associated with the Eleusinian mysteries. Lovecraft did not begin to correspond with Clark Ashton Smith until 1922, so if any of his acquaintances was meant to be referenced by the surname Smith, it might have been Charles W. ("Tryout") Smith of the *Tryout*. Perhaps Lovecraft described Iacchus Smith as a youth of fifteen to emphasize the advanced years of his real friend.

6. Note the similar phraseology used at the beginning of "The Statement of Randolph Carter": "I repeat to you, gentlemen, that your inquisition is fruitless. Detain me here for ever if you will; confine or execute me if you must have a victim to propitiate the illusion you call justice; but I can say no more than I have said already. Everything that I can remember, I have told with perfect candour" (*CF* 1.132).

7. At one point Goodguile declares: "I strongly desire to obviate any monotony of analogy in this tale." This follows a reference to "Tuesday, but not the one the man died of" which mystifies this reader.

few skulls and cross-bones lay in the foreground, while coffin plates, shreds of shrouds, and mattocks[8] which I instinctively knew appertained to gravediggers, scattered around loosely, completed the remarkable scene.

Mr. Goodguile misses his companion Smith but is confronted by the:

... hurried passing of an completely articulated skeleton, holding its nose, from whence the bright blue blood of a Colonial governor[9] streamed. And this was rather unique, because it had no nose!

Nervousness leads Goodguile to offend the Colonial governor by greeting him with "How's his ribs?" rather than "How's his nibs." The skeletonic governor's disappearance is followed by the appearance of a second skeletal figure:

I succeeded better, however, with the next bag o' bones, which came forth applying a skeleton hand to the base of a spinal column and groaning frightfully, which was the more peculiar, as it has neither lungs nor windpipe.

The second skeleton proceeds to inform Goodguile that his friend John Smith "is cleaning out Tomb 268."[10] The scene shifts immediately to that locale, where Goodguile remarks his friend's "shrunken eye sockets, his dropped jaw, as well as practically hairless cranium." As with the dead, his friend ("a youth who at 15 dwelt far from normalcy") covers his "flashing organs of sight" with pennies. He has only "a pile of unassorted bones in the corner" and "half dozen grinning wraiths" for company in

---

8. A hand tool with a long handle and a stout head used for digging, prying and chopping (Wikipedia).

9. Mr. Goodguile is silent regarding the identity of the Colonial governor. Of course, New England had numerous cemeteries containing the remains of colonial governors.

10. Miniter may have chosen the tomb number randomly or it may reflect an actual tomb she (and possibly Lovecraft) had visited. The number 268 (prime factorization $2 \times 2 \times 67$) is the smallest integer the product of whose digits ($2 \times 6 \times 8 = 96$) is six times the sum of its digits ($2 + 6 + 8 = 16$). The odd numbers (269 and 271) are a prime pair.

"the noisome atmosphere of the sepulcher."

Smith bids his friend to absquatulate;[11] "this ain't no place for a feller with cold feet" he declares. As means of exit, Smith points to "a ladder dripping with ichor,[12] whatever that is, and bordered by encrustations of nitre."[13] Echoing the injunctions addressed to Loveman in his dream, Smith bids Goodguile: "Make yourself scarce, cut sticks, fly the coop, go way back and sit down, 23 [14] for you, advance to the rear, vamoose!" Ending: "Good God, Goodguile, get out or I will kick you out!" Before fleeing, Goodguile remarked: "At the same time he employed a gesture which in a flash made plain to my understanding the cause for flight of the second fleeing skeleton."

Goodguile's flight through the "cenotaphs, slabs, mausoleums, urns, icy hands and marble hearts" is so long that he nearly misses breakfast at his boarding house. His friend and fellow boarder Smith is absent as evidenced by his napkin sitting in its ring with "cranberry sauce stain outward." Goodguile drops knives and spoons to the floor, flings a plate through the window, and spills his coffee on the table cloth. He protests:

> I am able to remain calm in the face of any number of ghosts, nor is the miasmal gas of disinterment in the least displeasing to my olfactory organs, but I must admit that seeing my friend's absence, with the odor of Ancient Greece,[15] possibly from frying potatoes, was too much.

The story concludes:

---

11. To leave suddenly or in a hurry.

12. In classical Greek mythology, the fluid that flowed in the veins of the gods and other immortals. More generally, a watery or blood-tinged discharge.

13. Potassium nitrate, found as a soft, white highly soluble mineral in caves and arid climates.

14. "23 skidoo" was an early 20th-century American slang phrase meaning to be forced to leave by another person (Wikipedia).

15. The sense of smell plays a large role in the story. Tomb 268 is described as an "abode of corruption." The tomb has a "noisome atmosphere." The "miasmal gas of disinterment" does not offend the narrator's olfactory organs. The first skeleton (the Colonial governor) which runs past Mr. Goodguile manifests symptoms of olfactory distress by bleeding blue blood from a nose he does not possess.

Just as I lapsed into unconsciousness the landlady's raucous voice issued as from a necrophagus[16] shadow. And this is what it said: "You fool, he's got indigestion from a supper of Grilled Bones!"

Inside Tomb 268, Smith had brandished "the thigh bone of a remote ancestor." We can probably assume that both the blue-blooded colonial governor and the second skeleton fled from the horrendous sight of Smith's gnawing the bones of his own ancestors in Tomb 268. The colonial governor is so shocked he has a bleed from his nonextant nose, while the second skeleton is apparently about to move his nonextant bowels in shock. There is clearly an association of the noisome odors of the tomb with indigestion and the potentially resulting regurgitation or defecation.

The absence of Smith from the boarding house breakfast table is enough to send the not-easily-disturbed Goodguile into a fit. Apparently, Smith meant what he said when he enjoined Goodguile to leave *instanter*. It seems apparent that Smith will never return to join his friend at the boarding house table, but that he must dwell henceforth with his ancestors in Tomb 268. Unless the raucous-voiced landlady is in fact his co-conspirator, and has prepared him a late-night supper from bones abstracted from the ancestral tomb. She is said to emerge from a necrophagus [*sic*] shadow, so maybe she is in cahoots in providing Smith with the diet he requires.

This short send-up of Lovecraft's writing and of "The Statement of Randolph Carter" in particular[17] was apparently received in good spirit by Lovecraft. Despite strongly dissimilar literary tastes and personalities, he and Miniter remained friends. Lovecraft was one of the few amateur journalists invited to visit Miniter at the home of Evanore Olds Beebe (1858–1935)[18] in

---

16. *Necrophagous* means deriving nutriment from decaying animal matter.

17. Another Lovecraft story with a strong burial place setting, "The Tomb," did not receive its first publication in W. Paul Cook's *Vagrant* until March 1922. However, Miniter might have heard it read at a Hub Club meeting. Joshi (*IAP* 307–8) notes the strong connection of "Falco Ossifracus" with "The Statement of Randolph Carter."

18. "Maplehurst," 782 Monson Road, was originally built by George Mixter as

Wilbraham. He stayed an entire week in July 1928, and soaked up the local sights and legendry, some of which appeared in his story "The Dunwich Horror." After Miniter died, Lovecraft wrote an appreciative essay ("Mrs. Miniter—Estimates and Recollections"; *CE* 1.378–86) that first appeared in Hyman Bradofsky's *Californian* for Spring 1938. His fictional tribute to Miniter and her Wilbraham birthplace, "The Dunwich Horror," first appeared in *Weird Tales* for April 1929. Whether Miniter herself ever had the opportunity to read this story may be doubted. She caught something of the personality and the style of Lovecraft in "Falco Ossifracus." She also used Lovecraft (H. Theobald, Jr.—"The Man with the Long Chin") in her unfinished novel *The Village Green* (77–208). But "Falco Ossifracus" will undoubtedly remain her most well-remembered portrait of Lovecraft and his work.

References

Derie, Bobby. "'Falco Ossifracus' (1921) by Edith Miniter." Available at deepcuts.blog/2019/06/03/falco-ossifracus-1921-by-edith-miniter/.

Glare, P. G. W., ed. *Oxford Latin Dictionary*. Oxford: Oxford University Press, 1982. [*OLD*]

Halley, Matthew R. "Audubon's Bird of Washington: Unravelling the Fraud That Launched *The Birds of America*." *Bulletin of the British Ornithologists' Club* 140 (2020): 110–41. Available at bioone.org/journals/bulletin-of-the-british-ornithologists-club/volume-140/issue-2/bboc.v140i2.2020.a3/Audubons-Bird-of-Washington--unravelling-the-fraud-that-launched/10.25226/bboc.v140i2.2020.a3.full

Lovecraft, H. P. *Miscellaneous Letters*. Edited by David E. Schultz and S. T. Joshi. New York: Hippocampus Press, 2022.

Miniter, Edith. *Dead Houses and Other Works*. Ed. Kenneth W. Faig, Jr. and Sean Donnelly. New York: Hippocampus Press, 2008.

---

a tavern in the 1830s. Miniter had helped to lecture on Beebe's antiques there during the celebration of the Wilbraham sesquicentennial in 1913.

———. *The Village Green and Other Amateur Writings*. Ed. Kenneth W. Faig, Jr. and Sean Donnelly. New York: Hippocampus Press, 2013.

"Ossifrage." *McClintock and Strong Biblical Encyclopedia*. Discussion of the biblical ossifrage. Available at www.biblicalcyclopedia. com/O/ossifrage.html.

Briefly Noted

Several important tokens of Lovecraft's ascending worldwide fame have appeared over the past year. First, Lovecraft is to be included in the Bibliothèque de la Pléiade, the most prestigious series of books published in France, which includes all the classic French writers dating back centuries. It is rare, but not unheard-of, for non-Francophone writers to be included in this series, and Lovecraft has made the grade. Next, Lovecraft's name continues to be dropped in a number of contexts that one might not expect. The *New York Times* ran an article on the parallels between artificial intelligence (AI) and the shoggoth (Kevin Roose, "Why an Octopus-like Creature Has Come to Symbolize the State of A.I.," 30 May 2023). In response to this, Mike Calia of CNBC ran an article, based on an interview with S. T. Joshi, that corrected some errors in the *Times* article and expounded Lovecraft's own views of the shoggoth ("The World's Top H. P. Lovecraft Expert Weighs In on a Monstrous Viral Meme in the A.I. World," cnbc.com). Most recently, one of the *New York Times'* conservative columnists, Ross Douthat, compared the prospect of Donald Trump's in these terms: ". . . his second term was foretold in the Necronomicon, written in eldritch script on the Mountains of Madness and carved deep, deep into the white stones of the Plateau of Leng" (18 June 2023).

The Disgusting Thing on the Doorstep

H. P. Lovecraft's Sexuality and the Science of Revulsion

Dylan Henderson

Few authors have appeared as fictional characters as often as H. P. Lovecraft has. Brilliant, eccentric, and opinionated, he has presented writers with a ready-made character, whose distinctive personality sometimes seems better suited to fiction than to reality. For the most part, contemporary depictions of Lovecraft portray him as reserved, dignified, and scholarly—if, perhaps, somewhat socially awkward. A few authors, however, intrigued by Lovecraft's unconventional lifestyle, have drawn a very different picture. In Paul La Farge's 2017 novel *The Night Ocean*, for instance, Lovecraft is depicted as a closeted homosexual who, despite his claims to the contrary, is obsessed with sex. Secretly reveling in his excesses, La Farge's Lovecraft records each act in a lurid diary dubbed the *Erotonomicon* and eventually falls in love with his teenage protégé R. H. Barlow. Though his work is fictional, La Farge uses *The Night Ocean* to suggest that Lovecraft's relationship with Barlow was far too intimate to be platonic. And, undoubtedly, their relationship does invite a number of questions. Was Lovecraft a homosexual? Were he and Barlow lovers? And if so, how does this affect our understanding of Lovecraft and his work? While La Farge's bold depiction of Lovecraft encourages a thoughtful re-examination not just of the author's life but of his fiction, it is contradicted by Lovecraft's frequent assertions on the topic. Recent research into the science of disgust, however, offers readers a new way of thinking about Lovecraft's sexuality that is in accord with his stated views, his life, and his work.

I. An Ongoing Controversy

The Night Ocean may be fiction, but a number of scholars suspect that Lovecraft either repressed or hid his homosexuality. Research into the question began in earnest in 1966 when J. Vernon Shea (who had corresponded with Lovecraft for about six years in the 1930s) provided a Freudian interpretation of the author's work. Theorizing that Lovecraft's sea-born monsters reflected his subconscious feelings toward women, Shea speculated that his late friend might have been a latent homosexual. Robert M. Price would revisit the subject in his landmark 1982 essay "Homosexual Panic in 'The Outsider,'" which compares that story to the emotional trauma many gay men experience as they grapple with their own identities. Since then, interest in the issue has exploded, resulting in dozens of conference papers, journal articles, and blog posts exploring homosexuality, masculinity, and androgyny in Lovecraft's life and work (Matolcsy; Pace; Johnson; Muise). In 2014, in the first book-length work on the subject, *Sex and the Cthulhu Mythos*, Bobby Derie rejects the theory that Lovecraft was a homosexual, though he does not deny that his relationships with men and women invite speculation (46).

For those who do believe that Lovecraft was a homosexual, the evidence lies in his biography, specifically in his relationship with his mother, a "touch-me-not," whose attitude toward her son was such that Lovecraft once described it to his wife as "devastating" (Davis 152–53); his indifference to sex, which his wife, Sonia, had to initiate (Everts 19); his marked preference for male companionship before, during, and after his marriage; and his unusual friendship with young Barlow, whom he visited in Florida in 1934 and again in 1935. Having sifted through this evidence, Stanley C. Sargent (whose interpretation Derie praises though ultimately rejects) has maintained that Lovecraft struggled his entire adult life to repress his homosexuality. From Sargent's perspective, the evidence, though circumstantial, is simply too abundant to ignore. It follows, moreover, a familiar pattern that Sargent claims is too well established to be coincidental. Some might dismiss this as speculation, but Sargent supports his contention with perceptive readings of "The Outsider" and "The Dunwich Horror," both of which, according to Sargent, express Lovecraft's "extreme feeling of being an isolated monster." Growing up in rural Ohio, Sargent himself experienced similar feelings, and for him Lovecraft's tales of cosmic horror contain a very human sense of isolation, what Sargent calls the "abject horror of recognizing you are gay in a very anti-gay world."

As thought-provoking and emotionally compelling as these readings are, they beg the question: Why the sudden interest in Lovecraft's sexuality? What difference does it make to La Farge or Sargent or any of Lovecraft's readers? It is not, I would suggest, a coincidence that interest in Lovecraft's sexuality has grown alongside an awareness of his racism. As readers learn more about his prejudices, they find him increasingly difficult to understand as an individual. A cerebral person with no interest in sex or romance, Lovecraft would seem almost robotic were it not for his surprisingly passionate hatred of foreigners and immigrants. To contemporary readers (specifically those unfamiliar with his correspondence), Lovecraft is a caricature of a human being, whose oddball mannerisms seem better suited to the printed page than the real world. If Lovecraft, however, were a homosexual man vainly struggling to repress a sense of self-loathing, an "extreme feeling of being an isolated monster," he would be less unfathomable to the modern mind. Instead of being a detached intelligence, Lovecraft would become a recognizable and sympathetic type, whose life, despite its superficial oddities, adhered to an established pattern. As a fictional Samuel Loveman explains in *The Night Ocean*, if Lovecraft "really did love Bobby, at least that would mean he was human" (28). In that sense, the ongoing debate about homosexuality in Lovecraft's life and work is not just about understanding Lovecraft's sexuality; it is about understanding Lovecraft.

And yet, Lovecraft complicates matters by stating repeatedly in his letters that, from childhood on, he had no interest in sex of any kind. According to a letter to Frank Belknap Long, he viewed intercourse as an uninteresting function of biology: "Ending with the medical books of my physician-uncle, I knew everything there is to be known about the anatomy and physiology of reproduction in both sexes before I was eight years old; after which curiosity was of course impossible. The entire subject had become merely a tedious detail of animal biology" (*SL* 1.305). Most small children find the details of our "animal biology" endlessly fascinating, but it seems that Lovecraft, at an early age, developed a strong aversion to the human body and its functions. In a later letter, which retells the same story, Lovecraft claims that, after reading about reproduction, he began to view sex as a "prosaic mechanism—a mechanism which I rather despised or at least thought non-glamourous because of its purely animal nature & separation from such things as intellect & beauty" (*JVS* 220). Of course, Lovecraft's professed lack of interest could be an artistic pose, an attempt to depict himself as an aesthete devoted to "intellect & beauty," but his early poetry (which mocks the romance writer Fred Jackson for his sentimentality, lambastes the poet Walt Whitman for his licentiousness, and teases his friend Alfred Galpin for his love affairs) reinforces the impression of Lovecraft created by his letters.

As for male homosexuality specifically, Lovecraft condemns it repeatedly, labeling it a "repugnant" form of sexuality. In a discussion with August Derleth, for example, he contends that homosexuality should be proscribed, not because it is unethical, but because it is disgusting: "So far as the case of homosexualism goes, the primary & vital objection against it is that it is naturally (physically & instinctively—not merely 'morally' or aesthetically) repugnant to the overwhelming bulk of mankind" (*ES* 545–46). Lovecraft goes on to claim that he could not even *imagine* engaging in homosexual intercourse: "I hate both physically normal adultery (which is contemptible sneaking treachery) & paederasty—but while I might enjoy (physically) or be tempted toward adultery, I simply *could not* consider the abnormal state without physical nausea" (*ES* 546). Even though Lovecraft had several close friends who were homosexuals (including Loveman and Barlow), he was seemingly unaware of their orientation. How he would have reacted is unknowable, but when he met an openly gay man in Cleveland in 1924, he responded with loathing, calling him "that precious sissy" and claiming that he disliked Lovecraft because he was "too horrid, rough & mannish for it!" (JFM 63). Of course, the cerebral Lovecraft was not particularly rough or mannish, and his somewhat hysterical reaction to "that precious sissy" may be a pathetic attempt to paper over his own inadequacy. Indeed, one can hardly fault contemporary readers for raising an eyebrow at Lovecraft's hyperbolic denunciations of homosexuality. And yet, with so little evidence, scholars cannot ethically reject Lovecraft's assertion that he was a heterosexual (though uninterested in sex). To do so would be to claim that scholars know Lovecraft better than he knew himself.

Believing Lovecraft to be the best judge of his own nature, S. T. Joshi and others have maintained that Lovecraft was what we would now call asexual, his interest in sex—with anyone—being negligible. From Joshi's perspective, there is abundant evidence in both Lovecraft's letters and in his ex-wife's memoirs that he was nominally heterosexual, though his interest in romance, eroticism, and even physical affection was obviously limited. After examining Lovecraft's childhood and his belated response to Sonia's advances, Joshi concludes that "his emotions had clearly been stunted in this direction" (IAP 424). Donovan Loucks, who runs The H. P. Lovecraft Archive, takes a different tack on his website, noting that "Lovecraft, like many intellectuals, focused his attentions and efforts on mental, rather than physical, pursuits, and simply didn't have very strong sexual interests at all." From Loucks's perspective, there is nothing curious or even particularly noteworthy about Lovecraft's sexuality. Indeed, Loucks seems to praise Lovecraft for channeling his sexual desires into "mental, rather than physical, pursuits." As for Lovecraft's alleged homosexuality, Loucks considers this a "myth," which he refutes on his website. Derie, who writes about the subject persuasively and at length in Sex and the Cthulhu Mythos, concurs. He regards the theory that Lovecraft was a homosexual as speculation, noting that there is no evidence that Lovecraft ever had or wanted a homosexual relationship (44). Derie's point is well taken, and yet he errs in labeling Lovecraft sexually "indifferent" (44), for Lovecraft described sex not as uninteresting, but as repulsive and disgusting, as a "mechanism which I rather despised."

II. The Nature of Disgust

Considering the biographical and textual evidence presented above, recent developments in the field of psychology and neuroscience may provide readers with a better understanding of Lovecraft's sexuality and how it affected both his life and his work. In 2011, psychologists Richard J. Stevenson, Trevor I. Case, and Megan J. Oaten sought to understand the relationship between sex and disgust. Since sex, they argued, invariably involves fluids and odors that would be disgusting in other contexts, it is unclear why people have sex at all. Hypothesizing that arousal temporarily inhibits disgust, the researchers conducted an experiment, which required participants (some of whom had viewed erotica) to rate their responses to a series of revolting experiences, such as touching pea soup, listening to someone vomit, and smelling rotten fish. As expected, participants who had examined the erotic images beforehand found the experiences significantly less disgusting, thereby demonstrating that, for some at least, disgust diminishes with arousal.

This landmark experiment inspired a flurry of follow-up studies that sought to confirm or expand its findings (Borg and de Jong; van Overveld et al.; Lee et al.; Andrews et al.; Al-Shawaf et al.; Zhang et al.; Oaten et al.). A research team led by Arthur Andrews, for instance, found that, just as arousal inhibits disgust, induced disgust can inhibit arousal. Someone, in other words, whose disgust has already been triggered may subsequently find it more difficult to become aroused. If that is so, it raises questions about those on the left and right of the bell curve—those, that is, who are abnormally sensitive or resistant to disgusting stimuli. The earliest studies examined individuals without a history of sexual dysfunction, but recent studies have focused on those initially overlooked, including the unusually sensitive, who have complicated the conclusions offered by Stevenson and others. In 2015, a team led by Diana Fleischman found that, while women who are not sensitive to disgust become even *less* sensitive when aroused (as Charmaine Borg and Peter J. de Jong demonstrated), women who are sensitive to disgust become even *more* so when aroused.[1] This suggests that, while arousal releases most individuals from the inhibitions their disgust imposes upon them, disgust in "highly disgust-prone individuals" may serve as a psychological barrier that prevents them from enjoying sex (Fleischman et al.). Perhaps it could also explain why, for Lovecraft, sex was a mechanism to be despised.

III. *Prone to Disgust*

Unlike the theory that Lovecraft was a homosexual, which causes as many complications as it resolves, the idea that he was a "highly disgust-prone individual" explains many of his eccentricities. Most importantly, it explains why Lovecraft avoided sex with his wife and why, both before and after his marriage, he showed no interest in forming sexual relationships. Keep in mind that Lovecraft did not simply eschew heterosexual intercourse, as an asexual or homosexual individual might be expected to do; he avoided *all* physical contact. Instead of hugging or kissing his wife, he would, Sonia claims, "wrap his 'pinkey' finger around mine and say 'Umph!'" (152). His physical interaction with his wife was seemingly limited to his finger, the appendage furthest from "himself." If Lovecraft were unusually sensitive to disgust, it would be no surprise that, while married, he was happiest when conversing with his wife through the mail. It may also be noteworthy that, when he was a small child, his worst nightmares involved being touched: the night-gaunts that haunted his childhood dreams tortured him by carrying him through space while *tickling* him "with obscene clutch that titillates and stings" (AT 88).

A hypersensitivity to potentially disgusting stimuli would also explain Lovecraft's extreme reaction to both homosexuality (the thought of which inspired "physical nausea") and heterosexual intercourse, the very mention of which upset him. Indeed, in his letters that touch on the issue of sexuality, Lovecraft never fails to express how much intercourse repulses him. When, for instance, discussing eroticism in literature with Rheinhart Kleiner, Lovecraft claims that he initially opposed its depiction in part

---

1. All the participants in Fleischman's experiment were women. It is unclear whether or not men would be affected in the same way.

"because of the acknowledged repulsiveness of direct erotic manifestations, as felt by all races and cultures and expressed in reticence to a greater or lesser degree" (*RK* 177). Three years later, in a letter to Long from 1924, Lovecraft dismisses his friend's views on pornography as an affectation, noting that "there's nothing beautiful or artistick about it, any more than the idealisation of certain ultimate digestive processes would be" (*SL* 1.305). Lovecraft's elevated language masks the severity of his response, but he is claiming that the depiction of sex can be no more "beautiful or artistick" than the act of defecation.[2] Nor did Lovecraft's marriage noticeably soften his views. In a letter to Bernard Austin Dwyer from 1932 discussing Arthur Machen's views on sex, Lovecraft insists that, to someone freed from religious orthodoxy, illicit sex is nothing more than a "rather prosaic and unfortunate species of organic maladjustment—no more frightful, and no more interesting, than a headache, a fit of colic, or an ulcer on the big toe" (*MWM* 471). Lovecraft's point may be valid, but note the metaphor he uses: he compares the sexual "filth and perversion" that so upset Machen—and which excites and titillates so many others—to "an ulcer on the big toe," a truly repulsive image. While he was married, the very idea of sex upset Lovecraft so much that, according to his ex-wife, his friends would tease him by starting conversations on the topic, knowing that such talk bothered him (quoted in Everts 19). Such reticence, of course, could be the result of Lovecraft's puritanical temperament, but the inverse may also be true. That is, his puritanical temperament could be the result of his sensitivity to disgust.

After all, in other aspects of his life, Lovecraft displayed just

---

2. The upcoming publication of Lovecraft's correspondence with Long promises to shed additional light on the subject. In March 2022, Joshi, who is co-editing the correspondence for Hippocampus Press, posted one of Long's replies to Lovecraft to his blog. In it, Long denounces Lovecraft's views in the harshest terms possible, calling him a "sick man as far as sex sanity is concerned" and claiming that he views women as "a kind of inferior chamber pot for the reception of products akin to urine." What, exactly, Lovecraft wrote that prompted this reply is unknowable, for Lovecraft's epistle does not survive, but Long himself was clearly shocked by it: "As for your conception of coitus," he writes, "my GAWD."

such a sensitivity. As is well known, he *loathed* fish and seafood of all kinds, the smell of which made him nauseous. Many people, of course, dislike the smell of fish, but Lovecraft's hatred for it defies all reason. E. Hoffmann Price describes how Lovecraft once took him to a restaurant famous for clams, ordered for him, and then, before leaving his friend there, remarked, "while you are devouring this *God-damned* stuff, I'll cross the street to eat a sandwich, well away from the odor of steamed clams" (51). Considering how important manners, etiquette, and hospitality were to Lovecraft, his unwillingness to sit through a single meal with a friend from out of town speaks volumes. Lovecraft's remarks, now so hotly debated, about foreigners and immigrants also seem partly inspired by a sense of physical repulsion. In one of his most infamous diatribes, Lovecraft describes a visit to Chinatown and the sense of disgust it inspired:

> My gawd—what a filthy dump! I thought Providence had slums, and antique Bostonium as well; but damn me if I ever saw anything like the sprawling sty-atmosphere of N. Y.'s lower East Side. We walked—at my suggestion—in the middle of the street, for contact with the heterogeneous sidewalk denizens, spilled out of their bulging brick kennels as if by a spawning beyond the capability of the places, was not to be sought. At times, though, we struck peculiarly deserted areas—these swine have instinctive swarming movements, no doubt, which no ordinary biologist can fathom. Gawd knows what they are . . . a bastard mess of stewing mongrel flesh without intellect, repellent to eye, nose, and imagination—would to heaven a kindly gust of cyanogen could asphyxiate the whole gigantic abortion, end the misery, and clean out the place. (MWM 97)

Admittedly, racist tracts often dehumanize others by describing them as dirty, but Lovecraft seems unusually fixated on the cleanliness of New York's slums, which were (as a result of poverty and overcrowding) undoubtedly unhygienic. Note that he describes the neighborhood as a "filthy dump" with a "sty-atmosphere" and suggests that he and his companion walk in the middle of the street to avoid contamination. One should not overlook the passage's virulent xenophobia, but one cannot fight the impression that Lovecraft is hypersensitive to the disgusting stimuli that, regardless of the race of its inhabitants, is a feature of every slum.

A possible explanation for Lovecraft's reactionary outlook lies, yet again, in recent research involving disgust. In 2014, a research team led by Woo-Young Ahn used an MRI to capture participants' responses to disgusting imagery. They then compared these responses to a survey on political issues that the participants had completed. They found that conservatives, far more so than liberals, reacted strongly to disgusting images. The results were so clear that one of the researchers, when discussing his findings with Kathleen McAuliffe of the *Atlantic*, claimed that "my jaw dropped." The researchers could even predict a participant's ideology by looking at the resulting images. Previous research had found a correlation between political ideology and "negativity bias," the consensus being that conservatives have a stronger reaction than liberals to threatening and disgusting stimuli (Oxley et al.; Smith et al.; Hibbing et al.), but by using brain scans as opposed to surveys, the experiment confirmed what these earlier studies had only suspected: physiological differences in the brain partially account for ideological differences in individuals. If, as this research suggests, a sensitivity to disgust correlates with political conservatism, the reverse may also be true: Lovecraft's reactionary sentiments may be another indication that he was a "highly disgust-prone individual."

Lovecraft's fiction provides an additional piece of evidence, for disgust, much more so than fear, is a hallmark of his work, which features repulsive individuals (such as the "slatternly, almost bearded Spanish woman" [CF 2.12] in "Cool Air"), grotesque hybrids (such as Wilbur Whateley whose abdomen was dotted with "a score of long greenish-grey tentacles with red sucking mouths" [CF 2.439]), unclean places (such as the district of Red Hook, that "babel of sound and filth" [CF 1.484]), bodily contamination (which causes Arthur Jermyn to commit suicide), biological impurities (visible in Joe Sargent of Innsmouth, whose "long, thick lip and coarse-pored, greyish cheeks seemed almost beardless except for some sparse yellow hairs that straggled and curled in irregular patches" [CF 3.170]), and loathsome monstrosities (such as the offspring of Yog-Sothoth, which is "like jelly, an' made o' sep'rit wrigglin' ropes pushed clost together . . . great bulgin' eyes all over it . . . ten or twenty maouths or trunks a-stickin' aout all along the sides, big as stovepipes, an' all a-tossin' an' openin' an' shuttin'" [CF 2.462]). Foul smells, moreover, appear in almost every story, the word "foetid" being one of the most common descriptors in his oeuvre, appearing in, by my count, thirteen of his major works.

Recent scholars have claimed that Lovecraft's hatred of the Other inspired such passages, thus supporting Michel Houellebecq's claim that "racial hatred provokes in Lovecraft the trancelike poetic state in which he outdoes himself by the mad rhythmic pulse of cursed sentences; this is the source of the hideous and cataclysmic light that illuminates his final works" (107). It may be that Lovecraft's associates the feminine, non-white Other with contamination and corruption, but this interpretation fails to explain why some of his stories, which have no connection to race at all, are equally fixated on disgust. To put it simply, poetic descriptions with a "mad rhythmic pulse" abound in Lovecraft's work; a *few* touch on race, but *all* involve loathsome sights, which are so disgusting they hold the writer spellbound. In *At the Mountains of Madness*, for instance, Lovecraft describes a shoggoth as "that less conceivable and less mentionable nightmare—that foetid, unglimpsed mountain of slime-spewing protoplasm" (CF 3.146). Lovecraft is not venting his race hatred here. Instead, he seems mesmerized by the nastiness of this foul-smelling, continuously ejaculating slime. The explanation offered by Houellebecq also fails to account for another noteworthy attribute of Lovecraft's fiction: his reticence about the human body. As Roland Hölzing notes, Lovecraft's characters almost never eat or drink (184). Nor, for that matter, do they smoke or cough or vomit or urinate. Of course, Lovecraft, as a writer, was uninterested in such quotidia and, for that matter, in characterization itself, but even so, his characters are "clean" to the point of being mechanical or otherwise inhuman, which, by contrast, makes the earthy nature of his monstrosities all the more revolting.

IV. That Foul Thing on the Doorstep

No story demonstrates this hypersensitivity better than "The Thing on the Doorstep," which many consider evidence of Lovecraft's latent homosexuality. Noting that Derby and Ephraim are, in a sense, in a homosexual relationship, more than a few scholars have suggested that "The Thing on the Doorstep" is an exploration of sex, gender, and identity and, possibly, an expression of Lovecraft's repressed homosexuality. Joel Pace, for instance, asserts that the story implies a "homoerotic link between Edward and Dan as well as Edward and Ephraim (through Asenath)" (114). Robert H. Waugh goes even further, arguing that the story is primarily about sexual desire. Even Joshi, who maintains that Lovecraft was a heterosexual with a sluggish sex drive, asks, "is this marriage [between Derby and Asenath] homosexual?" (*IAP* 931). That question is all but unavoidable, for the sexual dynamics of the story loom so large that they threaten to overwhelm the narrative, in the process generating a number of questions that Lovecraft never answers: Does Ephraim (in his daughter's body) have sex with Derby? Is Derby attracted to Asenath (the only woman, it seems, he has ever loved) because she is really a man? If Lovecraft were a latent homosexual, who explored his own sexuality through Derby and his relationships with Ephraim, Asenath, and Upton, the questions raised by "The Thing on the Doorstep" would be quickly and tidily resolved. And yet, as tempting as such an interpretation might be, it succeeds through misdirection—by replacing Lovecraft's interests with those of contemporary readers. If readers focus on the actual text, a different story emerges, one with little interest in sex, gender, or the nature of attraction.

Despite the desire of contemporary audiences to read "The Thing on the Doorstep" as an exploration of sexuality, intercourse is completely absent from the story. As Joshi notes, Lovecraft never once touches on Derby and Asenath's sex life, nor does he ever discuss what any of the characters think or feel when they switch genders. "If," Joshi concludes, "someone were to write a story on this basic premise today, it is unlikely that such issues would be avoided" (*IAP* 931). For his comic book *Providence*, Alan Moore did just that, and as predicted, he does not avoid the issue of sex: in his version, Ephraim temporarily exchanges souls with Robert Black so that he can rape Asenath's body (which is now, of course, inhabited by Black). Lovecraft's version is, by contrast, almost shockingly chaste. And yet, he does make a perfunctory attempt at answering the question readers have found so puzzling: why is Derby initially attracted to a woman with a man's personality or soul? If, as Derby claims, Upton "ought to have known the difference" (CF 3.346) between him and Asenath, should not Derby have known the difference between Asenath and Ephraim? Upton's claim that Derby was "wildly taken with her appearance" (CF 3.330) (Asenath being "dark, smallish, and very good-looking" [CF 3.329]) provides us with Lovecraft's answer: like so many inexperienced lovers, Derby is too distracted by his partner's physical appearance to notice their fundamental incompatibility. Such an answer, which Lovecraft dashes off so quickly, may seem insufficient to contemporary readers, but it is the only one he offers.

Moore and others could argue that the conspicuous absence of sex in the story indicates just how repressed Lovecraft was. He was so repressed, in fact, that he wrote a story about sex without even realizing it! Such theories are popular in part because they provide readers with endless opportunities to speculate, to search for subconscious clues, to reimagine Lovecraft's alien gods as "a lot of cocks and pussies crawling round" (Moore, *Neonomicon*, ch. 3). They also elevate the role of literary critics, transforming them from perceptive readers into clairvoyants "wresting truths from the hidden depths of resisting texts" (Best and Marcus 13). In any case, there is textual evidence that Lovecraft was well aware of the sexual implications of his story and worked to downplay them while still keeping the basic plot intact. In 2013, Joshi published the passages Lovecraft cut from his original draft, including the following paragraph:

> He [Dr. Hathorne] had been summoned one Candlemas to the lonely Crowninshield place; & could not feel easy after what he had seen. Fortunately, it was dead. He had known monstrous births before—but when monstrosity takes certain directions, there are questions one has to ask oneself . . . questions about people, & about the universe itself. Candlemas is nine months af-

ter the Witches' Sabbat, & country legend has much to say about it. Were not Innsmouth folk said to keep the Sabbat? Where were the Derbys last May-Eve? Dr. Hathorne allowed that if he were Edward Derby he would leave Asenath while the leaving was good. He was never quite specific, though, until that night at the last when the horror came to my doorstep. Now he will back me up in trying to do what must be done. ("Passages" 174)

Asenath/Ephraim did not just have sex in Lovecraft's draft: she/he had a stillborn "monstrosity" of some sort (having been impregnated by either Derby or some sort of Lovecraftian monster). Clearly, Lovecraft realized that sex and reproduction *could* play a major role in the story, but it is also clear that he did not want them to. Joshi suggests that Lovecraft eliminated the paragraph because "this development was too sudden in its evocation of weirdness" (174), but its removal also suggests that Lovecraft fully realized the questions the relationship raised and, not wanting them to overshadow the rest of the story, worked to forestall them by expunging sexuality from his draft. In that sense, the finished version recalls "The Dunwich Horror," another tale devoid of any mention of sex even though its very plot hinges on Lavinia Whateley's unholy impregnation.[3] By removing any hint of sexual intercourse from "The Thing on the Doorstep," Lovecraft preserved the story he wanted to tell—a story not about sex or gender (topics in which he never expressed much interest) but about exchanging personalities, a topic that surfaces in many of Lovecraft's stories, including the first major story he wrote ("The Tomb") as well as the last ("The Haunter of the Dark"). It could be that his father's mental breakdown inspired this interest, but then again, such an idea is innately interesting and has roots deep in the horror genre. Of course, if Lovecraft wanted to steer his readers away from the

---

3. Much like "The Thing on the Doorstep," "The Dunwich Horror" presents readers with a scenario—the rape of a human woman by a gargantuan and, judging by the appearance of its offspring, shockingly bizarre monstrosity—so outrageous that it almost demands that the author comment upon it. And yet, the story, which relegates Lavinia to a comparatively minor role, passes over the subject, an indication that Lovecraft's interests lay elsewhere.

topic of sexuality, he did not quite succeed, but the textual evidence suggests that he avoided raising the very questions contemporary readers have been unable to overlook.

But if "The Thing on the Doorstep" is not an exploration of sexuality, what is it? If Lovecraft shows no interest in sexual dynamics, what issues does he explore? The answer is his sensitivity to—and fascination with—disgust. As the title itself indicates, the moment of horror occurs when Asenath's corpse arrives at Upton's door. When it does, Lovecraft displays no interest in the bizarre gender reversal taking place, for Derby is, at that very moment, trapped inside his wife's body. Indeed, Lovecraft does not assign the figure a gender at all, referring to Asenath's corpse as a "thing" in the title and as an "it" in the text (CF 3.357). Instead, Lovecraft dwells on the loathsomeness of Upton's experience:

> It was only afterward that I read the last half of this paper, for I had fainted at the end of the third paragraph. I fainted again when I saw and smelled what cluttered up the threshold where the warm air had struck it. The messenger would not move or have consciousness any more.
>
> The butler, tougher-fibred than I, did not faint at what met him in the hall in the morning. Instead, he telephoned the police. When they came I had been taken upstairs to bed, but the—other mass—lay where it had collapsed in the night. The men put handkerchiefs to their noses.
>
> What they finally found inside Edward's oddly assorted clothes was mostly liquescent horror. There were bones, too—and a crushed-in skull. Some dental work positively identified the skull as Asenath's. (CF 3.357)

With a master's touch, Lovecraft evokes a sense of revulsion, forcing the reader not just to visualize the decomposing corpse that has disintegrated until it is a "mostly liquescent horror," but to smell the "warm air" that wafts over it. Lovecraft seems obsessed with such scenes: corpses that disintegrate in front of the reader also appear in "The Shunned House," "Cool Air," "The Colour out of Space," and "The Dunwich Horror." Curiously, they do not merely rot, but liquefy, becoming in the case of Wilbur in "The Dunwich Horror" "a sticky whitish mass on the painted boards" (CF 2.441).

Such stomach-churning scenes result in a curious paradox, which appears throughout Lovecraft's oeuvre: routine but potentially disgusting experiences are conspicuously absent from the "real world" as Lovecraft depicts it, though the fantastical elements that intrude into this world are invariably and *extraordinarily* repulsive. It is as if Lovecraft (who could not even stand to listen to stories about sex) could not bring himself to write about the human body and the "tedious details of its animal biology," creating instead a fictional environment that seems oddly clean or perhaps even lifeless. And yet, such strong feelings naturally provoke a counterreaction. Just as someone with arachnophobia will stare, spellbound, at a spider, Lovecraft cannot help but gorge himself on the very loathsomeness he struggled to avoid, in the process creating scenes, like the climax to "The Thing on the Doorstep," that are infinitely more disgusting than anything a person would encounter in reality. Just as Lovecraft, in his New York tales, could not help but fixate on the city he wanted to escape, he also cannot resist creating on the page that which he shunned everywhere else. And thus, a man who could not sit in a restaurant that steamed clams writes of the smell created by warm air blowing over a liquefying corpse.

By downplaying Lovecraft's tortured fascination with disgusting stimuli, scholars are not just overlooking the episodes he chose to stress and ignoring an important facet of his personality; they are missing the effect these passages have on the reader. To read Lovecraft's fiction—to read anyone's—is to enter into an imaginary world, only distantly related to the real world, which reflects the author's preferences and perspective. No matter how devoted to realism an author may be, he cannot recreate the world, in all its complexity, on paper. Thus, the pieces the author does include tell the reader something about that author's view of the world—or what the world should be. Lovecraft, confronted by a world of "reservoirs, billboards, and concrete roads, power lines, garages, and flamboyant inns, squalid immigrant nests and grimy mill villages" ("The Whisperer in Darkness" [CF 2.508]), retains what he perceived as elegant (the fanlights, diamond-paned windows, and gambrel roofs of Old New England) and discards the squalor and grime.

In that sense, Lovecraft's fiction is a continuation of his lifelong attempt to replace the alienating norms and inventions of the twentieth century (which he so memorably describes as "cubes and cogs and circles .... segments and squares and shadows [. . .] rotogravures .... radio ..... Babel ..... Bedlam" ["An Account of Charleston," *CE* 3.82]) with the familiar relics of his childhood, "the ponderous furniture & paintings & clocks & books which help to keep 454 always in my dreams" (*LFF* 1.168). The result is a fictional world that is both beautiful and strangely sanitary. Even the characters themselves seem clean, for Lovecraft has scrubbed away life's messiness, banishing what Julia Kristeva calls the abject, those visible signs of our own corporeality, from view. Thus, sex in Lovecraft's work is not so much absent as it is unimaginable. And then, suddenly, into this sanitized space, which he has so thoroughly purified, the loathsome intrudes, staining and blackening everything beyond salvation. Therein lies much of the potency of Lovecraft's work. To read it is to witness the corruption of the world, the fall of Eden. It is to watch as a perfect world, as Lovecraft envisioned it, is spoiled.

V. Conclusion

Of course, one could dismiss such a theory as armchair psychology. Joshi does exactly this when he points out that "it is mere armchair psychoanalysis to say that he [Lovecraft] somehow sublimated his sex urges into writing or other activities" (*IAP* 515). And Joshi, no doubt, is correct. When Moore claims that Lovecraft's work consists of nothing but "cocks and pussies," his analysis tells us more about Moore than it tells about Lovecraft. And yet, Lovecraft encourages readers to analyze his works from a biographical perspective when he writes himself into his own stories. When he creates a character like Derby, a weak-willed man who rashly marries a strong-willed woman, readers cannot help but be shocked when Derby later claims that his wife is actually a man who is trying to steal his body. For better or for worse, Lovecraft cannot be divorced from his work. For those seeking to understand him and his fiction, the theory of latent homosexuality provides an answer, but considering Lovecraft's dislike of physical affection and his sensitivity to disgust (both of which appear in "The Thing on the Doorstep"), ongoing research into "disgust-prone individuals" provides us with a tempting alternative.

Works Cited

Ahn, Woo-Young, et al. "Nonpolitical Images Evoke Neural Predictors of Political Ideology." *Current Biology* 24 (2014): 2693–99.

Andrews, Arthur R., et al. "Correlational and Experimental Analyses of the Relation Between Disgust and Sexual Arousal." *Motivation and Emotion* 39 (2015): 766–79.

Best, Stephen, and Sharon Marcus. "Surface Reading: An Introduction." *Representations* 108 (2009): 1–21.

Borg, Charmaine, and Peter J. de Jong. "Feelings of Disgust and Disgust-Induced Avoidance Weaken Following Induced Sexual Arousal in Women." *PLoS ONE* 7, No. 9 (2012), journals.plos.org/plosone/article?id=10.1371/journal.pone.0044111. Accessed 17 July 2022.

Davis, Sonia H. "Memories of Lovecraft." In S. T. Joshi and David E. Schultz, ed. *Ave atque Vale: Reminiscences of H. P. Lovecraft.* West Warwick, RI: Necronomicon Press, 2018. 152–53.

Derie, Bobby. *Sex and the Cthulhu Mythos.* New York: Hippocampus Press, 2014.

Everts, R. Alain. "Howard Phillips Lovecraft and Sex; or, The Sex Life of a Gentleman." *Nyctalops* 2, No. 2 (July 1974): 19.

Fleischman, Diana S., et al. "Disgust versus Lust: Exploring the Interactions of Disgust and Fear with Sexual Arousal in Women." *PLoS One.* 10, No. 6 (2015), journals.plos.org/plosone/article?id=10.1371/journal.pone.0118151. Accessed 17 July 2022.

Hibbing, John R., et al. "Differences in Negativity Bias Underlie Variations in Political Ideology." *Behavioral and Brain Sciences* 37 (2014): 297–307.

Hölzing, Roland. "Lovecraft: A Gentleman without Five Senses." *Lovecraft Annual* No. 5 (2011): 181–87.

Houellebecq, Michel. *H. P. Lovecraft: Against the World, Against Life*. 1991. Tr. Dorna Khazeni. London: Gollancz, 2008.

Johnson, Brian. "Paranoia, Panic, and the Queer Weird." In Sean Moreland, ed. *New Directions in Supernatural Horror Literature: The Critical Influence of H. P. Lovecraft*. New York: Palgrave Macmillan, 2018. 253–78.

Joshi, S. T. "Excised Passages from 'The Thing on the Doorstep.'" *Lovecraft Annual* No. 7 (2013): 171–77.

———. "March 17, 2022: An Intriguing Letter by Frank Belknap Long." *S. T. Joshi's Blog*, stjoshi.org/news2022.html. Accessed 17 July 2022.

Kristeva, Julia. *Powers of Horror: An Essay on Abjection*. Tr. Leon S. Roudiez. New York: Columbia University Press, 1982.

La Farge, Paul. *The Night Ocean*. New York: Penguin Press, 2017.

Lee, Ellen M., et al. "Effects of Subjective Sexual Arousal on Sexual, Pathogen, and Moral Disgust Sensitivity in Women and Men." *Archives of Sexual Behavior* 43 (2014): 1115–21.

Loucks, Donovan K. "Myth: Lovecraft Was a Homosexual." *The H. P. Lovecraft Archive*, 14 May 2011, www.hplovecraft.com/life/myths.aspx#homosexual. Accessed 17 July 2022.

Lovecraft, H. P., and August Derleth. *Essential Solitude: The Letters of H. P. Lovecraft and August Derleth*. Ed. David E. Schultz and S. T. Joshi. New York: Hippocampus Press, 2008. 2 vols. [Abbreviated in the text as *ES*.]

———. *Letters to Family and Family Friends*. Ed. S. T. Joshi and David E. Schultz. New York: Hippocampus Press, 2020. 2 vols. [Abbreviated in the text as *LFF*.]

———. *Letters to J. Vernon Shea, Carl F. Strauch, and Lee McBride White*. Ed. S. T. Joshi and David E. Schultz. New York: Hippocampus Press, 2016. [Abbreviated in the text as *JVS*.]

———. *Letters to James F. Morton*. Ed. David E. Schultz and S. T. Joshi. New York: Hippocampus Press, 2011. [Abbreviated in the text as *JFM*.]

———. *Letters to Maurice W. Moe and Others*. Ed. David E. Schultz and S. T. Joshi. New York: Hippocampus Press, 2018. [Abbreviated in the text as *MWM*.]

———. *Letters to Rheinhart Kleiner and Others*. Ed. S. T. Joshi and David E. Schultz. New York: Hippocampus Press, 2020.

[Abbreviated in the text as *RK*.]

McAuliffe, Kathleen. "Liberals and Conservatives React in Wildly Different Ways to Repulsive Pictures." *The Atlantic,* March 2019, www.theatlantic.com/magazine/archive/2019/03/the-yuck-factor/580465/. Accessed 17 July 2022.

Matolcsy, Kálmán. "The Innsmouth Thing: Monstrous Androgyny in H. P. Lovecraft's 'The Thing on the Doorstep.'" *Gender Studies* 1 (2004): 171–79.

Moore, Alan (w), Jacen Burrows (p), and Juanmar (i). *Neonomicon*. Rantoul: Avatar Press, 2011.

———. *Providence*. Rantoul: Avatar Press, 2017. 3 vols.

Muise, Peter. "Lovecraft Had to Have a Secret Life." *Gay and Lesbian Review* (July–August 2017), www.glreview.org/article/lovecraft-had-to-have-a-secret-life/. Accessed 17 July 2022.

Oaten, Megan, et al. "The Role of Disgust in Male Sexual Decision-Making." *Frontiers in Psychology* (2019), www.frontiersin.org/articles/10.3389/fpsyg.2018.02602/full. Accessed 17 July 2022.

Overveld, Mark van. "The Sexual Disgust Questionnaire; A Psychometric Study and a First Exploration in Patients with Sexual Dysfunctions." *Journal of Sexual Medicine* 10 (2013): 396–407.

Oxley, Douglas R., et al. "Political Attitudes Vary with Physiological Traits." *Science* 321 (2008): 1667–70.

Pace, Joel. "Queer Tales? Sexuality, Race, and Architecture in 'The Thing on the Doorstep.'" *Lovecraft Annual* No. 2 (2008): 104–37.

Price, E. Hoffmann. "Howard Phillips Lovecraft." In Price's *Book of the Dead: Friends of Yesteryear: Fictioneers and Others*. Sauk City, WI: Arkham House, 2001. 43–69.

Price, Robert M. "Homosexual Panic in 'The Outsider.'" *Crypt of Cthulhu* 1, No. 8 (Michaelmas 1982): 11–13.

Sargent, Stanley C. Interview by Peter A. Worthy. *Mythos Online,* 1997, www.web.archive.org/web/20010511063836/http://geocities.com/Athens/forum/4162/sargent.html/. Accessed 17 July 2022.

Al-Shawaf, Laith, et al. "Disgust and Mating Strategy." *Evolution and Human Behavior* 36 (2015): 199–205.

Shea, J. Vernon. *H. P. Lovecraft: The House and the Shadows*. 1966. West Warwick, RI: Necronomicon Press, 1982.

Smith, Kevin B., et al. "Disgust Sensitivity and the Neurophysiology of Left-Right Political Orientations." *PLoS One* 6, No. 10 (2011): 1–9.

Stevenson, Richard J., et al. "Effect of Self-Reported Sexual Arousal on Responses to Sex-Related and Non-Sex-Related Disgust Cues." *Archives of Sexual Behavior* 40 (2011): 79–85.

Waugh, Robert H. "The Ecstasies of 'The Thing on the Doorstep,' 'Medusa's Coil,' and Other Erotic Studies." *Lovecraft Annual* No. 4 (2010): 136–62.

Zhang, Jing, et al. "Moral and Sexual Disgust Suppress Sexual Risk Behaviors among Men Who Have Sex with Men in China." *Frontiers in Psychology* (2017), www.frontiersin.org/articles/10.3389/fpsyg.2016.02045/full. Accessed 17 July 2022.

Briefly Noted

Cadabra Records continues its recording of Lovecraft's works. To date, it has issued readings of "The Hound" and "The Music of Erich Zann" (2016), "The Lurking Fear" (2016), "Dagon," "The Cats of Ulthar," and "The Music of Erich Zann" (2018), *At the Mountains of Madness* (2020), "Beyond the Wall of Sleep" (2021), and "The Shadow out of Time" (2022). All were read by Andrew Leman, with liner notes by S. T. Joshi. A reading of *The Case of Charles Dexter Ward* is forthcoming. Leman read "The Lurking Fear" and "The Dunwich Horror" at the Nightlands Festival (2–3 June) held in Hammonton, NJ.

The Esoteric Order of Dagon amateur press association recently celebrated its fiftieth anniversary. It was founded in June 1973 by Joseph Pumilia and Roger Bryant and has generated a substantial amount of Lovecraft scholarship, much of it subsequently disseminated in other print or online venues. Such leading figures in Lovecraft scholarship as Ken Faig, Jr., Dirk W. Mosig, J. Vernon Shea, Ben Indick, Donald R. Burleson, David E. Schultz, and Steven J. Mariconda have been members; some continue to be members to the present day. S. T. Joshi has been its official editor since 1987.

A Ghoul's Progress: On Art, Ekphrasis, and Image in "Pickman's Model"

Andrew Paul Wood

Of all the rhetorical exercises of the ancient world, few have been so widely revived discussed (and, dare I say it, misunderstood) in contemporary critical discourse than ekphrasis—the creative, vivid description of an image. The *Merriam-Webster Dictionary* and OED give the date of the earliest known use of the word in English as 1715, though it is a relatively recent inclusion in those and other dictionaries, and it is unlikely that Lovecraft would have used the word or been aware of it. He was, however, a master of ekphrasis's use.

Most often this image is a work of art, either real or imagined. The Hellenistic sophists Philostratus the Elder (190?–230? C.E.) and Philostratus the Younger (3rd century C.E.), *grand-père et grand-fils*, each produced a collection of descriptions of (probably imaginary) artworks in gallery settings—the defining examples of ekphrasis separated from a larger narrative as a literary form in its own right. Confusingly both works have the same name: *eikones* in Greek and *imagines* in Latin. For the Philostrati these descriptions were not merely literary *topoi*, but philosophical meditations on the epistemology and ambiguity of seeing that drew on the Cynic and Stoic schools. Paintings are treated as complex literary texts, framed as a lesson in artistic appreciation (Shaffer 303).

This narrow definition of ekphrasis as a description of an artwork is the most widely expressed one in the post-medieval period, but this was not always the case. Any sufficiently vivid description that causes the reader or listener to imagine the sce-

ne from words alone could be an ekphrasis. The rhetorician
Hermogenes of Tarsus, writing during the reign of the Roman
emperor Marcus Aurelius, describes ekphrasis thus:

> Ekphrasis is an account with detail; it is visible, so to speak, and
> brings before the eyes that which is to be shown. Ekphrases are
> of people, actions, times, places, seasons, and many other
> things. ... The special virtues of an ekphrasis are clarity and
> visibility; the style must contrive to bring about seeing through
> hearing. However, it is equally important that expression should
> fit the subject: if the subject is florid, let the style be florid too,
> and if the subject is dry, let the style be the same. (Baxandall 85)

A magnificent example of this intuitive understanding of ekphrasis in Lovecraft, unrestricted to describing an artwork, is his
description of the monstrous naked corpse of Wilbur Whateley
in "The Dunwich Horror" (1928), expressing the three qualities
most prized by the rhetoricians of antiquity: *enargeia* (vividness),
sapheneia (clarity), and *phantasia* (mental image) in abundance
(cf. Zeitlin 17). It is pure, unsubtle nightmare fuel, executed
with the kind of forensic exactitude one might apply to describing a sculpture.

In his study of Cervantes, Fredrik de Armas supplies this
more broadly analytical definition:

> In terms of form and function, ekphrasis can be *allegorical, em-
> blematic, decorative,* or *veiled;* and it can serve as a *rhetorical or
> mnemonic device* (or both). ... In terms of pictorial models and
> how these are used, ekphrasis can be *notional* (based on an im-
> agined work of art), or *actual and true* (based on a real work of
> art). It can also be *combinatory* (combining two or more works of
> art), *transformative* (changing some elements of the art work in-
> to others that can be connected to the original ones),
> *metadescriptive* (based on a textual description of a work of art
> which may or may not exist), or *fragmented* (using parts of a
> work). Ekphrasis can conform to the pause in the narrative to
> describe an object (descriptive ekphrasis), or it can tell the story
> depicted in the art work and even expand on the incidents
> (narrative ekphrasis). (21–22)

Throughout Lovecraft's oeuvre we can find examples of nearly all these variants to one degree or another. Although ekphrasis had long existed as a narrative technique and literary exercise—Homer's account of the shield of Achilles in the *Iliad* being the earliest—it is Virgil's *Aeneid* and the description of the murals of Dido's temple of Juno that provide the first surviving examples of a narrator describing a work of art through the eyes of the protagonist. Here Virgil allows Aeneas' evaluations of quality and biases inform our experience of what he sees (Putnam 243). This does not mean, however, that the reader must completely relinquish agency; as is frequently the case in Lovecraft, the reader is often contextually more aware of what the author is alluding to than the protagonist is—a *prolepsis* or foreshadowing. "Ekphrasis," as Michael Trussler observes, "creates a kind of ontological miniature that signals a world beyond the confines of the text" (261).

Lovecraft had a wonderfully visual imagination, lavishing it with purple embellishment on things that are so alien to experience that they would defy the descriptive abilities of a lesser imagination. Indeed, describing things as indescribable but often describing them anyway, in precise detail, is an identifiable Lovecraftian trope. It is almost as if Lovecraft is trying to cast his stories with the quotidian acceptance of gods and monsters in the tradition of the epic. This tendency, in my opinion, sometimes diminishes the atmosphere of his creations a little too much, dispelling the fug of terror with too much direct light. Lovecraft also very much enjoyed the visual arts. His love of art and facility with descriptive language converge in his use of ekphrasis in several of his stories but is particularly interesting in "Pickman's Model." This is, not least, because one of the themes of the story is the psyche of the driven artist and the lengths—at least as a Gothic-Romantic trope—they will go to in pursuit of their art. It is a well-established conceit in the works of two of Lovecraft's models, Hawthorne and Poe.

"Pickman's Model," written in 1926 and published the following year, is the tale of the Boston artist Richard Upton Pickman, painter of horrifying and fantastically grotesque images.

His work is technically brilliant but so graphically realistic that his membership of the Boston Art Club is withdrawn, and he and his paintings are shunned by Boston's art community. One suspects there is an echo here of Lovecraft's real-life attempts to promote Clark Ashton Smith as an illustrator to *Weird Tales*. The narrator, Thurber, Pickman's friend, relates to another acquaintance, the silent Eliot, following Pickman's mysterious disappearance, his visit to the latter's secret studio in the slums of Boston, leading to a horrid revelation.[1]

Pickman probably represents Lovecraft's own view of his work, always more artistically ambitious than the establishment gave him credit for, a creative spirit apart from conventional literature. This is more explicit here than in the similarly themed "Music of Erich Zann." In "Pickman's Model," through the character of Thurber, Lovecraft adopts the role of a connoisseur, both to demonstrate his own aesthetic credentials and to establish a baseline of what may be regarded a rational, *normal* response to art and the fantastical grotesque. The criticisms of Pickman's art by the Boston establishment recall (and anticipate) similar criticisms directed at Lovecraft's fiction throughout his life and beyond, such as Edmund Wilson's 1945 review eight years after Lovecraft's death, which described his writing as "hackwork" and dismissing *Weird Tales* and *Amazing Stories*, "where [Lovecraft's stories] ought to have been left" (Wilson 288). The preference for figuration and Old Masters chimes with what Jason Ray Carney detects in the use of ekphrasis by Lovecraft, Smith, and Howard, as a deliberate attempt to subvert modernism and modernity.

With that baseline established, Lovecraft progressively diverges from it to create an atmosphere of increasing weirdness and the *Unheimlich*. As Vivian Ralickas observes, this is probably a deliberate stratagem on Lovecraft's part, to set a tone of anti-

---

1. Although the name Pickman belongs to an established real-world Boston family of note—for example, Edward Motley Pickman (1850–1938), who gave his name to the Edward M. Pickman Concert Hall at Bard College's Longy School of Music in Cambridge—one may read a pun in the title: pick the model of which man is to become.

humanist cosmicism ubiquitous in the oeuvre. The typical Love-craft story seeks to undermine comfortable consensus reality—the reader's and the narrator's false sense of identity—and lays bare the vulnerability of the human sensorium and sanity in the face of our ingrained impulse to ascribe meaning and agency to things. Despite the Lovecraftian protagonists' self-delusion about a moral, non-arbitrary universe, ultimately they are inca-pable of maintaining an objective appreciation of either the gro-tesque or even the beautiful (Ralickas 297). Mystery is often a product of Lovecraftian ekphrasis, suggesting that mystery plays a role in Lovecraft's aesthetic theory of art (Ralickas 299). This is not a new spin on ekphrasis, as something very similar occurs in Canto 33 of Ariosto's *Orlando Furioso* (1532) describing a pic-ture gallery created by the wizard Merlin.

Indeed, it is not the grotesque aspect of the ghoul that is ter-rifying, but, as Ondřej Šmejka notes, the in-world ontological existence of the ghoul, despite the atmosphere of distance culti-vated by the ekphrasis of an a priori denial of such a possibility, even hypothetically (Šmejka 76). Thurber initially seeks to ra-tionalize the uncanny in the story, as if description can control it. This is why the use of ekphrasis is so effective in the story: as Peter Wagner puts it, "Ekphrasis, then, has a Janus face: as a form of mimesis, it stages a paradoxical performance, promising to give voice to the allegedly silent image even while attempting to overcome the power of the image by transforming and in-scribing it" (13).

Through Thurber's exposition to the silent reader surrogate Eliot, we learn that he is interested in and presumably knowl-edgeable about "weird art," having met Pickman while writing a monograph on the subject. He describes himself as "fairly hard-boiled," "middle-aged and decently sophisticated" (CF 2.66[b]), and draws attention to his emotional sturdiness having experi-enced the horrors of the trenches of France in the First World War, although this has left him with a phobia about under-ground spaces (Lovecraft, *More Annotated* 219). He is unwitting-ly setting himself up for Lovecraft to pull a metaphorical rug out from under him. Given this stolidity, S. T. Joshi and David E.

Schultz regard his descent into hysteria "implausible" (205), but perhaps Lovecraft is suggesting that it is the posture of sanity and reason in the face of cosmic horror, once shown to be real, that is the implausibility.

> You know, it takes profound art and profound insight into Nature to turn out stuff like Pickman's. Any magazine-cover hack can splash paint around wildly and call it a nightmare or a Witches' Sabbath or a portrait of the devil, but only a great painter can make such a thing really scare or ring true. That's because only a real artist knows the actual anatomy of the terrible or the physiology of fear—the exact sort of lines and proportions that connect up with latent instincts or hereditary memories of fright, and the proper colour contrasts and lighting effects to stir the dormant sense of strangeness. I don't have to tell you why a Fuseli really brings a shiver while a cheap ghost-story frontispiece merely makes us laugh. There's something those fellows catch—beyond life—that they're able to make us catch for a second. Doré had it. Sime has it. Angarola of Chicago has it. And Pickman had it as no man ever had it before or—I hope to heaven—ever will again. (CF 2.57–58)

Thurber's defense of Pickman recalls Lovecraft's appraisal of Poe in "Supernatural Horror in Literature," written at the same time (Joshi and Schultz 205). James Machin detects in Lovecraft the influence of Walter Pater (1839–1894) and his theories regarding the consolation of aesthetics, which Machin suggests was partly Lovecraft's strategy in psychologically processing an arbitrary and meaningless universe. Lovecraft, having demonstrated his mastery of critical and technical vocabulary to his satisfaction through the proxy of Thurber, takes the opportunity to insert an unorthodox list of some of his favorite artists of the weird, exhibiting his art-historical literacy and biases, and giving his story some anchoring realism in the same way dropping references to historical and fictional texts does. Later he mentions another artist:

> You recall that Pickman's forte was faces. I don't believe anybody since Goya could put so much of sheer hell into a set of

features or a twist of expression. And before Goya you have to go back to the mediaeval chaps who did the gargoyles and chimaeras on Notre Dame and Mont Saint-Michel. (CF 2.58)

Lovecraft deftly primes the informed reader with what sort of artist Pickman is, and more importantly, how to visualize Pickman's paintings informed by ekphrasis. While the grotesque, the uncanny, and the frightening had established itself as a genre in the visual arts by the late eighteenth century, it was in around 1800 that it gained previously inconceivable prominence in the popular cultural imagination. Canvases became populated with witches, demons, ghosts, the mentally ill, dream imagery, hell, and apocalyptic visions. Francisco Goya (1746–1828) and Henry Fuseli (1741–1825) belong to this period, and the engraver and illustrator Gustave Doré (1832–1883) was an heir to that tradition, though much more of a neoclassicist.

Goya is an interesting case. His earnest depictions of the horrors of war and his society, once placed in an art gallery, become aestheticized in a way that the artist had probably not intended. Likewise, Thurber exhibits confusion in his attempt to understand Pickman's paintings as aesthetic objects rather than a kind of veneration of an outside reality. It is difficult to know whether Lovecraft had actually seen works by these artists in the flesh, though it was certainly possible. The Rhode Island School of Design Museum holds an extensive collection of Goya etchings and a Thomas Burke engraving of Fuseli's infamous *The Nightmare* (1783). The latter clearly inspired the sentence, "Occasionally these things were shown leaping through windows at night, or squatting on the chests of sleepers, worrying at their throats" (CF 2.64). The Metropolitan Museum of Art holds a number of Fuseli drawings that Lovecraft might have seen during his New York period. Given the inclusion of illustrators in the list, however, one suspects Lovecraft's main exposure to the other artists was through reproductions in books.

Doré is ubiquitous in the period through his illustrations in popular editions of the Bible, *Paradise Lost,* and *Don Quixote.* Doré also has an impeccable weird provenance, being used in a story by M. R. James (1862–1936). This occurs in "The Mezzotint" (1904), in which the rustic retainer remarks:

> "No, Sir. Why, the pore child, I recollect once she see a Door Bible, with pictures not 'alf what that is, and we 'ad to set up with her three or four nights afterwards, if you'll believe me; and if she was to catch sight of this skelinton here, or whatever it is, carrying off the pore baby, she would be in a taking. You know 'ow it is with children; 'ow nervish they get with a little thing and all. But what I should say, it don't seem a right pictur to be laying about, sir, not where anyone that's liable to be startled could come on it. (49)

Sime is, of course, Sidney H. Sime (1865–1941), Lord Dunsany's preferred illustrator, who belongs to a group of illustrators and artists I shall call the post-Beardsley school in that they are clearly heavily influenced by the Decadent-Symbolist version of Pre-Raphaelitism and Arts and Crafts design of Aubrey Beardsley (1872–1898). This category includes Harry Clarke (1889–1931), Austin Osman Spare (1886–1956), Alastair (Hans Henning Baron von Voight, 1887–1961), Wallace Smith (1888–1937) among others. The Chicago-based Anthony Angarola (1893–1929) also fits within this group, being clearly influenced by Beardsley and Clarke.

Lovecraft's interest in Angarola is something of a paradox. It seems highly unlikely that prudish Lovecraft would have responded favorably for the highly erotic work Angarola is best known for, Ben Hecht's *The Kingdom of Evil: A Continuation of the Journal of Fantazius Mallare* (1924). Yet he clearly knew Angarola's work enough to use it as a point of reference in a simile for the debauched cultic orgy in "The Call of Cthulhu"; he wrote to Richard Ely Morse in 1932: "Sorry to hear that Angarola is dead. He almost illustrated my 'Outsider'—that is, he read it & told Wright he'd like to illustrate it just after the present illustration had been made & purchased!" (*Letters to Hyman Bradofsky* 37). In the end the story was illustrated by Angarola's student and alleged mistress Belle Goldschlager (later Baranceanu, 1902–1988) in *Weird Tales*, April 1926.

Returning to the subject of ekphrasis, in describing Pick-

man's paintings Lovecraft draws on tropes of grotesque or Gothic art that are so familiar as to suggest that he has a real-world
model at least partly in mind. There is, for example no shortage
of Goya etchings and Fuseli drawings, supernatural and satirical,
that might furnish the basis for the following description:

> There was one thing called "The Lesson"—heaven pity me,
> that I ever saw it! Listen—can you fancy a squatting circle of
> nameless dog-like things in a churchyard teaching a small child
> how to feed like themselves? The price of a changeling, I sup-
> pose—you know the old myth about how the weird people leave
> their spawn in cradles in exchange for the human babes they
> steal. Pickman was shewing what happens to those stolen
> babes—how they grow up—and then I began to see a hideous
> relationship in the faces of the human and non-human figures.
> He was, in all his gradations of morbidity between the frankly
> non-human and the degradedly human, establishing a sardonic
> linkage and evolution. The dog-things were developed from
> mortals! (CF 2.65)

There is a strong echo of the pseudo-science of physiognomy
here, which, like its sister pseudo-science, phrenology, was
popular from the seventeenth century into the nineteenth century as a way of determining character. The French artist
Charles Le Brun (1619–1690) around 1671 produced a series of
illustrations showing human types compared with the animals
they resembled in face and personality.

Here, too, Lovecraft implies a connected cycle of images. It is
fairly typical of ekphrastic description to outline the artist's
schema, which in this case sounds like a ghoulish recapitulation
of Hogarth's series of eight paintings A Rake's Progress (1732–
34), which were engraved in 1734 and published in print form in
1735. It is perhaps unsurprising that we find an admiring Lovecraft placing Hogarth with Goya in a letter to William Lumley in
1931: "Another artist who went even farther than Hogarth in
depicting human bestiality is the Spaniard, Goya" (Letters to
Woodburn Harris 446). Call it "A Ghoul's Progress." The sequence continues:

And no sooner had I wondered what he made of their own young as left with mankind in the form of changelings, than my eye caught a picture embodying that very thought. It was that of an ancient Puritan interior—a heavily beamed room with lattice windows, a settle, and clumsy seventeenth-century furniture, with the family sitting about while the father read from the Scriptures. Every face but one shewed nobility and reverence, but that one reflected the mockery of the pit. It was that of a young man in years, and no doubt belonged to a supposed son of that pious father, but in essence it was the kin of the unclean things. It was their changeling—and in a spirit of supreme irony Pickman had given the features a very perceptible resemblance to his own. (CF 2.65)

In this instance ekphrasis serves to emphasize the mundanity of the scene, attempting to bridge intervening Enlightenment cynicism to focus on the reality of the changeling for the superstitious seventeenth century. It brings forth a sense of the futility of Christianity to defend against this ancient phenomenon. Ekphrasis also serves to hint that the scene may be more real and historical than the erstwhile protagonist and reader surrogate might initially suppose. For all that the foreshadowing here is somewhat heavy-handed, it is a marvelous vignette, like something from the pages of Nathaniel Hawthorne inset as a story within a story. The "changeling" is emphatically a proxy for Pickman, the atavism of a portrait recalling a similar scene in *The Case of Charles Dexter Ward* (1927) and the sequence continues to progress.

Dances in the modern cemeteries were freely pictured, and another conception somehow shocked me more than all the rest— a scene in an unknown vault, where scores of the beasts crowded about one who held a well-known Boston guide-book and was evidently reading aloud. All were pointing to a certain passage, and every face seemed so distorted with epileptic and reverberant laughter that I almost thought I heard the fiendish echoes. The title of the picture was, "Holmes, Lowell, and Longfellow Lie Buried in Mount Auburn". (CF 2.66–67)

This sounds a great deal like a merging of two Goya paintings, *Men Reading* and *Women Laughing*, both companion pieces painted between 1819 and 1823. The image suggests the tradition of *vanitas* or *memento mori* painting, that fame is fleeting and ultimately dust as it is intimated that the corpses of these great New England poets no longer lie beneath their monuments but were long since devoured by the ghouls. It mocks the cultural pretentions of the modern world and perhaps allegorizes Lovecraft's xenophobic anxieties about possible cultural dilution and erosion through immigration. The illusion of sound implied by the silent painting is an intimation of the descriptive painterly skill of Pickman.

> Gad, how that man could paint! There was a study called "Subway Accident", in which a flock of the vile things were clambering up from some unknown catacomb through a crack in the floor of the Boylston Street subway and attacking a crowd of people on the platform. Another shewed a dance on Copp's Hill among the tombs with the background of today. Then there were any number of cellar views, with monsters creeping in through holes and rifts in the masonry and grinning as they squatted behind barrels or furnaces and waited for their first victim to descend the stairs. (CF 2.66)

The title "Subway Accident" suggests a newspaper headline rather than a painting, which may have inspired the idea. One may presume that Lovecraft chose the Boylston Street station because the line was built hard by Boston's old Central Burying Ground, as discussed in a 1894 report by Dr. Samuel Abbott Green (1830–1918), former mayor of Boston and the librarian for the Massachusetts Historical Society, to the Boston Transit Commission. Regarding the "cellar views," Sidney Sime produced a number of compositions depicting underground chambers and caverns populated by monstrous creatures, typically with mysterious entrances and portals not otherwise involved in the narrative in dramatic, multi-point perspective. Examples of this include *Kai* (1906) and *He Felt as a Morsel* (1912). To an extent, one is also reminded of images such as the eerie engraving of werewolves standing upright by a churchyard wall, produced by Maurice Sand (1823–1889) to illustrate the *Légendes Rustiques* (1858) of his mother George Sand (1804–1876).

The most concrete example where Lovecraft appears to be providing an ekphrasis of a known real-world painting is the following, which is widely accepted to be based on Goya's *Saturn Devouring His Son* (1820–23) with the addition of the canine features of a Lovecraftian ghoul:

> It was a colossal and nameless blasphemy with glaring red eyes, and it held in bony claws a thing that had been a man, gnawing at the head as a child nibbles at a stick of candy. Its position was a kind of crouch, and as one looked one felt that at any moment it might drop its present prey and seek a juicier morsel. But damn it all, it wasn't even the fiendish subject that made it such an immortal fountain-head of all panic—not that, nor the dog face with its pointed ears, bloodshot eyes, flat nose, and drooling lips. It wasn't the scaly claws nor the mould-caked body nor the half-hooved feet—none of these, though any one of them might well have driven an excitable man to madness. (CF 2.69)

This is an example of the rhetorical technique *hypotyposis* or *diatyposis*—a vivid evocation intended to appeal to the eye rather than the ear in order to inspire an intense emotional response—in this case, one of terror and revulsion (cf. Morales 77). As the original is in the Prado in Madrid, Lovecraft can only have seen this grisly work in reproduction. It is interesting to consider that Clark Ashton Smith's story "The Colossus of Ylourgne," published a few years later in 1934, makes similar ekphrastic use of a Goya painting: in Smith's case Goya's *The Colossus* (1808), likewise in the Prado. Smith also gets name-checked as an artist in "Pickman's Model." In my opinion, the line "gnawing at the head as a child nibbles at a stick of candy" is perhaps one of the most vivid and evocative things Lovecraft ever wrote.

Although Goya dispensed with the mappable space of classical linear perspective, letting the viewer's perception oscillate between a sense of deep, dark space and shallow pictorial flatness, the thing that makes Goya's art so terrifying is his technical precision, his draftsmanship, and his grounding in some kind of naturalism. Irrespective of the outlandishness or supernaturality of the scene, Goya's inventiveness derives from selective observation of actual physical types of his time, usually in mockery of superstition and theocracy. Goya, for all his depictions of horror and nightmare, was a product of Enlightenment thought struggling to gain a foothold in priest-ridden, Inquisition-haunted Spain. This compromise between realism and the unreal has much in common with Lovecraft's own complicated relationship with realism and fantasy, and Goya's cynicism has much in common with Lovecraft's. They are a perfect pairing.

Graham Harman, betraying a lack of understanding of what Picasso and Braque were actually about, attempts to make a case for Lovecraft's prosody being a kind of "literary cubism" (234), because of its use of allusions, innuendo, and ambiguity in offering an oblique access to a higher cosmic reality. Color is analogous, and "formless" is a frequently used adjective. That said, Lovecraft tends to describe the individual parts of his narratives in unflinching realistic detail, eschewing impressionistic effects once he had gotten out from under the shadow of Dunsany.

Acknowledging the gaps in reality and perception is not the same thing as abstraction, and formlessness does not mean the literal lacking of form, as it is a form in itself. Sean Elliot Martin interprets "Pickman's Model" as a critique of the Imagist movement characterized by Ezra Pound, James Joyce, and Amy Lowell (68n36). This is certainly plausible, and yet, for all Lovecraft's florid vocabulary and narrative obfuscations, he wielded his prose with all the precision of an eighteenth-century naturalist describing a new species of butterfly.

Lovecraft's aesthetic preferences in the visual arts likewise prioritize realism, naturalism, and descriptive accuracy. In his letters he tends to be scathing of Modernist art and only references it in his fiction when he requires an analogy for something truly alien as in At the Mountains of Madness (1931):[2] "Those who see our photographs will probably find its closest analogue in certain grotesque conceptions of the most daring futurists" (CF 3.88); and "The Call of Cthulhu," where he juxtaposes the

---

2. Fully a third of the narrative is conveyed in ekphrastic form.

"vagaries of cubism and futurism" with the "cryptic regularity, which lurks in prehistoric writing" (CF 2.23). Throughout "Pickman's Model" Lovecraft emphasizes the realism of Pickman's paintings, not just because it makes the denouement possible, but because that is how he approached his own writing:

> It was the technique, Eliot—the cursed, the impious, the unnatural technique! As I am a living being, I never elsewhere saw the actual breath of life so fused into a canvas. The monster was there—it glared and gnawed and gnawed and glared—and I knew that only a suspension of Nature's laws could ever let a man paint a thing like that without a model—without some glimpse of the nether world which no mortal unsold to the Fiend has ever had.
>
> . . . Their art was the art that convinced—when we saw the pictures we saw the daemons themselves and were afraid of them. And the queer part was, that Pickman got none of his power from the use of selectiveness or bizarrerie. Nothing was blurred, distorted, or conventionalised; outlines were sharp and life-like, and details were almost painfully defined. And the faces!
>
> It was not any mere artist's interpretation that we saw; it was pandemonium itself, crystal clear in stark objectivity. That was it, by heaven! The man was not a fantaisiste or romanticist at all—he did not even try to give us the churning, prismatic ephemera of dreams, but coldly and sardonically reflected some stable, mechanistic, and well-established horror-world which he saw fully, brilliantly, squarely, and unfalteringly. God knows what that world can have been, or where he ever glimpsed the blasphemous shapes that loped and trotted and crawled through it; but whatever the baffling source of his images, one thing was plain. Pickman was in every sense—in conception and in execution—a thorough, painstaking, and almost scientific *realist*. (CF 2.69, 67)

Even so, Lovecraft had a complicated relationship with literary realism, writing to Frank Belknap Long that he disliked Henry Fielding's *Tom Jones* (1749) and failed to find any beauty in realism (SL 1.282), but this pertains more to social—or, rather, sexual—realism than to naturalism or mimesis per se. The dynamic and horrific scenes in the described paintings are a counterpoint of the otherwise conventional and expected mundanity of Pickman's studio. The descriptions of the paintings set up the studio as a kind of "Chapel Perilous" where Thurber will be forced to confront and contest the horror of extra-contextual reality.

Thurber marvels at the way Pickman has seemingly given realism to what is presumed fantasy, and morbid fantasy at that, describing it in terminology more appropriate for mimesis, only for it to be revealed at the denouement that it is painted from life. Or at least, undeath. Diana Shaffer calls this the "appeal to wonder" inherent in ekphrasis (308). Like Philostratus, Thurber praises the painter for his technical virtuosity and stimulus to the imagination, but ultimately seems more fascinated by its sentiment. This is an upending of the traditional paradox of art so realistic it deceives the eye into thinking it real. Rather it deceives the narrator into thinking what turns out to be in-text reality is fiction, reading beyond the phenomenology of the painting into transcendental cosmic horror, but interpreting it as fantasy.

So vivid are Lovecraft's Pickman ekphrases, in part emphasized by his narrational assertion of their realism, that a number of artists have over the years attempted to interpret them visually, superimposing another layer of interpretation on the narrative. "Pickman's Model" is already a narrative onion of relationships and meta-relationships between creator and audience, description and interpretation, mimesis and invention. There is a kind of nested matryoshka doll-like *mise en abyme* at play. The reader understands that they are reading fiction. In that fiction a narrator relates to a fictional audience his descriptions of paintings which he at first thought were fictions. The paintings themselves are descriptions of a horrific preternatural reality. It is ekphrasis that binds these layers together.

Steven J. Mariconda's 1993 survey of objects in Lovecraft's work, "H. P. Lovecraft: Art, Artifact and Reality," mines the author's letters extensively for a philosophy of aesthetics to support the premise that art "enables us to see reality as it truly is" (12).

As Ralickas points out, this neglects the responses of characters within the narrative to these objects and what their critical function within the Lovecraftian text (298–99). That critical stratum in Lovecraft's work is often conveyed through ekphrasis, particularly in the case of "Pickman's Model," and it is through ekphrasis that Thurber indirectly describes the corrosive process of revelation inflicted on him through his fetishistic gaze. This is analogous to a similar process of revelation via ekphrasis and fetishistic gaze in "The Picture in the House" (1920).

Ekphrasis is ultimately an essential functional and pragmatic component of the narrative machinery of "Pickman's Model" and of Lovecraft's oeuvre as a whole.

Works Cited

Baxandall, Michael. *Giotto and the Orators*. Oxford: Oxford University Press, 1971.

Carney, Jason Ray. *Weird Tales of Modernity: The Ephemerality of the Ordinary in the Stories of Robert E. Howard, Clark Ashton Smith, and H. P. Lovecraft*. Jefferson, NC: McFarland, 2019.

de Armas, Fredrik. *Ekphrasis in the Age of Cervantes*. Lewisburg, PA: Bucknell University Press, 2005.

Harman, Graham. *Weird Realism: Lovecraft and Philosophy*. London: Zero Books, 2012.

James, M. R. *Collected Ghost Stories*. 1931. Ware, UK: Wordsworth, 1992.

Joshi, S. T., and David E. Schultz. *An H. P. Lovecraft Encyclopedia*. 2001. New York: Hippocampus Press 2004.

Lovecraft, H. P. *Letters to Hyman Bradofsky and Others*. Ed. David E. Schultz and S. T. Joshi. New York: Hippocampus Press, 2023.

———. *Letters to Woodburn Harris and Others*. Ed. S. T. Joshi and David E. Schultz. New York: Hippocampus Press, 2022.

———. *More Annotated Lovecraft*. Ed. S. T. Joshi and Peter Cannon. New York: Dell, 1999.

Machin, James. "Lovecraft, Decadence and Aestheticism." In Clive Bloom, ed. *The Palgrave Handbook of Contemporary Gothic*. London: Palgrave Macmillan, 2020. 1223–27.

Martin, Sean Elliot. "H. P. Lovecraft and the Modernist Grotesque." Ph.D. diss.: Duquesne University, 2008.

Mariconda, Steven J. "H. P. Lovecraft: Art, Artifact and Reality." *Lovecraft Studies* No. 29 (Fall 1993): 2–12.

Morales, Helen. "Phantasising Phryne: The Psychology and Ethics of 'Ekphrasis.'" *Cambridge Classical Journal* 57 (2011): 71–104.

Putnam, Michael C. J. "Dido's Murals and Virgilian Ekphrasis." *Harvard Studies in Classical Philology* 98 (1998): 243–75.

Ralickas, Vivian. "Art, Cosmic Horror, and the Fetishizing Gaze in the Fiction of H. P. Lovecraft." *Journal of the Fantastic in the Arts* 19, No. 3 (2008): 297–316.

Shaffer, Diana. "Ekphrasis and the Rhetoric of Viewing in Philostratus's Imaginary Museum." *Philosophy and Rhetoric* 31 (1998): 303–16.

Šmejka, Ondřej. "Azathoth Negative: H. P. Lovecraft and the Unrepresentable Vistas of Ontology." M.A. thesis: Anglo American University, 2015.

Trussler, Michael. "Literary Artifacts: Ekphrasis in the Short Fiction of Donald Barthelme, Salman Rushdie, and John Edgar Wideman." *Contemporary Literature* 41 (2000): 252–90.

Wagner, Peter, ed. *Icons-Text-Iconotexts: Essays on Ekphrasis and Intermediary.* New York: de Gruyter, 1996.

Wilson, Edmund. *Classics and Commercials: A Literary Chronicle of the Forties.* New York: Farrar, Straus, 1950.

Zeitlan, Froma I. "Figure: Ekphrasis." *Greece and Rome* (Second Series) 60 (2013): 17–31.

The Pop Cultural Lovecraft: Two Snapshots

Duncan Norris

On 20 February 2020 the British Film Institute (BFI) published on its website a list of "10 Great Lovecraftian Horror Films," written by critic and cultural commentator Anna Bogutskaya. As one might expect given the title, format, and publishing locale, it was a habitual mixture of the almost mandatory older inclusions (*Alien*, 1979; *The Thing*, 1981), genre choices that were box-office disappointments but widely beloved by later audiences (*Event Horizon*, 1997; *The Cabin in the Woods*, 2011), more esoteric but still relatively mainstream fare such as *In the Mouth of Madness* (1994) and *Annihilation* (2018), an outlier in *The Mist* (2007), a non-Western entry in Japanese-language *Uzumaki* [*Spiral*] (2000), an indie, *The Endless* (2017), and oddity in *True Detective* Season 1 (2014), which, while it has a single continuous story with the same writer and same director for all eight episodes, is obviously not a feature film. The foregoing is not meant as a criticism of Bogutskaya's choices. Most lists upon the topic, including mine, would have much crossover with the above selections, and I personally like almost all, and love many, of the cited examples.

But the point of this examination is not to wax poetical about the merits of films one likes. Instead it is to use Bogutskaya's list as a starting point to examine the effects, perceptions, and interconnections of Lovecraft in modern pop culture.

Perhaps most obviously, none of the above films is based on a Lovecraft story,[1] which is telling in itself. The *great* in "Love-

---

1. An argument could be made that John W. Campbell's novella "Who Goes There?," which is the basis for *The Thing*, is a riff—or less kind terms—on

craftian" does not need to spring direct from the font, it seems. Given the very deliberate way in which Lovecraft creates his menaces, so deeply shadowed and buried in half-glimpses, negative impressions, and results rather than confrontations, it is far from coincidental that those drawing upon his work in the visual medium of cinema seem to find greater success with his ideas and atmosphere than in projection of his monstrous beings on screen.

Yet therein lies a paradox. "Lovecraftian" in the BFI listing is specifically grounded upon the adaptation of the ideas of others. *Annihilation* (2014) is based upon Jeff VanderMeer's novel of the same name. *The Thing*—technically a remake of—*The Thing from Another World* (1951), by director John Carpenter's own stated mission, extends to John W. Campbell's novella "Who Goes There?" (*Astounding Science Fiction*, August 1938) draws on the paranoid and transformative elements that make the tale so effective, and that are absent in director Christian Nyby's[2] version. *The Mist* is based on a Stephen King novella of the same name,[3] while *Uzumaki* is a manga serial subsequently issued in various bound editions, although at the time the film was made the manga had not been completed. Also important to this idea of literary origins is the fact that the terminology and iconography associated with Robert W. Chambers's *The King in Yellow* (1895)—whose reputation and survival into the twenty-first century is due almost entirely to Lovecraft's praise of it and arrogation of several terms of Chambers into his own work—play a key if subtle part in *True Detective*. Further germane to the issue, *True Detective* is the name of a very famous and extremely long-lived pulp magazine, which actually began in Lovecraft's day in 1924 as *True Detective Mysteries*.

Filmmaking is inherently a cooperative endeavor, and as such influences are naturally abundant; yet for these films, such connections are more specific. Co-writer of *Alien* Dan O'Bannon ad-

---

Lovecraft's *At the Mountains of Madness*, but that ground need not be re-trod here, and this very point feeds into the topic under discussion.

2. And perhaps Howard Hawks. Again that ground need not be re-trod here.

3. First published in the anthology *Dark Forces* (1980), but referenced here from the more commonly accessible lead story in *Skeleton Crew* (1985).

mitted that *The Thing from Another World* was one of a plethora of important inspirations on his script, whereas *The Cabin in the Woods'* entire premise is awash in the iconography, plot beats, character tropes, and details of previous horror films as an entire genre. By design its audience is expected to be familiar with all these aspects,[4] which inform the ultimate revelation that all such elements are part of an elaborate ritual of pain, suffering, and human sacrifice being orchestrated for the entertainment and appeasement of slumbering ancient gods. Even more to the point is the art of famous Swiss surrealist and core creator of the biomechanical genre of art, H. R. Giger, that suffuses *Alien* and links it back to the Lovecraftian quite specifically, the exhibition that drew the notice of director Ridley Scott to Giger's work being the familiar name of *Necronomicon*. This is a chicken-or-egg question: would *Alien* be truly Lovecraftian were in not for the nightmarish infusion of Giger to create the genuinely alien? The sequel *Aliens* (1986), also highly respected as a science fiction action/horror hybrid, again uses Giger's designs, although its deeper Lovecraftian credentials might be questioned. The Lovecraftian element is again filtered directly through another artist's interpretation of his work into a third creation.

The interpretation issue is interesting if sometimes thorny. VanderMeer's work, about an alien intrusion into our world from space that takes the form in part of a malign and intelligent color, instantly strikes the reader with broad similarities to Lovecraft's "The Colour out of Space," and this effect is played into by director Alex Garland, who sought to make a movie based more on the book's atmosphere—a very Lovecraftian dictum—rather than on a literal or faithful adaptation. However, VanderMeer claimed not to have even read "The Colour out of Space" before writing his novel, hence the connection is more likely a cryptomnesic assimilation through pop culture and associated writ-

---

4. I suspect at least a part of the reason for its failure commercially is that the key demographic for the horror film in cinema—the teenage audience—is the one least likely to have the depth of background in horror films that *The Cabin in the Woods* demands of a viewer. The film is more enjoyable if one is more familiar with horror films.

ings.[5] Perhaps Lovecraft's shadow is grown so long that people do not know they stand in its shade.

King by contrast has openly and long acknowledged his debt to Lovecraft, and *The Mist* is about an unexplained—or rather underexplained—mist with horrors lurking in its depth spreading across a rural community, trapping a mixed group of survivors in a supermarket. Concerning the monstrous denizens of the mist, King specifically states that they "were no Lovecraftian horrors with immortal life" (p. 138). This clearly shows King's perception of the Lovecraftian, which is simultaneously correct (Cthulhu infamously combines back into its hateful original form after being run down by the *Alert* in "The Call of Cthulhu"), popular, and wildly inaccurate: many a strange being comes to a grisly fate in the original corpus of Lovecraft's tales.

The trend perception of Lovecraft and his constructions is echoed in the other movies on the list. *In the Mouth of Madness* is the only work named that is a direct homage to Lovecraft, using not only the names of his creations and his ideas central to the plot, but also snippets of his actual text as dialogue. The premise of the film is the hunt by an insurance investigator for the work and person of a missing author, a clear Lovecraft expy,[6] told in flashback after the investigator's incarceration in an asylum. As might be imagined by the stereotypically Lovecraftian setup,[7] it is also a very metatextual work, with the malign author of the film writing at the bidding of the Old Ones unknowingly, a charge

---

5. For a deeper analysis of this topic, see my "The Reverberation of Echoes: Lovecraft in Twenty-First Century Cinema," *Lovecraft Annual* No. 15 (2021): 190–93.

6. A neologism of fandom, a condensation of "exported character" with a suffixed "y," and which refers to a fictional character who is a stand-in or replica for someone from a different work or who represents a real person.

7. I deliberately use *stereotypical* rather than *typical*. Despite the popular perception, generated in part by its overuse in Lovecraftian pastiches and other media as well as numerous associations with madness in his wider corpus, only two original Lovecraft stories—"The Tomb" and "The Rats in the Walls"— have an asylum narrator, with that also being a possible interpretation for "The Festival." Don't come at me about "The Thing on The Doorstep." Note that Lovecraft stated in a letter to August Derleth of 11 March 1934 that the narrator was in Arkham Gaol (*Essential Solitude* 626).

made against Lovecraft even in his own lifetime, and the movie ends with the character in the film watching the film we just saw as it rewrites reality and brings about the end of the world. Significant too is that John Carpenter is the only director with more than one film on the list.[8] Carpenter is a known fan of Lovecraft, making references to him from his earliest films, one of which starred Dan O'Bannon, the co-writer of *Alien* with whom Carpenter attended film school. Equally importantly, *In the Mouth of Madness* is the third film in Carpenter's informal Apocalypse Trilogy, starting with *The Thing* and followed by *Prince of Darkness* (1987). The latter, with its mixture of black magic ideation and quantum physics, is a popular choice for inclusion in great Lovecraftian film lists.

The Cabin in the Woods is a huge homage to the horror film, filled with literally hundreds of blatant and subtle references to the genre, and its specifically Lovecraftian credentials only become truly apparent at the end, when all is revealed to be a form of amusement for all-powerful gods, and with the destruction of the world resulting from what would in most instances be seen as the correct moral choice. The appearance of Sigourney Weaver, who rose to fame in *Alien*, at the last certainly helps cement the idea of Lovecraftian connections, albeit at a remove and metatextually. But Lovecraft is not merely a part of the panoply of monsters on display. It is his creations, and more importantly his ideas of cosmic horror and the unimportance of humans to the wider universe, that ultimately take centre stage.

Yet even this dark conclusion pales in comparison to the emotionally devastating and unflinching brutality of the ending of *The Mist*, which has one of the grimmest finales in a mainstream movie, one not present in the original novella. The nihilism that is a core component of cosmic horror and Lovecraft's vision of an uncaring universe, along with the bitterest ironies that suffuse

---

8. The star of *In the Mouth of Madness*, Sam Neill, is a key figure in *Event Horizon*, but given Neill's broad and extensive filmography this is not particularly significant. Others might disagree: his *Possession* (1981) is seen by some as indirectly influenced by Lovecraft. Deeply allegorical, it is certainly filled with surreal madness and a horribly memorable squid-monster.

his work, is on full display in the crushing finale, in which the surviving main character kills all the others, irrevocably trapped in the mist in their useless car. He shoots them as a form of mercy given the horrors that surround them, and the victims include his own young son. He has insufficient ammunition to commit suicide himself, and he is almost immediately rescued by forces pushing back the mist. In his semi-catatonic despair, the woman from the beginning of the film passes him by; he had shamefacedly refused to accompany when she went out into the mist to recover her own child, now safely in her arms.

Event Horizon has a more distantly related but still clear pedigree with Lovecraftian connections.[9] The debt it particularly owes to *Alien*, and especially *Aliens*, is small yet distinct, and *Event Horizon* itself is highly influential on the famously Lovecraftian *Dead Space* video game series. The set-up for the film is a classic horror premise: the answering of a distress call from a vessel thought long lost. Like *Alien*, it is very much a haunted house tale in space, in this case fused with a Gothic nightmare—often quite literally. The spaceship is deliberately designed to invoke Gothic architecture—specifically Notre Dame Cathedral—and the disturbing aesthetic is carried throughout the production design and other aspects in varying degrees of subtlety.[10] For example, many of the doorways are shaped in the classic anthropoid coffin design, whereas the engineering area where the gateway/drive is located—termed a containment—holds a secondary double meaning; the conflation with medieval

9. Like most films under discussion, *Event Horizon* has more influences and homages other than Lovecraft—the scene of the exploding tank and corridor of blood instantly evokes the famous elevator of blood scene Stanley Kubrick's adaptation of *The Shining* (1980)—but it is the Lovecraftian aspects that are of primary concern here.

10. For those who might question how much of this is intentional, it should be noted that in a quick, unremarkable scene boarding the gravity-less *Event Horizon*, a wristwatch is briefly seen floating past camera along with other debris. It is an Omega Speedmaster Professional, which was the watch worn during the first American Gemini spacewalk and by Neil Armstrong on his famous moonwalk. Observant viewers will also note that the Aboriginal Flag has replaced the Union Jack on Sam Neill's Australian Flag insignia on his uniform.

demonology is even more prominent in the shooting script, wherein it is called a containment seal. There are frequent nods to classic horror tropes of such settings, such as the distress call being in Latin, the docking bay being number XIII, or with the nearby atmosphere of the planet the ship is about to burn up in, despite theoretically being in space, effectively turning the environment of space into that of being inside a storm.

The deeper plot, involving the opening of a gateway to a different dimension—"Hell is only a word. The reality is much, much worse"—in the belief that it will allow instantaneous travel has seen *Event Horizon* being widely adopted by fans of the Warhammer 40,000 (40K) setting as a prequel set inside their very specific milieu. This deeply layered conceptual universe is founded originally upon a miniatures-based tabletop war-game that has grown exponentially into a notable fixture in its industry and with a huge production arm with numerous spinoff games, hundreds of books, video games, a feature film, and an enormous proliferation of fan works.[11]

The setting involves a notorious grim-dark—the term derives from the endless pairing of the words in early 40K material—far future where the human race has conquered the stars as a totalitarian theocratic empire whose founding principle is xenocide, but who are the good guys in a universe where malign aliens, mutants, cultists, and far worse threaten at every turn. Such travel as is roughly presented in *Event Horizon* is possible; but the Warp, as it is known in 40K, is likewise the habitation of daemons who pose an omnipresent threat both to travelers and those inside the material universe they ever strive to enter.[12] The setting of 40K is deeply infused from all manner of science fiction, fantasy, and historical analogy—most everything makes an appearance in some form eventually—but Lovecraft is a core element of the

---

11. At the time of writing a television show is announced as being in pre-production with Hollywood heavy hitter Henry Cavill as lead and executive producer.

12. Purists will note that the theory of dimensional travel in *Event Horizon* is not precisely like that of navigating the Warp in 40K, but these elements certainly have a closer kinship than most such systems.

fictional universe, both in broad trends and specific references and deliberate nods as acknowledgment; the dead but never dying God-Emperor of Mankind guides humanity through the Warp via the light of his psychic emanation, the Astronomicon.

Uzumaki and *The Endless* are far more Lovecraftian in feel— the dread of the unknown and a cosmic sense of terror, and utter helplessness in the face of incomprehensible horrors—than in other connections. *Uzumaki* deals with a series of deaths and malign incidents in a small Japanese community connected with the motif of a spiral. *The Endless* follows survivors of a UFO cult returning to their old community for some semblance of closure after receiving a videotape from their former comrades. The strangeness that pervades both films is difficult to convey in mere description. It is challenging to point to specific instances of what makes the films objectively Lovecraftian, but the consensus is near universal, and has been confirmed by the creators of both works, is a conscious decision. *True Detective* is Lovecraftian around the edges, with hints about strange cults and deeper truths about the universe underlying the ritual murder investigation that is the central premise of the story, which is told in flashback as the key participants are being called upon to retell the events leading to several deaths, about which all know they are lying.

The BFI list is weighted toward more modern productions: one film each from the late 1970s and the 1980s, two each from the 1990s and 2000s, and four less than ten years old at the time the list was composed. This is a typical artefact of internet lists, which commonly skew to newer films given their key demography both as authors and readers. Although far from universal,[13] broad consensus holds *Alien* as the starting point of the widely acknowledged and celebratedly Lovecraftian in cinema. Many of the fondly remembered Lovecraftian films that begin to become a genre unto itself following *Re-Animator* (1985) are frequently more personally liked than held up to larger acclaim, and often are lacking Lovecraftian elements other than arrogation of his

---

13. For example, some people do genuinely like Daniel Haller's film adaptation of *The Dunwich Horror* (1970), or any of a number of early offerings, such as *The Haunted Palace* (1963) and *Die, Monster, Die!* (1965).

names and the barest skeletons of his tales. Opinion is inherently subjective, but what is not is that so many more Lovecraftian movies have been produced since the late 1990s. Thus, even if one's ratio of terrible through excellent films remains unchanged, more great Lovecraft films are being made.

Of the films on the BFI list only *Alien* was a box office hit, although by analogy *True Detective* Season 1 was a much-acclaimed and popular series upon preliminary screening. Specifically, several of the BFI films were noted flops, and with the exceptions cited, none was considered a great success commercially upon initial release, although several have gone on to be long-term moneymakers on various home media or turned profits due to lower production costs. Seemingly, Lovecraft's commercial failings follow him from beyond the grave: cosmic horror is intrinsically ill-suited to a mass audience. Counterintuitively, many of the films on the list have had sequels or remakes. *Alien* has become a franchise, one that crosses over into the equally popular *Predator* series: indeed, *Alien* is almost a subgenre unto itself, with numerous clones and copies proliferating, including further copies of its own sequel, and a huge amount of physical merchandise and ancillary materials in such media as books, comics, and video games. *The Thing* is of course a remake and had a further 2011 prequel using the same name; both *The Mist* and *Uzumaki* had later television series made from their source material; and *True Detective* continued for two more seasons, albeit with different cast and stories, and significantly less acclaim. *The Endless* was itself a sequel and had an additional exploration of its universe in another tangential sequel film, while *Annihilation* was probably planned for one—it is part of a trilogy of books—but such failed to manifest itself after the poor performance of the initial outing. The perpetual (and, in truth, largely wishful thinking and internet rumor) *Event Horizon* sequel talk keeps fans ever hopeful.

So what does all the forgoing begin to tell us in a snapshot about Lovecraft in the twenty-first century? First, whatever problems are had with issues surrounding Lovecraft the man, his influence is so pervasive that his removal from the horror genre is simply impossible. The interwoven threads that lead to so much of modern horror and science fiction has so many tendrils and traces, sometimes even entire supportive beams, built upon Lovecraft generationally that he had become part of the ineradicable foundation.

Second, it informs us that people are still deeply interested in his ideas, with both artists and consumers receptive to such. It is not merely the constant remaking of Bram Stoker's *Dracula* (1897) in varying levels of faithfulness to the source material or bold modern reinterpretation that it seems people feel the need to do every few years. People are still engaging with Lovecraft's creations specifically, and his conception broadly; it continues to resonate, and new constructions, rather than mere recrudescences of his work, continue to be fashioned. In fact, as patently demonstrated by the BFI list and forming a wonderful illogicality, it is not Lovecraft's own work directly that seems to make the best adaptations of his work. The very thing that imbues Lovecraft's work with such longevity is nigh impossible to translate directly, and as such the creative wellspring never runs dry.

Third, it speaks of the possibilities, of the depth and breadth connected with Lovecraft. *Aliens* is considered seminal for the powerful female character of Ellen Ripley, and popularized the idea of the science fiction "used future" aesthetic, while *The Mist* is enough of an homage to monster movies of the 1950s that a black-and-white version was released to heighten the connection. *Annihilation* continues in *Alien*'s wake with a diverse all-female team leading the exploration of the alien effect zone in the film. *True Detective* is straight police procedural in which the supernatural is only teasingly hinted at. *Uzumaki* is explicitly supernatural without any real explanation. *In the Mouth of Madness* breaks reality by showing us the character watching the very film he is in. *The Endless* is a surrealistic journey of escapees from a cult returning to face their fears, while *Event Horizon* is a basic science fiction action thriller when not a harrowing horror ordeal. They are all highly distinct from one another, yet are broadly under the same cosmic horror umbrella. The Lovecraftian universe shows no signs of having an end.

*

The other extreme of ephemerality is that ubiquitous clothing item of the twenty-first century, the T-shirt. Still largely an undergarment in Lovecraft's day, it has grown in exposure, acceptance, and popularity since World War II to be globally omnipresent. In addition to its basic utility, the T-shirt has become an endless canvass for all manner of expression: cultural, political, and artistic as well as a group identifier, status symbol, and proclamation of intent or belief. While high end fashion companies do make T-shirts, its origins as a working-class garment, habitual popularity among the younger members of society, low cost, and the relative ease of manufacture as concerns fabric printing, even at the personal level, means that pop culture dominates the imagery and wordage of the T-shirt. It is not surprising that Lovecraft is much represented in the words and imagery on display on such a medium, and this provides a distinctive window into wider ideas and perceptions of Lovecraft and his work in the community as a whole.

There are many areas of art and creation that stem from Lovecraft—pictorial art in particular—but there is a noticeable transition onto other media, including T-shirts. The T-shirt presents a unique cultural insight due to its fundamental features, including the need for a relative simplicity of ideas and design, a certain recognizability (even if only to the initiated), and intrinsically public demonstration of affiliation. Lovecraft has certainly become a part of this wider trend. Without seeking such out, I have randomly come across Lovecraftian T-shirts in numerous unexpected places, such as those being sold in a store in Stockholm, Sweden, worn by an anthropologist at a dig in eastern Poland, sported by a reveler at a medieval festival in Brisbane, Australia, and on a local man walking down the street is a small town in western Kenya.

My strategy for this monograph was to start with hard data, using a statistical model to gain empirical evidence in the form of a tabulation of the most common tropes, words, and images found on Lovecraftian T-shirts. This swiftly proved to be a difficult and, ultimately, fatally flawed model. A simple search of "Lovecraft" on two of the more popular pop culture T-shirt websites, teefury.com and teepublic.com,[14] revealed more than 5000 options at the former and some 1800 at the latter. Even though the higher figure reflects an enormous number of examples of replication—the same image on a great number of different items other than T-shirts—the latter are almost all distinct and individual images and designs, and even this limitation is not a natural conclusion, but rather merely reflects the fullest volume of listing available on the site, 50 pages each displaying 36 images.[15]

Adding to the volume are images that are clearly Lovecraftian in origin but not picked up under the basic search parameters. There is also a crossover in designs—both in copying and variations on very specific themes and the literal work of the same creator being sold at both sites simultaneously. While obviously voluminous, such a statistical model could still hold great merit, save for the difficulties of classification. I chose some very basic categories, both from common-sense and what were obviously thematic commonplaces. Of the twenty categories the latter includes images of Lovecraft, Cthulhu, the *Necronomicon*, Miskatonic University, and textual quotations; the thematic offerings included the comical, puns, Japan, cats, and crossovers with other elements.

It quickly became apparent that such a model would be un-

---

14. References to all merchandise companies in this essay are not endorsements or reflections of quality, but are merely germane to the topic at hand. Nor are the listings designed to be definitive or even an attempt a full coverage; they were simply chosen to help illustrate the larger picture. Likewise, I have tried to name the artists when their original work is specifically mentioned, but given the ubiquitous usage of pseudonyms, blatant copyings, and the wide dissemination of such images, not all are easily traceable and I apologize in advance for any omissions, misattributions, or errors.

15. For comparison, the name Stephen King fills the pages at teepublic at 1800, as does Cthulhu, while Poe has 1535, Harry Potter 1414—including some that are actively attacking his creator, J. K. Rowling. Her name, rather than her creation, brings only about 500; Tolkien has 708, although *The Lord of the Rings* brings a full 1800; Clive Barker has around 400—mostly for his film adaptations—while Lovecraft's friends and fellow titans of *Weird Tales* Robert E. Howard and Clark Ashton Smith have, respectively, around 720—most for Conan and again referencing the film or Marvel Comics versions (about the same as for *The Wizard of Oz*) and 11.

wieldy and unhelpful. Many designs fell into a great number of categories, others fell into none, some were highly subjective: what constitutes a comical depiction is often not at all clear,[16] not to mention the *kawaii*[17] element that was found in many designs. Certain images are Lovecraftian only by the viewer's decision to make them so—Lovecraft did not invent tentacles, after all—and others contained tiny elements of one category that was clearly not the key aesthetic or focus of the depiction, such as a tiny Cthulhu in a larger dominant image. Furthermore, there are a plethora of Lovecraft shirts available that are merely printing upon a T-shirt of extant designs, images, or quotations in a specific style font. Ultimately there are just so many T-shirts that one can find a great number on almost any chosen Lovecraftian aspect, including many that make strange bedfellows. For example, there is a recurrent theme of Lovecraftian fish restaurants and seafood products, playing upon his association with tentacles in the popular perception and at humorous odds with his famous detestation of such fare. Such seems far more connected than the involvement of Lovecraft and his creations with images of alcohol brands—occasionally representing actual products—despite his complete abstinence from intoxicating drinks stronger than coffee, and a rather puritanical distrust of alcohol in general.

Thus, instead of a hard-data approach, a more intrinsically subjective version and analysis drawing from smaller models must of necessity be offered. That said, it is abundantly clear that Cthulhu itself is by a significant margin the most popular Lovecraftian image to be depicted on T-shirts. This is perhaps

16. For example, the name H. P. Lovecraft done in the style of the HP Sauce logo clearly is supposed to be so, but what about an Arkham Sanatorium T-shirt (probably), or the Lovecraft Mysterious Mythos Comic Cover T-shirt picturing a man getting strangled by a killer plant in the precise style of a '50s comic, or the Poe and Lovecraft Vampire Hunters offering that is drawn dark and broody?

17. A Japanese term that is translated into English as "cuteness" but refers to a larger aesthetic of an entire cultural trend with an emphasis on loveable, childlike, vulnerable, adorable, shy, pretty, and innocent, of which Hello Kitty is the best-known example in the West. A typical T-shirt of such a nature is Jerry Fleming's depiction of a friendly looking Cthulhu with pink cheeks holding the Earth close above the caption Cuddler of Worlds.

unsurprising, for a number of reasons. Lovecraft's own writings were of course given a unification by August Derleth under the banner of the Cthulhu Mythos, and this idea has penetrated far enough into popular culture that many would recognize Cthulhu without ever having read Lovecraft's work. And Cthulhu is, of all Lovecraft's creations, unarguably the most recognizable, being the only such entity to be described in detail and to appear as a living entity in a story as well as having a depiction drawn by the author's own hand. The imagery, pared down to tentacles trailing from a humanoid face, is also something that lends itself to easy replication and recognition, which is an essential trait for memetic distribution and easy parody.

Perhaps the most interesting part of this imagery is how divorced it is from the horrific Cthulhu as a pop culture icon on T-shirts. On teefury, of the 36 images under the first page search for "Cthulhu," only a single one is a straight horror image of it, and the majority are actively comical. Teepublic with the same parameters has an arguable six horror images of 36,[18] including one that is a slight variation on that solitary example on teefury. The ratio increases toward the more horror-oriented as one scrolls further pages on both sites, yet the overall comic preponderance of the offerings remains. Showing the difference between sites, a wider search for "Lovecraft" continues the overwhelmingly comical, or at the least far from horror, offerings on teefury while teepublic has a far greater abundance of horror imagery. Such general distinction holds true for various other sites and the internet as whole. It is important to note that, despite the foregoing statement, there are a huge number of dark, horrific, and clearly malign Lovecraftian images on T-shirts, with the entities and ideas of Lovecraft created with dedicated seriousness.[19] Yet the comical images undoubtedly hold the larg-

---

18. Repeated searches on different days gave slightly different ratios to the results, but the overall trend remained constant.

19. For example, the artist Azhmodai, whose work in this context is mentioned herein several times for more humorous T-shirts, has in the more than 250 designs he offers at teepublic a great number of more traditional and horrific interpretations of Lovecraft's work, while on the same site EmptyIs (Sandro

est swath of the territory; there are a surprisingly large number of variant images playing on the juxtaposition of the word call, and its modern connection with the telephone, and Cthulhu.

It is interesting to observe that the horror imagery and the comic are often very similar in theme but differing in tone. Two random examples on the same page at teepublic are Anna-Maria Jung's "Forbidden Books can be Fun!" and Redbug's "Lovecraft T-Shirt." Both depict Lovecraft with an open *Necronomicon* and Cthulhu looming behind him, but Jung's is in a cartoon style with the caption that titles the work—drawing on ideas of campaigns of the promotion of books to children—above the image; Redbug's image is done with a distinct realism, giving it the air of menace Jung's lacks by design. These depictions are a good entranceway to how Lovecraft the man is seen through this specific pop cultural lens. Natural variants of photographs of Lovecraft are used as the template for images of him, as straight depictions, photomontages, or the basis for drawings.

Yet the most common additions to Lovecraft's own image are with him reading the *Necronomicon*, accompanied by tentacles, with various cabalistic-style iconography or shadowed by his creations. This defictionalization of his work and blending of the author back into his own creations show the perception of Lovecraft as creator but also hint at the reality of his creations, the very element of verisimilitude Lovecraft strove for in his work, which is now a monster long escaped its summoner's control. Significantly, the most common cabalistic image used in these T-shirts is the star inside a circle motif, creating a seal or sigil, found on the cover of the Simon *Necronomicon* (1977), a fictional grimoire presented as the real *Necronomicon* from which Lovecraft was drawing.

The defictionalization of Lovecraft in T-shirts is part of a wider process, both with his writings specifically and with pop culture in general. Lovecraft's work, having many recurrent unique locations and with these having a real-world grounding and template, as well as the air of reality generated inside his work, lends

---

Fazlinovic) offers 42 separate Lovecraftian designs, all character studies or tarot cards, which are without exception horrific.

itself perfectly to such merchandising. The most common is apparel from the campus of Miskatonic University, ranging from entirely straight examples that would pass unnoticed next to those offered by genuine institutions[20] through those with stealthily hidden aspects in Latin mottos such as *astra inclinant, sed non obligant, timendi causa est nescire,* or *mare nos vocat,*[21] dates such as 1890 or 1937 (Lovecraft's birth and death years) or 1922 (publication of "Herbert West—Reanimator," the first work to mention Miskatonic University), or references to specific departments relevant to the stories and wider mythology, most especially the expeditions to Antarctica that initiate the events in *At the Mountains of Madness.*

At the opposite end of absent verisimilitude are more patently unreal or comic elements such Arkham Bazaar's Miskatonic University Spiritualist Club with Lovecraftian figures incorporated into a Ouija board, one of many college apparel T-shirts with images of Cthulhu or other Lovecraftian monstrous aspects placed in the depictions, or promoting less reputable teaching departments such as Necromancy. Other Lovecraftian locales get similar treatments, including more esoteric ones such as R'lyeh or Yuggoth, often blended in with more traditional tourist paraphernalia such as the Greetings from Innsmouth postcard replication or the local bait and tackle shop there. Likewise there is extrapolation and conflation of event, organizations, and people from the Lovecraftian universe, which results in T-shirts such as for the Esoteric Order of Dagon,[22] the Church of the Starry Wisdom, Marsh Refinery, Joe Sargent's Omnibus Service, Roger's Wax Museum, and the Pickman School of Art.

---

20. I was once politely questioned by a puzzled American gentleman from New England as to the exact whereabouts of the Miskatonic University, Arkham, Mass. on my T-shirt.

21. "The stars incline us, they do not bind us," "Ignorance is the cause," and "The sea calls us" respectively. The first given is actually a famous quotation concerning astrology.

22. Which is itself defictionalized as a both an occult Order—in fact, there are a number who claim the name—and title of the long-running H. P. Lovecraft Amateur Press Association.

This blending in T-shirts of Lovecraft with other elements takes three mains forms, although it should be noted that these are not hard boundaries and sometimes bleed into one another.[23] The first is to place the Lovecraftian into an existing template, a process commonly done with numerous other unrelated elements and omnipresent in modern T-shirt designs. A few examples include Straight Outta R'lyeh[24] (done in the style of iconic Straight Outta Compton logo connected with the band NWA, which logo is itself a mockery derived from the Parental Advisory sticker concern offensive language that was placed upon such albums as NWA sold), Cthulhu Buster (Cthulhu in the Ghostbusters logo), Lovecraft Original Recipe (with Cthulhu in place of the icon of Colonel Sanders of Kentucky Fried Chicken, above the initial HPL instead of KFC), Cthulhu in Théophile Steinlen's iconic "La Chat Noir" poster, "My child is an honor student at Miskatonic Elementary School," "Keep Calm and Call Cthulhu," or "I ♥ craft" and "I ♥ NY arlathotep," "My parents went to Innsmouth and all I got were these weird dreams" and "I went to Innsmouth and all I got was this debilitating madness," the latter four all playing on the ubiquitous tourist shirts from major cities across the world. Others utilizing this same formula of replacement into existing material largely focused upon words—the love in Lovecraft gives a particularly wide scope to such endeavors—include "I Love craft beer," "I Love crafting," "Love the Craft," "Make Lovecraft Not War," and "Live, Laugh, Lovecraft," the last named having a particularly wide number of variants. Such items offer little by way of profounder analysis, save to point out that there is obviously a market for a blending of such elements.

The second form is the mixing of Lovecraft with elements that are clearly not Lovecraftian. This is frequently, although far from ubiquitously, done with a comedic intent and has all manner of curious imaginings and juxtapositions. Cthulhu hybridized with all manner of traditional Christmas imagery is a perennial

---

23. Again I want to make clear that these are not value judgments on the art or creations, merely a means to separate what different elements might mean for the wider context.

24. Or Dunwich, Arkham, Innsmouth, Kingsport, Yuggoth, etc.

favorite, with an obvious seasonal boost in the appropriate period. "Cthulhista" by Andres Abel reimagines the hammer and sickle of Communism, with Lovecraft's Elder Sign branch replacing the latter in the image, while VP021's "Ogre Cthulhu" reimagines Shrek as Cthulhu. This "Thing A plus Thing B" trend—commonly referred to as a mashup—is particularly widespread and numerous. There are numerous interpretations of the creations of Lovecraft as the monsters from Maurice Sendak's 1963 children's classic *Where the Wild Things Are*, Cthulhu in the *Batman* (1989) film logo, fighting Godzilla or Kratos from the *God of War* video game series, religious imagery—stained-glass motifs are popular, as are alterations on perceived stereotypical Christian slogans, and pop cultural Satanism. Non-Christian religious imagery is largely absent, save for a prevalence of Cthulhu in the iconographic pose of the seated Buddha—as Cookie Monster from *Sesame Street*, in a Peanuts parody as Anna-Maria Jung's "Snoopthulhu," hating Mondays as Garfield, having the *Necronomicon* read by Curious George the Monkey in Eli Wolff's "NecroNoMonkey," or with the characters of the Simpsons depicted as "The Whateleys" in Azhmodai's creation.

Third are elements that are more profoundly thematic to Lovecraft and whose mixtures represent a richer—or at least more niche—appreciation of his work, or to use the parlance of fan culture, deep cuts. Some are deceptively simple, such as the H. P. Lovecraft Historical Society (HPLHS) standard "What part of Ph'nglui mglw'nafh Cthulhu R'lyeh wgah'nagl fhtagn don't you understand?"; Omega Man 5000's (Harry Gordon) "Accursed Inspiration," which depicts Lovecraft as a brain in a jar writing with pseudopods; tourist-style T-shirts from Exham Priory; Devil Olive's pictorial advertisements for "Pickman's Craft Butchery"; Little Cozy Nostril's (Kyle Bridgett) "Don't Hug the Gug" depicting the titular creature is a cartoony yet accurate way; Nick Beta's (Nicholas Betancourt) far less cutsie image under the legend "Ghast from the Vaults of Zin"; We Need A Signal's "Men of Leng" design, which features that title above a sword and shield in a classic role-playing game (RPG) style, with the shield decoration having a blue line across a large purple spider; or Hands Off My Dinosaur's (Teo Zirnis) cartoon image of Lovecraft in sunglasses going for a swim wearing a Cthulhu inflatable flotation device about his waist in "The Call of The Beach." There is a decided tendency toward wordplay in many T-shirts, Lovecraftian and otherwise, but Godfrey Temple's "Squamous" T-shirt—which features that word in a design with tentacles and a red eye above a progressively smaller font offering it as "Lingua Lovecratia" for "When saying scaly just isn't enough"—is a joke showing that some offerings have very deep roots, exhibiting Lovecraft's own alleged fondness for the word in his fiction, but more importantly portraying the metatextual awareness and perception that he did by fans.[25]

Images of the covers of issues of *Weird Tales* altered to emphasize their Lovecraftian connections are another binding of primary sources and original work. Armadillo Hat's such creation offers a depiction of *At the Mountains of Madness* dominating such a cover in the November 1931 issue: such would have been a likely date for the publication of this story had editor Farnsworth Wright not rejected it early in the year. Other designs too have layers within layers, such as a depiction of the Elder Thing from *At the Mountains of Madness* using the style and font of John Carpenter's *The Thing* (1982), a movie as just noted drawing from Lovecraft in numerous large and small ways, or the Miskatonic University Boxing Club T-shirt, which is stated as being founded in 1910, the date that Hebert West reanimates the dead boxer to such horrific results in his eponymous tale, details that will pass unnoticed save by the most devoted. Likewise with the image of Lovecraft portrayed as the member of a black metal band, with his name in an appropriately arcane and semi-

---

25. This perception is key: squamous is only used a single time in the entire corpus of Lovecraft's original work, in "The Dunwich Horror," although it will appear in two of his ghostwritten tales—"The Curse of Yig" and "Out of the Æons"—as well as his collaboration with E. Hoffmann Price, "Through the Gates of the Silver Key." Daniel Harms probably sums up the fan perspective in the foreword to his *Cthulhu Mythos Encyclopedia* (2008) wherein he states: "The creations of Lovecraft and other authors have had a resonance that derives from their ability to embody numerous meanings within an appealing, albeit horrific and often squamous, exterior" (xvii).

decipherable font, which is seemingly a rather generic jest—one can after all get a similar T-shirt featuring famous country singer Dolly Parton. Yet Lovecraft is for many in that very specific genre a seminal figure of influence: the nihilism of cosmic horror is a key element in much of the music and aesthetic of black metal.

Heavy metal has many tangents and connections to Lovecraft. Given that the standard garb of the metalhead is the black T-shirt, crossover is inevitable. There are the faux tour shirts such as H. P. Lovecraft's Necronomicon Tour (by Insomnia) and Cosmic Horror End of the World Tour (Azhmodai) with the bands being Mythos deities, the latter in the iconic fonts of genuine metal bands such as Motörhead, Ghost, and Slayer. Other mixed musical examples include Joy Division's iconic *Unknown Pleasures* (1979) cover art as Lovecraft Division Horror Pleasures, with the image of Lovecraft himself surrounded by four tentacles visible in the radio pulsar image that makes up the artwork; The Misfits' famous Crimson Ghost/Fiend Skull logo with added tentacles; or with the Beatles *Let It Be* (1970) cover used as a basic for a horror quartet of Lovecraft, Poe, Mary Shelley, and Bram Stoker in four individual frames creating a larger symmetrical whole under the Beatles font title of The Beasts.

Given the iconography and aesthetic of Lovecraft being such a part of the music and artwork of metal bands, such naturally turns up on the shirts. These can be simply a part of the name of the band itself, and in various levels of patentness, from commonly known creations such as Necronomicon and Azathoth through Arkham Witch, Darkest of the Hillside Thickets,[26] and Inquinok,[27] as a small sampling of a far vaster number. Cthulhu itself appears in numerous guises such as on Cradle of Filth's "Mother of Abominations" T-shirt (based upon the song of the same name about Lovecraft's most famous creation). Alestorm's 2015 Tour T-Shirt "Piratefest America" features an image of

---

26. Not a metal band, but a direct and rather obscure Lovecraft quotation, hence the point remains.

27. A variant on Inganok from *The Dream-Quest of Unknown Kadath*, which was offered as Inquanok in many earlier publications. The vocalist Krelian "changed the A to an I because I thought it looked better."

Cthulhu whose tentacles also resolve into cultists on the front, while the variant "Pirates Down Under" for the Australia and New Zealand tour also sports a pirate Cthulhu skull on the reverse, or Metallica's "Worldwired Europe Awakens" 2019 Tour T-shirt, which features Cthulhu tilting an hourglass; Metallica has famously been referencing Lovecraft in its work since its album *Ride the Lightning* in 1984, which features the instrumental "The Call of Ktulu" as the final track. Iron Maiden's 1985 *Live After Death*, whose iconic Derek Rigg cover features Lovecraft's name and most famous *Necronomicon* quotation on a gravestone, remains a popular T-shirt almost forty years after its release, while Michael Whelan's *Lovecraft's Nightmare A* graces the cover of the famed death metal album *Cause of Death* (1990) by Obituary and is naturally sold as a T-shirt, as well being the cover of the famous Del Rey/Ballantine paperbacks of Lovecraft's work. French metal Band The Great Old Ones, who (unsurprisingly) feature a number of Lovecraftian-based T-shirts, even offers a fairly straight image of Lovecraft as a large back patch deigned to be the centerpiece for the iconic heavy metal attire know as a battle jacket.

As noted, far from the totality of Lovecraft as T-shirt icon is dark, gritty, or highly specialized. "Monster Riffs," for example, just offers a highly kawaii Cthulhu playing a guitar. The Old Gent's love of cats is frequently referenced,[28] and Cathulhu [*sic*] is a recognizable figure in a number of different guises and designs by various artists, as is the Necronomicat. Likewise, Lovecraft's fondness for coffee is the source of a number of T-shirts, frequently juxtaposed with Cthulhu awakening and needing a cup, admixed with the Starbucks logo, or with Lovecraft's quotation about how "I like coffee exceedingly."[29] In recognition of their position as American masters, and Lovecraft's idolization of him, Poe and Lovecraft are often paired as a team, occasionally with other relevant authors as noted previously. A deeper cut along

---

28. The internet of course also (in)famously loves cats, so how much of such art derives from Lovecraft's ailurophilia or cat memes will probably forever remain an open question.

29. From a letter to J. Vernon Shea of 10 November 1931. See *Letters to J. Vernon Shea* 78.

such lines is reflected in Hafaell's (Rafael Pereira) "Poe's Night-mare," which juxtaposes Lovecraft's literary hero with Cthulhu.

As might be expected, quotations of Lovecraft on T-shirts, sometimes as part of a design, as a background feature, but most frequently as standalone words or with an image of Lovecraft himself, proliferate. Given the broad scope of Lovecraft's work, the chosen writings are narrowly selected, with Lovecraft's famous quotation from the *Necronomicon,* and the chant of the Cthulhu cultists, both in English and its ritual syllabic pronunciation, overwhelmingly in statistical domination. The openings of "The Call of Cthulhu" and "Supernatural Horror in Literature" are numerically popular, but other quotations become rapidly heterogeneous thereafter. Importantly, some things that seem like—and technically are—quotations, in particular the idea that "The Stars Are Right," are commonly coming from the adaptation of this phrase as a tagline by RPGs, making the connection paradoxically simultaneously direct and diffused. Likewise the adaptation of *fhtagn* in various uses, particularly as a comical synonym or substitution for swearing, is another technically quoted usage that feels in a vastly different spirit.

Interestingly, give the plethora of Lovecraftian film adaptations, they are poorly represented in the great majority of T-shirts, with the exceptions—outside of the mere reproduction of poster and promotional art—being the aforementioned *The Thing,* infamous video nasty *The Evil Dead* (1981),[30] and cult classic *Re-Animator.* The first two are more often referencing themselves than Lovecraft, with the Lovecraftian connections coming out as a consequence rather than directly from Lovecraft. Such secondary sources are true for the majority of these T-shirts, such as with those featuring Sutter Kane, the aforementioned Lovecraft expy of *In the Mouth of Madness. Necronomicon* depictions on T-shirts are dominated by the image deriving from the Simon

---

30. The extent to which *The Evil Dead* is Lovecraftian remains an open question, but given its importance to the perception of Lovecraft in broader pop culture due to the association with the *Necronomicon*—even though the evil book in the film series does not have that name attached until the second movie—it must of necessity be included in such lists.

Necronomicon or the book's appearances as seen in *The Evil Dead* franchise, or not infrequently an amalgamation of both. *Re-Animator* likewise is so divergent from Lovecraft that many of the iconic images and lines associated with it that make their way onto T-shirts, such as "Cat dead. Details later" or (most especially) the glowing green hypodermic needle, are in a like manner solely artifacts from the film rather than Lovecraft's original material. Other aspects divorce even further from Lovecraft, with Hank Tees' "Rhiannamator" T-shirt featuring the poster art of the film *Re-Animator* with Herbert West being replaced by famous singer Rihanna.[31] Exceptions and blendings exists, such as Nowhere Streetwears's near direct Lovecraft quotation from "Herbert West—Reanimator" that "Damn it! It wasn't fresh enough"[32] which replaces the "i" in "it" with a green glowing syringe, or advertising of the Pickman Hotel, Hobb's End,[33] New England, a locale from *In the Mouth of Madness,* but in total these are far less one common that might be expected.

Film connections are often blended more with recognizable logos in the manner previously described than any deeper engagement, such as Cthulhu Park done in the style of the Jurassic Park logo, or with Cthulhu in the *Jaws* (1975) poster. As ever, exceptions exist, such as Dream Shirts Inc.'s (Ivana Ivicevic) "H. P. Lovecraft's Necronomicon," which has him standing with the dread book before a bluish tringle gateway with emergent tentacles, which immediately evokes the poster art of Lovecraftian film *The Void* (2016), or "Lovecraft V8," which features the Old Gent's visage merging with a that of a ghoul in a side-by-side juxtaposition that instantaneously invokes both *The Thing* and *From Beyond* (1986). But, comparatively, such examples are a small part of the overall offerings. Television, being relatively

---

31. If this seems odd to the reader, consider further Joshua Chaplinsky's *Kanye West—Reanimator* (2015), an entire book retelling Lovecraft's tale as the journey of West to reinvigorate hip-hop, by reanimation. The cover image—based upon the film—is, naturally, available as a T-shirt.

32. The original has an emphasized *quite* before "fresh."

33. Itself a nod in the movie to the locale in the Lovecraftian film *Quatermass and the Pit* (1967).

scant on Lovecraft adaptations, has a proportionally limited appearance on T-shirts, with the exception being *Lovecraft Country* (2020). Its depictions are, however, largely in line with that of the films cited above, being self-referential more than drawing back more directly to Lovecraft.

As noted, Japan was one of my original categories, and with good reason. It is not simply due to Japanese language insertions, which are certainly far in excess of other languages that do likewise, such as Korean or Russian.[34] There was a particular abundance of Japanese imagery, both crossing over with pop cultural elements from Japan such as *My Neighbor Totoro* or Pokémon (there is after all an RPG blending of such with Lovecraft as *Pokéthulhu*), broader artistic styles, and riffs on famous Japanese works of art. This is far from exclusive to Lovecraft and his work, and represents wider Western societal trends in connection with Japanese pop culture, which is in and of itself significant. Lovecraft is being adapted into new media in new ways, rather than being left behind as an important but now bypassed relic. While outside the purview of the survey of T-shirts—and there are entire sections in Tokyo stores dedicated to Lovecraft T-shirts—Japanese pop culture itself has embraced Lovecraft, and it exerts a distinct influence in certain sections, while manga adaptations of his work are of such quality that they are now being translated back into English, as well as other European languages.

Another specific group with a notable representation is connected with the original RPG community. While not as omnipresent as other features, there is a noteworthy presence in the wider T-shirt offerings, most commonly and simply juxtaposing Cthulhu with the icosahedron die.[35] Given the importance of RPGs to the exponential increase of Lovecraft in popular cul-

---

34. This is from the perspective of an English-speaking Western audience (of one!). I am reliably informed that there is a particular interest and growth of Lovecraft in Spanish-speaking countries and Latin America, and there is a notable substratum of such artists in many of the T-shirt designs I encountered. However I feel I have insufficient grounding and connection to pursue such links in an academically relevant way, and will leave it to other hands.

35. Without its fancy linguistic pants, a common twenty-sided die, or D20.

ture, beginning with TSR's original *Deities and Demigods* (1980), a *Dungeons and Dragons* (D&D) supplement that featured the godlike beings of the Cthulhu Mythos, and Sandy Peterson's *Call of Cthulhu* (1981) [CoC] RPG, the connection is a natural one. The aforementioned frequent image of Lovecraft with a *Necronomicon* in his hand and Cthulhu behind him can be found as a variant, with the CoC RPG font and original cover scheme clearly the inspiration. There is even a T-shirt that simply offers the *Deities and Demigods* statistics page for Cthulhu, complete with image and opening paragraph of description as its whole design. Artefacts of these RPG elements—and their far more popular successors in video games—have slowly accreted into popular ideas of the Cthulhu Mythos, even among active readers of Lovecraft's work, and as such make their way naturally onto T-shirts. The Orne Library at Miskatonic University, the specific name of which is not in Lovecraft's original fiction, is a typical and popularly referenced locale of this type, and most larger companies in these fields such as Chaosium sell numerous T-shirts with their products, logos, and covers upon them.

Related to this phenomenon, the iconography of the games, and the popular portrayals of Lovecraftian monstrosities, such as the seal from the Simon *Necronomicon*, further infiltrate into the artistic depictions on T-shirts, both directly and as a base image for later interpretation. Perhaps the most prominent example is Nyarlathotep, who is underdescribed in a monstrous guise in Lovecraft's work but has a standard image in other derivative media, commonly derived from his depiction as the God of the Bloody Tongue in the seminal CoC *Masks of Nyarlathotep* (1984) campaign. All the above blending leads to curious elements, and multiple and ever distant layers of inspiration and influence. As exemplar, from Azhmodai comes the "Flayer SITU" T-shirt, which features the name Flayer written in the style of metal band Slayer, and Seasons in the Underdark in the font used for their 1990 album *Seasons in the Abyss:* the Lovecraft connection comes in the image betwixt the two captions, which is of a mind flayer. Formally known as an illithid, it is an iconic creature from D&D with a classic Cthuloid appearance of a humanoid skull and facial tentacles.

Creator Gary Gygax has stated that he specifically had Lovecraft in mind when he created the nightmarishly evil beings, and was inspired most directed by the tentacles on the cover of Brian Lumley's Cthulhu Mythos novel *The Burrowers Beneath* (1975).

From there begin more curious blendings. "The Elder Things and Mr. Chicken T-shirt" features an image of actor and comedian Don Knotts surrounded by a nest of tentacles, a reference to his breakout hit film *The Ghost and Mr. Chicken* (1966), a comedy that deals with a man having to spend the night in a haunted house. I feel confident in saying that this film is hardly one of great reputation, deep pop cultural memory, or prodigious influence in the twenty-first century. BRU design's "The Caulk of Cthulhu," featuring caulking gun with a vague tentacle upon the barrel surrounded by the design's title, shows how far afield such Lovecraftian T-shirts can venture, and the key the role of wordplay in many offerings. A more in-depth version on this niche subject is featured in Genki Gear's "Cthulhu Builders" design, which advertises Cthulhu & Sons building contractors and has a number of playful Mythos references in the depiction, including a suggestion to "take advantage of our eons of experience in working with non-Euclidean geometry!" The variant Lovecraftian "Respect your Elders" T-shirts offer some of Lovecraft's antediluvian horrors with that slogan, which originally derives as an antique piece of civil advice with long biblical antecedents but which was memeified into variant forms, which on T-shirts include old cars, clearly malign mummies, ancient trees, and bears.[36] Another deeper cut is an imposing depiction of Cthulhu in an astronaut's suit, a blending of the pseudo-scientific ancient astronauts theory with the fictional alien visitor to Earth: Erich van Däniken's *Chariots of the Gods? Unsolved Mysteries of the Past* (1968), whence derives the notion of such events in mass pop culture, is infamously plagiarized in many key ideas from other works and ultimately derives in large part from Lovecraft's fiction.

Jessica Jacobs's "Necronomicon Ex Mortis Pizza" T-shirt,

---

36. Circling back to the original biblical pronouncements, the latter refers to II Kings 2.23–34, in which a dire fate is given to children who mock the prophet of the Lord, in the form of two very aggressive she-bears.

which shows a (decidedly grim) slice of pizza with the face depicted on the book of the title from *The Evil Dead* franchise, is one of a number of images juxtaposing or blending food with Lovecraftian creations. Asian food styles and seafood dominate this category, with a number of famous brand logos of fast food, cereals, and condiments filling out most of the remainder, along with ice cream: whether this deliberately homages Lovecraft's love of the product or a happy coincidence is difficult to gauge. Other more marginal and individualist examples include Cave Dweller Collective's "Eldritch Cuts," which has a depiction of Cthulhu as per Lovecraft's own famous drawing but internally sectioned out with labels akin to a traditional meat cut chart for professional butchery of animals, and Yezplace's "CthulhuTomatoes," which depicts three real tomatoes with two protuberant growths face downward, making a basic Cthulhu image with the stalk attachment as an eye between the legend "Cthulhu Tomatoes Will Rule the Kitchen."

Even more frankly bizarre is the shirt offering the slogan "Lovecraft did not approve of titties," which is illustrative of the places where, thankfully, such T-shirts are not much represented: the closest would perhaps be J. L. Giles "Lovecraft Immersed" which depicts a lady, tastefully topless in a prone position, reading a book from which tentacles are emerging, or SlideRule You's "Call of Cthulyn" featuring a blending of an alluring Marilyn Monroe, in a single-piece white swimsuit, sporting cthulhoid tentacles and small wings, or similar variants featuring Monroe's iconic subway grating pose as the key image in "Cthulyn Monroe."

Also largely unrepresented are genuine political shirts. I have noted only a single authentic example, which offered an extended quotation from Lovecraft upon the Republican Party that begins "how can one regard seriously a frightened, greedy, nostalgic huddle of tradesman & lucky idlers who shut their eyes to history and science" and concludes "the Republican idea deserves the tolerance and respect one gives to the dead."[37] That said, there is a large number of mocking political T-shirts with

37. From a letter to C. L. Moore of c. August 1936. See *Letters to C. L. Moore* 151.

some variation of Cthulhu for President, frequently in the style of major political parties and under the slogan "Why Settle for the Lesser Evil?" All these originally sprang from the Cthulhu for President RPG game begun in 1996, although there are now endless individual variants, and with slogans and iconography updated to match the changing figures, designs, and slogans of the political landscape. "Greater Evil. Greater Old One. Greater America" is the slogan for Arkham Bazaar's "Cthulhu for President 2020," while "Doom We Can Believe In" and "The Great of Two Evils" are but a sampling of the variants on offer: a particularly grim jest in the modern age shows a representation of Cthulhu above the slogan "No Lives Matter." The latter brings up an element of the transitional inherent in T-shirts that feature connections to pop culture and current events. T-shirts such as WickedMofo's "Covid-19 Necronomicon Variant" or the long absent designs featuring Cthulhu as an element in the alleged Mayan 2012 extinction prophecy[38] are good examples as part of such a trend with a limited pop cultural shelf life.

The proliferation of Lovecraft as a T-shirt icon also has a curious secondary effect, which is the creation of the knock-off Lovecraft design. The humorous HPLHS original T-shirt referencing the near-unpronounceable syllables of the cultists from "The Call of Cthulhu" now has a number of imitators, and this is endemic to the T-shirt creation process, a consequence both of the nature of the internet and the lack of a controllable intellectual property as concerns Lovecraft's creations and work. Many of the T-shirts available offer variants of other works: there are numerous "Obey Cthulhu" in variants of the red and white Coca-Cola logo that feature a tentacle in place of the famous swirl, a black-and-white alternative, with others offering "Ia! Cthu-lhu" or "Cosmic Cthulhu Classic" as the key wording, and further and alternative derivations and variants in a green "Fear CoCthulhu," or "Things Go Better with Cthulhu," referencing a now long obsolete marketing campaign for Coca-Cola that began in the 1960s. As such T-shirts are of course deriving

---

38. Incorrect both as an event (obviously) and as something the Mayan Calendar predicted.

from an original template, they thus have similarity as a necessary part of their premises.

Less salutary, the copying of freer artistic expressions is often blatant in the extreme, and occasionally even acknowledged, for example with some *At the Mountains of Madness* expedition T-shirts acknowledging the debt to the previous creations, while others reference both such and the source with the printing on the back of Lagoon Corps' offering "Your Madness Is Not Complete, Until You Have Been To The Mountains." Given the generations of artists making Lovecraftian creations, yet often from limited technical descriptive material, there is an abundance of influence in such depictions, which often becomes even more noticeable with the frequent simplification of art necessitated for printing upon a T-shirt. Given the volume of material available, there is much that has not been discussed, such as offerings from conventions including those both highly Lovecraft-focused and more general, which still often incorporate Lovecraftian elements, specifically Lovecraft-oriented organizations—for example the annual H. P. Lovecraft Film Festival or the "I'm mad for the Lovecraft E-zine Podcast" T-shirt, which shows a straitjacketed figure making the declaration—or T-shirts from Lovecraft walking tours in Providence. Also largely glossed over in this examination are the thousands of instances of the simple printing of extant images of Lovecraft and associated creations as T-shirt fodder, sometimes from the source producer or creator but often coming from the merely entrepreneurial; commonly examples include old book covers and dust jackets,[39] internal illustrations, as well as iconic *Weird Tales* issues in which Lovecraft's stories were first published.

All the forgoing, of necessity a tiny slice of a far greater whole, demonstrates in microcosm the deep and lasting penetration of Lovecraft into pop culture in the twenty-first century. Whether in full earnestness or deep jest, explicit sourcing or the vaguest of third-hand referencing, inner need for expression or crass commercialism, Lovecraft's work continues to have a vital-

---

39. I feel compelled to remark on the T-shirt being sold with the John Holmes illustration for the cover of *The Shuttered Room and Other Tales of Horror* (1974), which describes a "science fiction melty green head."

ity, engagement, and connection with an amazingly diverse range of all manner of peoples, places, and ideas. Truly then, might it be said, that is not dead which can eternal lie . . .

Works Cited

Harms, Daniel. *The Cthulhu Mythos Encyclopedia*. Lake Orion, MI: Elder Signs Press, 2008.

Lovecraft, H. P. *Essential Solitude: The Letters of H. P. Lovecraft and August Derleth*. Ed. David E. Schultz and S. T. Joshi. New York: Hippocampus Press, 2008. 2 vols.

———. *Letters to C. L. Moore and Others*. Ed. David E. Schultz and S. T. Joshi. New York: Hippocampus Press, 2017.

———. *Letters to J. Vernon Shea and Others*. Ed. S. T. Joshi and David E. Schultz. New York: Hippocampus Press, 2016.

Briefly Noted

One of the most impressive editions of Lovecraft's work (both from a physical standpoint and from the standpoint of academic rigor) is *Fungi von Yuggoth und andere Gedichte* (*Fungi from Yuggoth and Other Poems*), issued by Deutsche Lovecraft Gesellschaft (a name that translates to "German Lovecraft Society"). The firm's website is worth examining for the wealth of information it provides on Lovecraft for German readers, as well as all manner of interesting merchandise. The *Fungi* edition includes a translation of S. T. Joshi's notes to the poems in question, taken from *The Ancient Track* (2nd ed. of 2013).

A large volume of Lovecraft's *Ensayos filosóficos* (philosophical essays), translated by *Lovecraft Annual* contributor César Guarde-Paz, has been published by AGON. Nearly a third of the book (184 pp.) is taken up with a detailed analysis of Lovecraft's philosophy by the translator. The essays themselves (relating to science, temprance, pure philosophy, politics, economics, and anthropology) are annotated far more exhaustively than in S. T. Joshi's edition of Lovecraft's *Collected Essays* (2004–06).

"The Dunwich Horror" and *Ghostbusters*

Ron L. Johnson II

H. P. Lovecraft's creation of the *Necronomicon* has influenced many forms of mass media and pop culture, for example, Sam Rami's 1981 film *The Evil Dead*. In the beginning of the movie, a group of friends along with the protagonist Ash J. Williams (Bruce Campbell) discovers a sinister antique book (*The Book of the Dead*) that can unleash daemoniac phantasms. The *Necronomicon* briefly appears in the horror movie *Jason Goes to Hell: The Finale Friday*, directed by Adam Marcus in 1993. And in the 1962 novel *Something Wicked This Way Comes*, Ray Bradbury depicts the character Charles Holloway going to a library to research the occult by reading mystical antique books because an evil force has come to his town with the traveling dark carnival. To protect his son, his son's friend, and the town, Charles Holloway feverishly reads through these ancient books.

In a recent article in the *Atlantic* titled "The Speech No President Should Have to Give," Tom Nichols makes reference to the *Necronomicon*. The article is about President Biden's "Soul of the Nation" address, which conveys how fanatical Republicans are compromising American democracy. The article points out how President Biden was flooded in an eerie vermilion light during his speech, which unintentionally made his podium look as if "it was set up for a reading from the *Necronomicon*." Also, in the *Ghostbusters* movies and cartoons, antique books are used for research to combat evil spirits.

Which brings me to my focal point: the 1984 movie *Ghostbusters*, produced and directed by Ivan Reitman and co-written by Dan Aykroyd and Harold Ramis, bears some striking resemblances to "The Dunwich Horror." The movie is basically about how apparitions have become a pesky problem in New York City, and the three original Ghostbusters—Egon Spengler (Harold Ramis), Ray Stanz (Dan Aykroyd), and Peter Venkman (Bill Murray)—are capturing these pervasive pests like sewer vermin. About forty-two minutes into the movie, the original three recruit one more Ghostbuster named Winston Zeddemore (Ernie Hudson).

Egon Spengler invents the Proton Packs to battle these pesky specters, just as Dr. Armitage uses the diary of Wilbur Whateley to create the powder of Ibn Ghazi. Dr. Armitage then develops a way to spray the powder out of a hose used for pesticides. Egon Spengler's Proton Pack inventions used to combat and trap ghosts seems derived from Dr. Armitage's hose, which sprays the powder onto the invisible brother of Wilbur Whateley. The major difference is that, in "The Dunwich Horror," the powder helps reveal the latent tentacled brother of Wilbur Whateley, so that Dr. Armitage, Professor Rice, and Dr. Morgan can see what they are battling against while chanting incantations. In the original *Ghostbusters* movie, the Ghostbusters use their Proton Packs to stun the ghosts so they can use their ghost trap and transport the specters to their containment unit, which is a place of captivity for the preternatural.

Although New York City's Environmental Protection Agency, led by Walter Peck (William Atherton), makes the Ghostbusters shut down the containment unit near the end of the film, it wreaks phantasmagorical havoc on the city because the incarcerated ghosts are liberated. Worrying about his love interest, Peter Venkman checks on Dana Barrett (Sigourney Weaver) in her apartment. Dana has become possessed by the Gatekeeper (a.k.a. Zuul, a minion of Gozer). In the intervening time, Egon and Ray find the Keymaster, who was known as Louis Tully (Rick Moranis) before becoming possessed by the Keymaster's sinister spirit (a.k.a Vinz Clortho, another minion of Gozer). The Keymaster and the Gatekeeper are names reminiscent of the *Necronomicon* excerpt from "The Dunwich Horror":

"*Yog-Sothoth* knows the gate. *Yog-Sothoth* is the gate. *Yog-Sothoth* is the key and guardian of the gate. Past, present, future, all are one through Yog-Sothoth" (CF 2.434).

In *Ghostbusters*, when Egon and Ray are studying the Keymaster and Peter Venkman is with the Gatekeeper, a.k.a. Dana Barrett, Dana is going through a sexual exorcism on her bed, and then she falls asleep. While the Gatekeeper appears to be sleeping and breathing heavily, Peter Venkman talks to Egon on the phone and says: "We got to get these two together." When the Gatekeeper and the Keymaster finally meet, Gozer enters Earth from its realm—just as Yog-Sothoth can unleash cosmic deities to enter Earth.

After the Keymaster and Gatekeeper are united, the Ghostbusters battle Gozer the Gozerian. Gozer, who is genderless, takes the form of a demonic woman with red eyes dressed in a white nylon leotard-like costume that looks as if Gozer may be ready for a Broadway horror-musical. When the Ghostbusters blast the female form of Gozer with their Proton Packs, she vanishes, and the Ghostbusters think they have defeated Gozer. Peter Venkman even says: "That wasn't so hard." And Winston celebratorily shouts: "We had the tools; and we had the talent!"

However, Gozer has not been destroyed yet. After a moment of celebration, the Ghostbusters are vocally introduced to "Gozer the Gozerian," "Gozer the Traveler," and "Gozer the Destructor." Instead of seeing Gozer, the Ghostbusters can hear Gozer's thunderous voice, and they can see the clouds light up in close unison with what Gozer is saying, as if Gozer is talking through the scintillating clouds. Gozer allows the Ghostbusters to pick their fate, so everyone tries to clear their head; but Ray Stanz cannot help thinking about how he used to roast Stay-Puft Marshmallows with his family.

After Ray accidentally thought of their "Destructor," the Ghostbusters have a comedic combat with The Stay-Puft Marshmallow Man; and then the Ghostbusters annihilate Mr. Stay-Puft with their Proton Pack beams by "crossing the streams" and by shooting the crossed streams into a gateway-portal that destroys both Stay-Puft and Gozer. In the aftermath of the defeated Stay-Puft Marshmallow Man, the Ghostbusters are covered in Stay-Puft matter—all except for Peter Venkman, who only has some sporadic splatters of the preternatural marshmallow matter, as this symbolizes that Dr. Venkman is the alpha male.

The city's denizens watch all this from below the skyscraper just as the Dunwich denizens watch Dr. Armitage, Professor Rice, and Dr. Morgan battle the son of Yog-Sothoth on top of Sentinel Hill, with some people watching through a telescope. When Curtis Whateley (relative to Wilbur Whateley and the son of Yog-Sothoth) catches a ghastly glimpse of Yog-Sothoth's son through the telescope, he faints because the Son hellaciously looks like a prodigious glob of tentacles with many mouths and half of a human face on top of the blob that resembles the grandfather, old Wizard Whateley.

The Ghostbusters start out as three scientists trapping New York City's ghosts, just as the "white-bearded" Dr. Armitage, the "stocky, iron-grey" Professor Rice, and "lean, youngish Dr. Morgan" battle the supernatural. In contrast to "The Dunwich Horror," the Ghostbusters hire a non-scientific member, Winston Zeddemore, to make a fourth Ghostbuster. However, as mentioned before, after the first forty-two minutes of the movie the Ghostbusters rid the city of many paranormal problems before their fourth member Winston Zeddemore joins.

And at the end of the movie, all four of the Ghostbusters ascend the enormous skyscraper to battle above the city, just as Dr. Armitage, Professor Rice, and Dr. Morgan in "The Dunwich Horror" climb Sentinel Hill to battle the son of Yog-Sothoth, a.k.a. brother of Wilbur Whateley, and son to Lavinia Whateley, and grandson to old wizard Whateley.

Many readers who are familiar with H. P. Lovecraft realize his widespread influence; however, the number of influenced mass media and artists is astronomical. If one analyzes different forms of pop culture, such as video games, cartoons, comic books, short stories, books, movies, and music (such as Metallica's song "Call of Ktulu" and "Dream No More"), the influence is eldritchly exponential.

The Year of the Red Moon: "Out of the Æons," Revisions, and Deep History

Francesco Borri

> Their main *immediate* abode is a still undiscovered and almost lightless planet at the very edge of our solar system—beyond Neptune, and the ninth in distance from the sun. It is, as we have inferred, the object mystically hinted at as "Yuggoth" in certain ancient and forbidden writings [. . .] But Yuggoth, of course, is only the stepping-stone. The main body of the beings inhabits strangely organised abysses wholly beyond the utmost reach of any human imagination. The space-time globule which we recognise as the totality of all cosmic entity is only an atom in the genuine infinity which is theirs. (CF 2.503)

This is a distinctive, inspired, and fascinating passage of one H. P. Lovecraft's most successful novellas, "The Whisperer in Darkness" (1930). Lovecraft was deeply influenced by the advances of his time. He unveiled a vastness and depth utterly defying every religious cosmology by billions of years; he turned the optimism held toward a brand-new world into a hopeless reflection on the horror of the human condition.[1] Lovecraft articulated the transforming question of scale: his dark and vast narrative of the unfathomable cosmos is thrilling and unforgettable. We can appreciate his ability to turn perspectives into what has been called anti-Humanism (Houellebecq), with Lovecraft restoring humanity to its marginal, insignificant, and utterly tragic role. Fritz Leiber averred that Lovecraft was a "literary Copernicus." In the opening passage, Pluto, which had been discovered by Clyde Tombaugh in 1930, was humanity's latest and remotest

---

1. See the essays collected *The Age of Lovecraft* (in Sederholm and Weinstock).

discovery. But for Lovecraft, it was merely a "stepping-stone" to abysses beyond comprehension; its very existence had been foretold in grimoires of ancient and arcane lore.

The narrative arc of many Lovecraft stories deals with what has become known as "Deep Time." It is a geological rather than a historical dimension, one of rocks, planets, and supernovas (Gould). It challenges time itself. It is the time of Cthulhu. Even today, many popular books aim to narrate a history of the universe or of the Earth in which human beings occupy only the last few pages or even lines of it (e.g., Hazen).

On other occasions, Lovecraft deals with a much shorter time—a human timeframe but one nevertheless wholly unbearable for individual existences. It is time spanning thousands of generations, which Daniel Lord Smail recently named "Deep History." The discipline of Deep History focuses on the distant past of the human species, encouraging scholars of such disciplines as genetics, linguistics, and primatology to cooperate with historians who typically deal in a more recent past. Smail describes a "time revolution" taking place in the second half of the nineteenth century in which biblical chronology finally collapses, leaving the stage to a "dark abyss of time" (42). In the nineteenth century, studies propounding the geological antiquity of Earth were rapidly followed by linguistics and archaeology drawing attention to the depth of human history. These discoveries went well beyond the previously accepted by biblical chronology of 5000 years B.C.E. Smail suggests that the concept of prehistory became a stratagem to cope with the deep dark chasms that had begun to open up in the presence of humanity. Indeed, it was an enormous time before history: a time that could have been conveniently left omitted from the records of human deeds because it occurred before the beginning of history.

Authors of fiction soon grasped the narrative potential of this turn in human chronology. As an admirer of Thomas Henry Huxley, Lovecraft shaped histories in which humans are only marginal players (*IAP* 212–13), following the trails blazed by such authors as Arthur Machen and H. G. Wells. Machen, who was one of Lovecraft's most important models (*IAP* 454–57), narrated the profound disturbance when confronted with the immensity of time, as recently discussed by Aaron Worth. It is well known that Lovecraft lifted single characters from Machen's fiction: the god Nodens, who appears in *The Dream-Quest of Unknown Kadath.* "The Strange High House in the Mist" (1926) borrowed the God of the Greater Abyss from "The Great God Pan" (1890; on the god, see Harms 200–201). Machen is also among the main influences of "The Call of Cthulhu" (1926; Joshi and Schultz 28–29). In "Out of the Æons" (hereafter referred to as "Æons"), a late story ghostwritten for Hazel Heald (1896–1961), Lovecraft seems to mimic Machen in describing a mummy stemming from the abysses of time:

> For one thing, there was a subtle, indefinable sense of limitless antiquity and utter alienage which affected one like a view from the brink of a monstrous abyss of unplumbed blackness—but mostly it was the expression of crazed fear on the puckered, prognathous, half-shielded face. Such a symbol of infinite, inhuman, cosmic fright could not help communicating the emotion to the beholder amidst a disquieting cloud of mystery and vain conjecture. (CF 4.454)

Herein I try to analyze the sources and composition of "Æons" together with its role in Lovecraft's other works.

I.

"Æons" is a short story Lovecraft developed for Hazel Heald that *Weird Tales* published in 1935. The story was often reprinted and ultimately collected in *The Horror in the Museum and Other Revisions* (1970). August Derleth introduced the volume by writing how the best of Lovecraft's revisions could stand comparison with his original material. Joshi observes that this is among the few of Derleth's intelligent statements regarding Lovecraft's work (Joshi, "Lovecraft's Revisions" 3; quoting Derleth ix).

Lovecraft's revisions are a mixed bag. Being the work to which Lovecraft sometimes applied his own prose or ideas, there is a different degree of involvement in every single fiction that remains largely unknown to us. As most of the original drafts submitted by the original authors are lost, we can only rely on internal analysis. Paramount in understanding Lovecraft's role as reviser are his letters to Zealia Brown Reed Bishop (1897–1968), discovered in 2014. The correspondence was published shortly thereafter by the H. P. Lovecraft Historical Society, as *The Spirit of Revision*, and resulted in a precious and elegant volume. The volume is a major accomplishment: Bishop was among Lovecraft's most important clients with the correspondence offering us an important vantage point for understanding Lovecraft's "spirit of revision."[2]

"Æons" is one of the five stories that Lovecraft wrote or revised for Heald, the others being "The Man of Stone" (1932); "The Horror in the Museum" (1932), "Winged Death" (1933), and "The Horror of the Burying Ground" (n.d.). All the stories (in CF 4) share similar settings and distinctive motifs stemming from Heald's own work or intentions, such as the fascination for museums and the idea of functioning brains entrapped in corpses or unanimated things (Joshi and Schultz 109). The latter became a successful trope in literature, notably developed by Bruno Schulz (1892–1942), Roald Dahl in "William and Mary" (1959), and Thomas Ligotti (206–7).

"Æons" is the most successful of the Heald stories. It is a work that Lovecraft would have called "complete recasting & re-writing" (*WH* 276), which was the ultimate in three kinds of involvement-scale developed by Lovecraft. Although Heald has said otherwise, it seems that "Æons" was written entirely by Lovecraft, but built on some of Heald's ideas. Lovecraft does not seem to have been fond of Heald as an author, lamenting, for example, the poverty of plot in "The Horror in the Museum" (*IAP* 838). In a letter to Clark Ashton Smith (26 March 1935), Lovecraft confirmed that the story was basically his own, stating "I *wrote* the damn thing!" (*Dawnward Spire* 594). Joshi maintains that "[t]here can be no questioning of Lovecraft's authorship from start to finish" ("Lovecraft's Revisions" 10). Due to its length and Lovecraft's investment in the work, "Æons" might

---

2. The letters to Bishop are reprinted in *Letters to Woodburn Harris and Others* (2022) and are cited from that edition (abbreviated as *WH*).

have been quite remunerative to Lovecraft, but he often said he could earn more by writing original fiction than by toiling over the work of another.

We are fortunate to have "Æons," but the story is far from the best of Lovecraft's works. I do not doubt its literary quality, nor do I question its relation to the rest of Lovecraft's works, but I would like to suggest that differences within his own works remain striking and pivotal. In fact, the tale, as in all revisions, was published under his client's byline. Even though the themes and plot stem from Lovecraft's pool of work, there is a fundamental difference in degree and salience. This offers us a suggestive vantage point by which to observe Lovecraft's works.

II.

"Æons" is built along many of Lovecraft's fictional tropes. It is an account of maritime voyages, showing the author's taste for adventure tales; it has an uncanny horror, which has both a local New England and a universal feel at the same time. It has an almost cosmic significance. What is happening now and has happened in the distant past are due to the reappearance of a millennia-vanished civilization. There is also the imaginary geography that has become characteristic of Lovecraft's fiction that includes Averoigne in France, a fictional historical province created by Clark Ashton Smith; the re-emerging sunken island along the route from Wellington, New Zealand, to Valparaiso, Chile; the Cabot Museum of Archaeology in Boston, for which Lovecraft offers a very precise location (Mt. Vernon Street, which is also fictional), among others.[3] In "Æons," we also find rich "Yog-Sothothery," featuring cosmic entities such as Tsathoggua, also developed by Smith and first featured in "Tale

---

3. The name Cabot is the Anglicized form of the name of the Venetian explorer Giovanni Caboto (known in the English-speaking world as John Cabot); it is a matter of opinion if the Italian origin of Cabot was supposed to add a further unsettling element announcing the things to come or not. Everybody remembers the short fiction "The Street" (1920; CF 1.113–21): "the single worst tale Lovecraft ever wrote" (IAP 340). It is suggestive that an actual Cabot's Museum was founded in 1945 at Desert Hot Springs.

of Satampra Zeiros" (*Weird Tales*, November 1931), but scooped by Lovecraft who used the entity in "The Whisperer in Darkness" (*Weird Tales*, August 1931); Shub-Niggurath, and, most important, Ghatanothoa, expressly created for "Æons." There is also his library of fictional grimoires, with the story containing one of the lengthiest excerpts from such tomes. The extract narrates a past immemorial: a Deep History staged thousands of years before the present.

The story allegedly is written by a late museum curator, Dr. Richard Johnson, whose report is based on a captain's log and some fictional newspapers and magazines: the *Boston Pillar* and the *Occult Review*, together with the lengthy section of Friedrich von Junzt's *Nameless Cults*. The first-person narrator is dead at the time his narrative is discovered ("[he] died suddenly and rather mysteriously of heart-failure on April 22, 1933" [CF 4.451]), a sinister omen of things to come.

The story opens in 1879 when the freighter *Eridanus* uncovers a mummy in a sunken Pacific island that surfaced as a result of volcanic activity. On the island, the crew discovers architecture of a primordial time: a "a massive stone crypt" (CF 4.452), an element found in many of Lovecraft's tales, beginning with "The Temple" (1920). In one corner of the vault "the frightful mummy crouched"; close by there "was a cylinder of an unknown metal containing a roll of thin, bluish-white membrane of equally unknown nature, inscribed with peculiar characters in a greyish, indeterminable pigment" (CF 4.452). The Cabot Museum's curator at the time, Pickman, a name clearly evoking that of the eccentric artist of Lovecraft's "Pickman's Model" (1926), is interested in acquiring the mummy, and travels to explore the site. No island is to be found because it has already sunk once again into "the watery darkness where it had brooded for untold aeons" (CF 4.453).

Lovecraft describes the mummies' hall by giving a richness of place names, typologies, and different epochs that trigger associations of vastness and depth that tantalize and upset the reader; it also reaffirms Lovecraft as name dropper, as suggested by Garofalo. The mummy is highly repulsive, as imagined in Robert M. Price's rendering for the cover of *Crypt of Cthulhu* No. 11

(1983). To describe the growing notoriety of the object, Lovecraft compares it to the so-called Cardiff giant (see Tribble). By mixing reality and fiction, Lovecraft gives strength and credibility to the tale and its many details.

Lovecraft apparently relished mummies as horror-tropes: in "Supernatural Horror in Literature" he writes favorably of Théophile Gautier's Egyptian-based fictions as well as of Sir Arthur Conan Doyle's "Lot No. 249." He himself cites mummies on a few occasions, particularly in such early writings as "The Nameless City" (1921), "The Hound" (1922), *The Case of Charles Dexter Ward* (1927), and "The Whisperer in Darkness." However, they always have a minor significance. It is suggestive that mummies figure prominently only in "Under the Pyramids" (1924), a novelette Lovecraft wrote for Henry Houdini, the only officially ghostwritten story in Lovecraft's career (Joshi, "Lovecraft's Revisions" 3)—i.e., one formally commissioned by a magazine.

Lovecraft introduces the main idea sustaining "Æons" as follows:

> Theories of a bygone Pacific civilisation, of which the Easter Island images and the megalithic masonry of Ponape and Nan-Matol are conceivable vestiges, were freely circulated among students, and learned journals carried varied and often conflicting speculations on a possible former continent whose peaks survive as the myriad islands of Melanesia and Polynesia. The diversity in dates assigned to the hypothetical vanished culture—or continent—was at once bewildering and amusing; yet some surprisingly relevant allusions were found in certain myths of Tahiti and other islands. (CF 4.455)

III.

At the core of "Æons" is a tale within a tale, the narrative of the sunken continent. Lovecraft's corpus includes stories dealing with time immemorial, such as the prehuman Pnakotic manuscripts (or fragments), introduced in the short story "Polaris" (1918), the first of Lovecraft's fictional grimoires. Historians such as Leopold von Ranke forcefully dismissed the possibility of narrating a history before the emergence of the oldest documents (Smail 45); yet pseudo-scientists, occultists, and science fiction writers aimed to the tell much more ancient stories. It was a chimera of an age where historical pessimism, nationalism, and racism blended with the positivistic expectation of finding narratives recording an immemorial past.[4]

In "Æons," the bygone drama is contained in a mysterious scroll that is found in the cylinder. The text is written with "large, bold hieroglyphs [that] could not be deciphered despite the transmission of photographic copies to every living expert in the given field" (CF 4.455–56). There were only "a few scholars, unusually versed in the literature of occultism and magic" (CF 4.456) who eventually were able to link the glyphs to other sources. Lovecraft records "the famous New Orleans mystic Etienne-Laurent de Marigny" (CF 4.458), a character who also appeared not long before in "Through the Gates of the Silver Key" (1932–33).

Echoes of the scroll's narrative were to be found in the "forbidden books": "obscure, and esoteric texts such as the 'Book of Eibon', reputed to descend from forgotten Hyperborea; the Pnakotic fragments, alleged to be pre-human; and the monstrous and forbidden 'Necronomicon' of the mad Arab Abdul Alhazred" (CF 4.456). The *Necronomicon* needs no introduction. The *Book of Eibon* was a creation of Clark Ashton Smith, and we know that many writers alluded to the fictional books of friends and colleagues as homage to one another. Lovecraft also mentioned the *Book of Eibon* in Heald's "The Man of Stone" and

---

4. The *Oera Linda Book*, written at the end of the nineteenth century, was a lengthy invented story written in Old Frisian. It narrates the fall of Atlantis stretching back to 2194 B.C.E. and proceeding all the way up to 803 C.E., when Charlemagne finally conquers the pagan North. The story recounts the lost Atlantean civilization, with Atlantis meaning *Alt Land*, the 'Old Country,' its downfall, and the migration of his inhabitant to the shores of the North Sea. The chronicle is a blatant hoax, however: up to the Second World War, it enjoyed a revival as a serious historical work, particularly by German-speaking nationalists and Nazis. The *Oera Linda Book* contained glyphs as well, which the first head of the SS Ahnenerbe, Hermann Wirth, tried to match with Scandinavian pictorial inscriptions to unfold a story older than any known at the time (Mees 152–60).

"The Horror in the Museum." The perfect match for the mysterious scroll was, however, yet another tome: the "odd geometrical designs" as "reproduced in the hellish and suppressed 'Black Book' or 'Nameless Cults' of von Junzt" (CF 4.459).

The *Black Book* was a creation of Robert E. Howard (1906–1936), featured in his stories "The Children of the Night" (1931) and "The Black Stone" (1931), the latter being "one of the best Lovecraftian pastiches ever planned" (Price, "The Burrower" 8). The book was written by the fictional character Friedrich von Junzt, a German traveler and explorer moving through Central Asia during the nineteenth century. Lovecraft mentions him and his work from time to time his stories. At Lovecraft's suggestion, August Derleth supplied the alleged German title for the tome (although with a minor mistake; see Joshi, *Rise, Fall* 152). Von Junzt even figures as a witness to the document in which Lovecraft grants Robert Bloch permission to kill the character Bloch shaped after Lovecraft (*Letters to Robert Bloch and Others* 142). The adoption of the *Black Book* is "[t]he most important instance of playful burrowing between Lovecraft and Howard" (Price, "Robert E. Howard" 230).

We have little information on the "hellish" book's story and topic: Robert M. Price suggests that Howard's essay "The Hyborian Age" was intended as stemming from von Junzt's work ("Robert E. Howard" 231). It is cited in Lovecraft's "The Dreams of the Witch House" (1932), wherein the workings of quantum physics are exposed. In "Æons," a long section of it is recorded together with its editorial history, which includes many beloved topoi, such the volume's editorial history from the first German edition (Düsseldorf, 1840; von Junzt dies horribly shortly afterwards), the English translation, and the reprint by Golden Goblin Press—a plot clearly modeled after "History of the 'Necronomicon'" (1927). Most suggestively, a copy of *Nameless Cults* was found in the Church of Starry Wisdom, as stated in the "The Haunter of the Dark" (1935). Together with von Junzt's magnum opus, the Church's library displayed tomes also mentioned in "Æons," although in slightly different forms, language, and editions:

He had himself read many of them—a Latin version of the abhorred "Necronomicon", the sinister "Liber Ivonis", the infamous "Cultes des Goules" of Comte d'Erlette, the "Unaussprechlichen Kulten" of von Junzt, and old Ludvig Prinn's hellish "De Vermis Mysteriis". But there were others he had known merely by reputation or not at all—the Pnakotic Manuscripts, the "Book of Dzyan", and a crumbling volume in wholly unidentifiable characters yet with certain symbols and diagrams shudderingly recognisable to the occult student. (CF 3.460)

It is suggestive that von Junzt's book clusters again (among others) with the *Book of Eibon* (i.e., *Liber Ivonis*), and the Pnakotic Manuscripts, perhaps related to the Pnakotic Fragments (Price, "The Pnakotic Manuscripts"). Lovecraft always staged his fantasies using existing literature: it is well known that Sir James George Frazer's *The Golden Bough* figures in "The Call of Cthulhu," together with Margaret A. Murray's *The Witch Cult in Western Europe,* a book that Lovecraft admired.

The *Book* or *Stanzas of Dzyan* was a creation of Helena Petrova (Madame) Blavatsky (1831–1891, the Russian-born occultist. Her great success *The Secrete Doctrine,* a multi-volume work that served as the basis of Theosophy, was nominally a commentary to the *Stanzas of Dzyan,* a text the author allegedly consulted while in a subterranean monastery of Tibet. The *Stanzas of Dzyan* was presented as the oldest book on Earth, preserved, like the cylinder-scroll, on its original support "a collection of palm leaves made impermeable to water, fire and air, by some specific unknown process" (Blavatsky 1.1). Theosophy was a modern religion, part of a broader occultist movement, imagining a hidden history of the world, a genealogy of races, forgotten continents, and secret, arcane knowledge. It exercised a powerful influence on the age, inspiring different arts, literature among them, and in particular the fantastic. Fritz Leiber notably suggested theosophic influences in Edgar Rice Burroughs's John Carter yarns; the same is true of some of Lovecraft's fantasies (Price, "HPL and HPB").

IV.

When writing of the lost continent, Lovecraft turned again to Deep History. The most successful early attempt was, by far, "The Rats in the Walls" (1923), one of his most iconic stories and the inspiration for endless projects, among them the acclaimed videogame *Darkest Dungeon*. The sense of depth is expressed when Delapore finds "some vault deeper than the deepest known masonry of the Romans [that] underlay this accursed pile" (CF 1.389–90).

But "Æons" is perhaps his boldest undertaking. The setting of the story develops in a landscape resembling his earliest Dunsanian tales, wherein he had created dreamlike allegories unfolding apparently in an ancient world filled with magic (*IAP* 332–54. Such stories as "The White Ship" (1919) or "Polaris" are delightful examples, although the latter was written before Lovecraft ever read Dunsany (Joshi, "Polaris"; *IAP* 888). Moreover, they were both composed as Lovecraft was just beginning to write fiction. But even if these older stories share elements with "Æons," they take place in an oneiric dimension, cast out of history. The setting of Polaris is not even on Earth—it unfolds in the center of the night sky. On the contrary, "Æons" is precisely framed within Earth's timeline, in forgotten Deep History.

Lovecraft introduces this aspect while narrating the growing fame of the mummy:

> The archaic whispers reflected in the "Black Book", and linked with designs and symbols so closely akin to what the mysterious scroll and cylinder bore, were indeed of a character to hold one spellbound and not a little awestruck. Leaping an incredible gulf of time—behind all the civilisations, races, and lands we know— they clustered round a vanished nation and a vanished continent of the misty, fabulous dawn-years ... that to which legend has given the name of Mu, and which old tablets in the primal Naacal tongue speak of as flourishing 200,000 years ago, when Europe harboured only hybrid entities, and lost Hyperborea knew the nameless worship of black amorphous Tsathoggua. (CF 4.460)

Mankind could not possibly have a chronology of this nature (Klein and Edgar). Yet this idea of an incommensurable antiquity for humanity was a vision of Lovecraft's age: "[n]ot only was humanity assigned an age of far greater antiquity than that conceded by science, but it was also integrated into a scheme of cosmic, physical, and spiritual evolution" (Goodrick-Clarke 20).

Lovecraft introduces a place lost in time: "here was mention of a kingdom or province called K'naa in a very ancient land where the first human people had found monstrous ruins left by those who had dwelt there before—vague waves of unknown entities which had filtered down from the stars and lived out their aeons on a forgotten, nascent world" (CF 4.460). Names (of places and people) are archaic and distant. Dunsany meticulously devised names to express the flavor of given historical landscapes (Joshi, *Unutterable Horror* 2.385); Lovecraft developed weird names intended to sound forsaken and alien. There is further interesting detail on K'naa society, created with some detail as having a sort of hierocracy and monarchy. The priest society again resonates with the occultist conception of societies ruled by priests and keepers of secret knowledge: the Austrian occultist Guido von List (1848–1919), one of the greatest inspirations of the Nazi Party, created a long-gone Aryan Empire (Goodrick-Clarke 56–65).

Here we have a milieu in which human beings and gods live together, as in "The Doom That Came to Sarnath" (1919): the spawn of Yuggoth that had once dwelt in the place has departed and is long gone, leaving behind a godlike creature: "their hellish god or patron daemon Ghatanothoa" (CF 4.460). Ghatanothoa, we learn, could turn creatures to stone with his gaze. This may have been Heald's idea: in "The Man of Stone," Mad Dan finds a copy of the *Book of Eibon* containing a formula capable of turning one to stone. In K'naa, a cult was dedicated to Ghatanothoa, commanding that twelve maidens and twelve warriors be sacrificed to the god every year in order to placate him.

The story is not very original in this regard: it is Greek mythology with tentacles. The petrifying gaze is that of the Gorgon; the annual sacrifice is that to the Minotaur of Knossos. (Ghatanothoa must have been much hungrier than the Minotaur, for he claimed twelve victims instead of seven.) Yet, in Lovecraft's stories, as in those of some occultists and pseudo-scientists, any redundancy was to be explained as coming from an earlier common source. Greek stories originated from Mu legends; the Minotaur and Gorgon were pale reflections of Ghatanothoa.

What follows is the story of T'yog, which covers the narrative and textual center of "Æons." T'yog is a "bold heretic" (CF 4.462) priest of Shub-Niggurath; he is ready to challenge Ghatanothoa because: "[i]n the end he felt sure that the gods friendly to man could be arrayed against the hostile gods, and believed that Shub-Niggurath, Nug, and Yeb, as well as Yig the Serpent-god, were ready to take sides with man against the tyranny and presumption of Ghatanothoa" (CF 4.462).

In this case, gods are benevolent to man. The sentence above was destined to become notorious as a result of the use that Derleth and his followers would make of it. It was probably meant to reflect the general fabulous atmosphere of the story, mirroring the Atlantean mythology of the day. Another German nationalist (and SS affiliate), Karl Maria Willgut (1866–1946), who gave himself the bombastic nickname Weisthor, also theorized a conflict between creeds in Atlantis that eventually brought the old continent to ruin (Goodrick-Clarke 177–191; Mees, 204–5).

The final moments of T'yog took place in "The Year of the Red Moon (estimated as B.C. 173,148 by von Junzt)" (CF 4.462), when the priest climbed the fortress of Yaddith-Gho armed with a spell granting him the power to overcome Ghatanothoa. However, his rivals deceitfully stole the spell so that T'yog went to his cosmic showdown emptyhanded, never to be seen again.

> None ever dared to defy it again. And so the ages rolled on, and King succeeded King, and High-Priest succeeded High-Priest, and nations rose and decayed, and lands rose above the sea and returned into the sea. And with many millennia decay fell upon K'naa—till at last on a hideous day of storm and thunder, terrific rumbling, and mountain-high waves, all the land of Mu sank into the sea forever. (CF 4.465)

The cult of Ghatanothoa continued to survive among different cults and was practiced in distant places. The narrative resumes

in the twentieth century with an unexpected rise in cultic activities that might be linked to von Junzt, the cylinder-scroll, and
T'yog. Mysterious strangers, mostly from Pacific regions, also
begin to visit the mummy. Lovecraft paints a gallery of stereo-
types to suggest the vastness of an underground creed crossing
regions and millennia.

In the final pages, two men are found dead in front of the
mummy, whose eye had finally opened. Within the mummy's
retina is an infinitely small image, which Dr. Johnson is able to
magnify: "for here, in the year 1932, a man in the city of Boston
was looking on something which belonged to an unknown and
utterly alien world—a world that vanished from existence and
normal memory aeons ago" (CF 4.476). Dr. Johnson is able to
peer into the fortress of Yaddith-Gho: even further magnifica-
tion reveals the monstrous shape of Ghatanothoa.

It comes as little surprise that the mummy is in fact poor
T'yog, petrified by Ghatanothoa's gaze. An autopsy reveals that
his brain is still alive and the priest has remained conscious the
whole time (almost 200,000 years!), condemned to spend eterni-
ty in a watery tomb.

V.

Stories of lost continents are rooted in the culture of the ancient
Mediterranean and gained prominence during the second half of
the nineteenth century. Their reach was immense, reflecting the
desire for new lands to uncover. At a time when the unknown
areas in geographical maps had almost completely disappeared,
expectations turned toward lands below the seas. By the end of
the nineteenth century developments in the theories of continental drift, which could be simplified around the figure of Alfred Wegener (1880–1930), who suggested that it was indeed
possible for land masses to rise and sink. The knowledge about an
area of land now submerged in the North Sea named Doggerland
seemed to grant scientific soundness to these myths. In 1897,
H. G. Wells made Doggerland the setting of his prehistoric tales.

Such suggestions gained momentum when Philip Scatler
published an article in 1864 that proposed the existence of a lost

supercontinent that he named Lemuria. Lemuria was a hypothetical land bridge running across the Pacific and Indian Oceans and linking Zeeland with Madagascar; it was named after the lemures populating the fringes of the oceans and ideally originating from a land mass in between. In only a few years, the same methods were applied to human culture, so that vestiges of ancient civilization perceived as similar in different continents but across the oceans legitimized the idea of a common origin: they all stemmed from a single, much older culture that had its epicenter in the immense water mass of the oceans. It is here that the origin emerged for the idea of lost continents and lost cultures as occupying a gray area between scientific research, metaphor, and occult thinking. Lost continents became a focus of theosophical views, where successive civilizations flourished and fell through Earth's long history.

In Lovecraft's day, theories flourished that imagined forgotten continents cradling lost cultures and secret knowledge, such as Atlantis, Lemuria, and Mu.[5] Lovecraft, being receptive to these speculations, mentioned a few in his fiction. In "Æons," Dr. Richards admits his "smattering" of knowledge of theosophical lore and his fondness for "Colonel Churchward and Lewis Spence" (CF 4.457).[6] Still more noteworthy, on 17 June 1926, Lovecraft wrote to Clark Ashton Smith:

> I've also been digesting something of vast interest as background or source material . . . the Atlantis–Lemuria tales, as developed by modern occultists & theosophical charlatans. Really,

---

5. Charles-Étienne Brasseur de Bourbourg, a scholar of Mesoamerican ancient civilizations, first mentioned the possible existence of land called Mu. The curious name stemmed from a misreading of a passage in the famous *Troano Codex*, today known as *Madrid Codex*, one of the three surviving Maya codices composed between the thirteenth and fifteenth centuries (Sharer and Traxler 126–29). Eventually, a "Land of Mu" was modeled by Augustus Le Plongeon as an alternative name for Atlantis: his work was pseudo-scientifical in nature and tainted by occult lore.

6. James Churchward wrote *Lost Continent of Mu, the Motherland of Man* (1926). Robert M. Price wryly observed that "Churchward's Mu was an Anglo-Saxon's paradise, a sort of super-Tahiti with an apartheid system" ("Monsters" 11).

some of these hints about the lost "City of the Golden Gates" &
the shapeless monsters of archaic Lemuria are ineffably pregnant
with fantastic suggestion; & I only wish I could get hold of more
of the stuff. What I have read is his "The Story of Atlantis & the
Lost Lemuria", by W. Scott[-]Elliot. (*Dawnward Spire* 106)

William Scott-Elliot's *The Story of Atlantis and The Lost Lemuria* was published in 1925 and comprised two booklets previously
issued separately. Scott-Elliot's ideas originated from Madame
Blavatsky's work. In *The Lost Lemuria*, the denizens of that race
inhabited the planet before there were human beings. They were
very tall, dark, and hermaphroditic. He characterized their com-
plexion poignantly: their heads "sloped forward and backward"
(Scott-Elliot 23), and their physical appearance could still be
seen in the great Moai stone carvings of Easter Island. Lovecraft's inhabitants of Mu resemble these Lemurians. Describing
T'yog, he wrote "but mostly it was the expression of crazed fear
on the puckered, prognathous, half-shielded face" (CF 4.454).
Scott-Elliot described Lemurians as follows: "[m]onsters they
bred. A race of crooked red-hair-covered monsters going on all
fours. A dumb race to keep the shame untold." Humans were
among the species with which the Lemurians had bred.

Inspiration for "Æons" may have also come from more mundane sources. William Fulwiler (20) has shown the influence of
Charles Fort, particularly in his *The Book of the Dammed* (1919),
in Lovecraft's development of Yuggoth. Indeed, ideas on Earth's
antiquity and its subsequent civilizations were often published.
Quite popular was the *Eis Welt Theorie,* the Ice World Theory of
the Austrian engineer Hans Hörbiger, a theory involving moons
striking the planet, successive Ice Ages, and the consecutive
downfall of civilizations; it was a theory beloved by Adolf Hitler.
Similar ideas are found in a lengthy article published in the *New
York American* on 20 October 1912 by Paul Schliemann, the
self-declared grandson of Heinrich Schliemann, the discoverer
of Troy, titled "How I Discovered Atlantis, the Source of All
Civilization." Schliemann wrote that his grandfather had recovered a vessel with a Phoenician inscription recording a King
Cronos of Atlantis. He announced that a book was soon to fol-

low, but one was never published. There is little literature on the topic: L. Sprague de Camp, writing in the 1950s, believed it to be a factual report, but it now seems that the whole article was a hoax (Joseph 245). Nevertheless, it reflects the discourse of the age: Atlantis was a lost world that had existed in a deep historical time; it was a just society, a heterotopia in a bleak vision of the present. Schliemann adds:

> [o]bjects then, perfectly similar and having unquestionably a common source were found in such widely separated countries as these. The objects themselves are not Phoenician, Mycenean nor Central American. What is the conclusion? That they came to both places from a common centre. The inscription on my objects gave that centre—It was Atlantis!

It is one of Lovecraft's beloved tropes:

> Yet the similarity of Egyptian and Mayan life and civilization is so perfect that it is impossible to think of it as an accident. We find no such accidents in nature or history. The only possibility is that there was, as the legend says, a great continent that connected what we now call the New World with what we call the old. Perhaps at this time what there was of Europe and America was populated with monsters. Africa possibly had a monkey-like negro race. Man in our sense had not overrun them. But there was a land where civilization as high as that we now know and perhaps higher was flourishing. Its outskirts were the edge of wilderness. It was Atlantis.

Schliemann broke the vase and from inside recovered a medal inscribed with hieroglyphs:

> On the obverse side was engraved in ancient Phoenician, "Issued in the Temple of Transparent Walls." How did the metal get in the vase? I do not know. The neck was too small for its insertion, but there it was and it had been imbedded in the clay of the bottom and my grandfather had evidently known it was there.

As Lovecraft was writing such tropes as civilizations lost in Deep History, sunken continents, and occult lore, then spread in the imagination and culture of the age as pseudo-sciences, religious doctrines, and nationalist vistas. He dismisses many these authors as "charlatans," but he was fascinated by grandiose depictions of the Earth's past proper to Theosophy and similar lore. It seems consistent with his complicated relationship with the occult, as drawn by Brian J. Reis. William Fulwiler wrote that "Æons" and the obscure "Bothon" (by Henry S. Whitehead) are the most theosophical of Lovecraft's stories (Fulwiler 20); I would add "The Mound" (1929–30) to the list. All these stories were revision work.

"Æons" contains several theosophically inspired tropes.

1) A lost and sunken civilization whose culture is inherited, although in fragments, by the primary civilizations in human history.

2) Friedrich von Junzt and his occultism. Robert E. Howard shaped von Junzt as his own Abdul Alhazred in "The Black Stone," wherein he offers a history of the author as a traveler and an explorer, acquainted with occult lore and lost and hidden civilizations, and portrays him as one who died horribly after returning from Mongolia.[7]

3) More questionable is whether "Æons" features the breeding of life with Ghatanothoa as being a creation of the Yuggoth spawn. The theme appears in At the Mountains of Madness with the Great Race creating the infamous shoggoths just as the Lemurians bred monsters (on shoggoths see Hams 257–58).

Lovecraft became outspoken after narrating the downfall of Mu following T'yog's misadventure with the continent's culture surviving

[. . .] in ill-fated Atlantis, and on the abhorred plateau of Leng [. . .] in the fabled subterranean kingdom of K'n-yan, [. . .] Egypt, Chaldaea, Persia, China, the forgotten Semite empires of Africa, and Mexico and Peru in the New World. That it had a

---

7. I have no positive evidence for this, but for me, the fictional author seems to be shaped after the Polish author and traveller Ferdynand Ossendowski, who published his first English book in 1921, the bestselling Beasts, Men and Gods, a report of his travels through Inner Asia (and Mongolia) in the aftermath of the Russian Revolution. Ossendowski blended occultist ideas with an account of Buddhist beliefs, referring to the subterranean kingdom of Agartha, where the King of the World reigned. This kingdom had supernatural powers that could be unleashed to destroy humanity. This warrants further investigation.

strong connexion with the witchcraft movement in Europe, against which the bulls of popes were vainly directed, he more than strongly hinted. It always survived somehow, chiefly in the Far East and on the Pacific Islands, where its teachings became merged into the esoteric lore of the Polynesian *Areoi*. (CF 4.465–66)

We grasp the idea of the deep antiquity of Earth and men, wherein humanity has undergone successive resets, with cultures of the past being legacies of an earlier age rather than developments. It is a view that has maintained some of its appeal, as can be seen in the success of such authors as John Anthony West and Graham Hancock.

Lovecraft drew on contemporary scientific and pseudo-scientific discourses to shape the fabric of his fictions, but he did so to varying degrees. In fact, I maintain that he skillfully molded revision work differently from his own tales.

VI.

Lovecraft's letters to Bishop focus on writing, genres, plot, and style. They convey his love for sharing the great knowledge of the editorial landscape of his day. There are many reading suggestions, ranging from Greek to French literature; his advice is dotted with amenities and pleasantries that demonstrate his patience as well as his ability and desire to keep clients.

Lovecraft was much more cautious in sharing his own literary characters and devices. His suggestions hint of the cosmic (WH 337), but such occasions are rare. Things changed slightly once Lovecraft began working on the story he renamed "The Curse of Yig" (1928), the first Bishop managed to get published. We may suppose Lovecraft's development and writing pervade the story. Yig was a snake god, which Lovecraft termed "a product of my imaginative theogony—for like Dunsany I love to invent gods & devils & kindred marvellous things" (WH 365). Yet the insight into his writing method stems from a letter written to August Derleth (*Essential Solitude* 146).

It is not surprising, but nevertheless unfortunate, that even while working on "The Mound" (since December 1929), Lovecraft never mentions his plot development with his client.

Therefore, we cannot distinguish the creative process of either. Lovecraft only warns Bishop on the correct spelling of imaginary names (*WH* 432). As a story, "The Mound" is similar to "Æons" (for an accurate discussion see *IAP* 745–48) and focuses on Deep History and lost civilizations, horrors of the past haunting the present. The story of a bygone time is again extracted from an ancient scroll inside a cylinder made of a peculiar material called Tulu-metal.

It seems Lovecraft developed a fictional world for his clients contiguous with but separate from his own. As with Bishop, Lovecraft made Heald write stories neighboring his fictional landscapes: we find books and characters of his own and those borrowed from friends. The revisions rarely feature important lore, such as the rare description of Yog-Sothoth in the "The Horror in the Museum" as "a congeries of iridescent globes, yet stupendous in its malign suggestiveness" (*CF* 4.436). If the *Necronomicon* kept Lovecraft's major stories together (Tyson 4–5), the same function in "Æons" is given to von Junzt's *Black Book*. Moreover, Lovecraft displays ad hoc creations that do not appear in the rest of his own tales, notwithstanding some major exceptions such as Shub-Niggurath, and Nug and Yeb to a minor extent (Murray). Robert M. Price named this minor "mythos" after the different authors for which Lovecraft revisited, in our case the "Heald Mythos" ("The Revision Mythos" 15). As Price remarked, the sunken Cyclopean fortress in Yaddith-Gho mirrors R'lyeh, with its non-Euclidean angles: "No human creature had ever climbed Yaddith-Gho or seen that blasphemous fortress except as a distant and geometrically abnormal outline against the sky; yet most agreed that Ghatanothoa was still there, wallowing and burrowing in unsuspected abysses beneath the megalithic walls" (*CF* 4.460–61). Ghatanothoa, in turn, is an analogue of Cthulhu:

> Even now I cannot begin to suggest it with any words at my command. I might call it gigantic—tentacled—proboscidian—octopus-eyed—semi-amorphous—plastic—partly squamous and partly rugose—ugh! But nothing I could say could even adumbrate the loathsome, unholy, non-human, extra-galactic horror

and hatefulness and unutterable evil of that forbidden spawn of black chaos and illimitable night. (CF 4.477)

It is not too callous to suggest that Ghatanothoa and Yaddith-Gho are a poor man's versions of Lovecraft's originals.[8]

Lovecraft is reluctant to feature his own trademark creations together with his cosmic philosophy in others' stories and finds confirmation in the spawn of Yuggoth that appears in "Æons": S. T. Joshi thoughtfully remarked how the spawn are not the fungi featured in "The Whisperer in Darkness" but instead an older breed of Pluto also mentioned briefly in that novella and developed for "Æons" ("Lovecraft's Other Planets" 6).

Not only are the characters lesser versions of Lovecraft's own, even the scale of the account is reduced. And it is here that Deep History comes into play. Although taking place at the dawn of human history, the story is human in character, just as it is in "The Mound": the deep and yet human chronological influence of Arthur Machen is apparent. While Lovecraft was working on his masterpieces, increasingly characterizing his narratives as horror-cum-science-fiction, "Æons" is a pronounced return to Dunsanian fantasies, strongly tinged by Clark Ashton Smith's work and Robert Howard's heroic fantasy.

Aside from setting and scale, revisions feature an array of tropes and tricks that Lovecraft normally avoided in his own fiction. We see the pervasive presence of occult lore; Lovecraft even returns to magic, among the weakest elements of his writings, yet featured in some of his most acclaimed fiction. Lovecraft never wanted to have the novella *The Case of Charles Dexter Ward* published. The spells of Joseph Curwen based on "essential saltes" have been dryly defined as "bad sci-fi" (Peter Straub in *H. P. Lovecraft: Fear of the Unknown;* Salonia). "Æons," like other revisions, finally moves along the "tongue in cheek" spirit (Fulwiler 23) that characterized his revisions, and which is mostly absent in his own writings. In "The Horror in the Museum," Rhan-Tegoth, another

---

8. Overlap between the two is clear. In the song "Sleep No More" (2013) by Metallica, besides listening to "Cthulhu Awaken" we also hear "You turn to stone," which is not a power of Cthulhu but of Ghatanothoa.

improbable Cthulhu-like god locked in the basement, which
"[o]ne would like to think [. . .] a self-parody of Lovecraft's own
mythos" (Joshi and Schultz 116; Harms 237–38). The story even
features Clark Ashton Smith as a character!

Finally, and most notably, the stories are dominated by a
"spirit of revision" that, I believe, should not be confused with
Lovecraft's own work, contrary to what August Derleth has asserted. In "Æons" there is a forgotten past is that measurable;
there are gods who act according to intelligible, almost human
patterns; there are even entities that acknowledge human beings
and are benign toward them. In this story, T'yog is so empow-
ered that he plans to fight a cosmic entity such as Ghatanothoa.
Like the infamous Black Magic quotation, this is the very stuff of
the "Derleth Mythos," even drifting into later Titus Crow's adventures.[9] As mentioned, it is in "Æons" that we find the sentence: "he [T'yog] felt sure that the gods friendly to man could
be arrayed against the hostile gods" (CF 4.462). It is not by coincidence that Derleth maintained that we should consider
Lovecraft's best revisions to "stand alongside" his own work (ix).
After all, Lovecraft wrote "Æons" for Heald, not for himself.
Lovecraft has the last word in the matter: "not much of my own
style gets into my revisions" (WH 338).

*

"Æons" is a sound revision work by Lovecraft, but its flavor is
bittersweet. It stands apart from Lovecraft's latest work, returning to Dunsanian and magical settings and plot. Readers will
find the story's tropes in a few of Lovecraft's other narratives,
but in different phases of his work; some were otherwise rejected
in other contemporary narratives while others were completely
dismissed by the time "Æons" was composed. The story is a sort of
Frankenstein-like creature; nevertheless, the pieces are granted

---

9. On Derleth, see Mackley. On Derleth's coloring of Lovecraft's work, see
Tierney; Mosig; Joshi, Rise, Fall 176–202; and, a bit more sympathetically,
Price, "The Lovecraft–Derleth Connection." See also a different interpretation
in Haefele, whose book must be handled with care. It nevertheless remains an
"heroic task," as Joshi wrote: stjoshi.org/review_haefele.html.

their own distinctive life and flavor, as Herbert West would have appreciated. They are developed into something new, which gives them some originality of their own.

Most importantly, "Æons" is cunningly meant to be a homage to Lovecraft written by another author. Lovecraft creates Heald's fictional word as contiguous with but separate from his own. This is a fundamental point in understanding "Æons" and, in my opinion, Lovecraft's revisions at large. Indeed, Lovecraft shaped terrestrial, almost provincial, human stories with themes exploited from occult lore and Deep History, rather than the science fiction and Deep Time characterizing his authored works.

I suspect that revisions may have been a sort of trial run for Lovecraft's own stories. "Æons" has indeed the flavor of the novella "The Shadow out of Time" (1934–35; see Fawver), which was written after "Æons" where even the similarity of the title makes it evident. "The Shadow out of Time" is among Lovecraft's more accomplished narratives, majestically expanding on some of the tropes in "Æons": the consciousness cast into distant ages; the horror of scale, where humanity is a part of successive civilizations or races, because we know that "[a]fter man there would be the mighty beetle civilisation" (CF 3.399.) It is the very essence of what Donald R. Burleson elegantly named "denied primacy" ("On Lovecraft's Themes" 136). It is a thrilling trope that could also be hailed with a sort of deliverance because recent books (e.g., Zalasiewicz) focusing on future geology develop the same vistas. Moreover, we find the recognition of Theosophy and occult lore, and even the idea "of chapters in human history whose existence no scholar of today has ever suspected" (CF 3.397): The Year of the Red Moon, indeed.

One final quotation may help in framing "Æons" within Lovecraft's works: "K'naa was a sacred place, since from its midst the bleak basalt cliffs of Mount Yaddith-Gho soared starkly into the sky, topped by a gigantic fortress of Cyclopean stone, infinitely older than mankind and built by the alien spawn of the dark planet Yuggoth, which had colonised the earth before the birth of terrestrial life" (CF 4.460). The Cyclopean stone fortress was "infinitely" older than the first continent's dwellers: here

Deep History meets Deep Time. The story written for Heald was merely a "stepping-stone" leading to the vaster, deeper, and darker fiction of Lovecraft.

Works Cited

Brasseur de Bourbourg, Étienne-Charles. *Manuscrit Troano: Études sur le système graphique et la langue des Mayas*. Paris: Impr. Impériale, 1869–70. 2 vols.

Blavatsky, Helena Petrovna. *The Secret Doctrine: The Synthesis of Science, Religion, and Philosophy*. 1888. Cambridge: Cambridge University Press, 2011. 3 vols.

Burleson, Donald R. "On Lovecraft's Themes: Touching the Glass." In David E. Schultz and S. T. Joshi, ed. *An Epicure in the Terrible: A Centennial Anthology of Essays in Honor of H. P. Lovecraft*. 1991. New York: Hippocampus Press, 2011. 139–52.

———. "Some Comments on the Lovecraft-Dunsany Influence," *Crypt of Cthulhu* No. 15 (Lammas 1983): 3, 29.

Carter, Lin (with Robert M. Price and S. T. Joshi). "H. P. Lovecraft: The Books." In Darrell Schweitzer, ed. *Discovering H. P. Lovecraft*. Holicong, PA: Wildside Press, 2001. 107–47.

Churchward, James. *The Lost Continent of Mu, the Motherland of Men*, New York: W. E. Rudge, 1926.

Derleth, August. "Lovecraft's Revisions." In *The Horror in the Museum and Other Revisions*. Sauk City, WI: Arkham House, 1970. vii–x.

Eco, Umberto. *Storia delle terre e dei luoghi leggendari*. Milan: Bompiani, 2013.

Fawver, Kurt. "'Present'-ly Safe: The Anthropocentricism of Time in H. P. Lovecraft's Fiction." *Journal of the Fantastic in the Arts* 20 (2009): 248–61.

Fort, Charles, *The Book of the Damned*. New York: Boni & Liveright, 1919.

Fulwiler, William. "Mu in 'Bothon' and 'Out of Eons.'" *Crypt of Cthulhu* No. 11 (Candlemas 1983): 20–24.

Garofalo, Charles. "Lovecraft the Name-Dropper." *Crypt of Cthulhu* No. 2 (Yuletide 1981): 9–10.

Goodrick-Clarke, Nicholas. *The Occult Roots of Nazism: Secret Aryan Cults and Their Influence on Nazi Ideology: The Ariosophists of Austria and Germany 1890–1935.* Wellingborough, UK: Aquarian Press, 1985.

Gould, Stephen Jay. *Time's Arrow, Time's Cycle: Myth and Metaphor in the Discovery of Geological Time.* Cambridge, MA: Harvard University Press, 1987.

H. P. Lovecraft: Fear of the Unknown. Dir. Frank H. Woodward. Wyrd, 2008.

Haefele, John. *A Look Behind the Derleth Mythos: Origins of the Cthulhu Mythos.* Odense: H. Harksen Productions, 2012.

Hallam, A. "Alfred Wegener and the Hypothesis of Continental Drift." *Scientific American* 232 (1975): 88–97.

Harris, Steven Marc. *Von Unaussprechlichen Kulten: A Preliminary History.* Monographs in Contemporary Metaphysics, 1. Buffalo, NY: Celestial Enlightenment Press, 1995.

Harms, Daniel. *The Cthulhu Mythos Encyclopaedia: A Guide to H. P. Lovecraft's Universe.* Lake Orion, MI: Elder Sign Press, 2008.

———, and John Wisdom Gonce III. *The Necronomicon Files.* Boston: Weiser, 2003.

Hazen, Robert M. *The Story of Earth: The First 4.5 billion Years, from Stardust to Living Planets.* London: Penguin, 2012.

Hörbiger, Hanns, and Phillip Fauth. *Glazial-Kosmogonie.* Kaiserslautern: Kayser, 1913.

Houellebecq, Michel. *H. P. Lovecraft : Contre le monde, contre la vie.* Monaco: Rocher, 1991. Tr. Dorna Khazeni as *H. P. Lovecraft: Against the World, Against Life.* San Francisco: Believer Books, 2005.

Joseph, Frank. *The Atlantis Encyclopaedia.* Franklin Lakes, NJ: Career Press, 2008.

Joshi, S. T. "Lovecraft's Other Planets." *Crypt of Cthulhu* No. 5 (Roodmas 1982): 3–11.

———. "Lovecraft's Revisions: How Much of Them Did He Write?" *Crypt of Cthulhu* No. 11 (1983): 3–14.

———. "On Polaris." *Crypt of Cthulhu* No. 15 (Lammas 1983): 22–26.

————. *The Rise, Fall, and Rise of the Cthulhu Mythos*. New York: Hippocampus Press, 2015.

————. *Unutterable Horror: A History of Supernatural Fiction*. 2012. New York: Hippocampus, 2014. 2 vols.

————, and David E. Schultz. *An H. P. Lovecraft Encyclopaedia*. 2001. New York: Hippocampus Press, 2004.

Joshi, S. T., ed. *Dissecting Cthulhu: Essays on the Cthulhu Mythos*. Lakeland, FL: Miskatonic River Press, 2011.

Klein, Richard G., and Blake Edgard. *The Dawn of Human Culture*. New York: John Wiley & Sons, 2002.

Kurlander, Eric. "Hitler's Supernatural Sciences: Astrology, Anthroposophy, and World Ice Theory in the Third Reich." In Eric Kurlander and Monica Black, ed. *Revisiting the 'Nazi Occult': Histories, Realities, Legacies*. Rochester: Boydell & Brewer, 2015. 132–56.

Le Plongeon, Augustus. *Queen Móo and the Egyptian Sphinx*. London: Trübner, 1896.

Lévy, Maurice. *Lovecraft ou du fantastique*. Paris: Union Générale d'Éditions, 1972. Tr. S. T. Joshi as *Lovecraft: A Study in the Fantastic*. Detroit: Wayne State University Press, 1988.

Leiber, Fritz. "John Carter: Sword of Theosophy." 1959. In L. Sprague de Camp, ed. *The Spell of Conan*. New York: Ace, 1980. 211–17.

————. "A Literary Copernicus." 1949. In Darrell Schweitzer, ed. *Discovering H. P. Lovecraft*. Holicong, PA: Wildside Press, 2001. 7–16.

Lovecraft, H. P. *The Annotated Supernatural Horror in Literature*. Ed. S. T. Joshi. 2nd ed. New York: Hippocampus Press, 2012.

————. *Letters to Robert Bloch and Others*. Ed. David E. Schultz and S. T. Joshi. New York: Hippocampus Press, 2015.

————. *Letters to Woodburn Harris and Others*. Ed. S. T. Joshi and David E. Schultz. New York: Hippocampus Press, 2022.

————, and August Derleth. *Essential Solitude: The Letters of H. P. Lovecraft and August Derleth*. Ed. David E. Schultz and S. T. Joshi. New York: Hippocampus Press, 2008. 2 vols.

————, and Clark Ashton Smith. *Dawnward Spire, Lonely Hill: The Letters of H. P. Lovecraft and Clark Ashton Smith*, ed. David

E. Schultz and S. T. Joshi. New York: Hippocampus Press, 2020. 2 vols.

Mackley, J. S. "The Shadow over Derleth: Disseminating the Mythos in *The Trail of Cthulhu.*" In David Simmons, ed. *New Critical Essays on H. P. Lovecraft.* New York: Palgrave Macmillan, 2013. 119–34.

Murray, Will. "On the Nature of Nug and Yeb." 1984. In S. T. Joshi, ed. *Dissecting Cthulhu.* Lakeland, FL: Miskatonic River Press, 2011. 139–47.

———. "Deconstructing Nug and Yeb." *Crypt of Cthulhu* No. 108 (Hallowmas 2017): 3–6.

Mees, Bernard. *The Science of the Swastika.* Budapest: Central European University Press, 2008.

Mosig, Dirk W. "H. P. Lovecraft: Myth-Maker." 1980. In S. T. Joshi, ed. *Dissecting Cthulhu.* Lakeland, FL: Miskatonic River Press, 2011. 13–21.

Price, Robert M. "The Borrower Beneath: Howard's Debt to Lovecraft in 'The Black Stone.'" *Crypt of Cthulhu* No. 3 (Candlemas 1982): 8–11.

———. "HPL and HPB: Lovecraft's Use of Theosophy." *Crypt of Cthulhu* No. 5 (Roodmas 1982): 3–9.

———. "The Lovecraft–Derleth Connection." *Lovecraft Studies* No. 7 (Fall 1982): 18–23.

———. "Monsters of Mu: The Lost Continent in the Cthulhu Mythos." *Crypt of Cthulhu* No. 5 (Roodmas 1982): 10–14.

———. "The Pnakotic Manuscripts: A Study." *Crypt of Cthulhu* No. 23 (St. John's Eve 1984): 38–42.

———. "Robert E. Howard and the Cthulhu Mythos." 1989. In S. T. Joshi, ed. *Dissecting Cthulhu.* Lakeland, FL: Miskatonic River Press, 2011. 224–32.

Reis, Brian J. "Structurally Cosmic Apostasy: The Atheist Occult World of H. P. Lovecraft." *Lux* 1 (2013): 1–16.

Romano, Marco, and Richard L. Cifelli. "100 Years of Continental Drift." *Science* 350 (2015): 915–16.

Salonia, John. "Essential Saltes: Lovecraft's Witchcraft." *Lovecraft Annual* No. 10 (2016): 53–74.

Scatler, Phillip. "The Mammals of Madagascar." *Quarterly Journal of Science* 1 (1864): 213–16.

Schliemann, Paul. "How I Discovered Atlantis, the Source of All Civilization." *New York American* (20 October 1912). https://levigilant.com/Bulfinch_Mythology/bulfinch.englishat heist.org/atl/AtlantisFound.html

Schultz, David E. "The Origin of Lovecraft's 'Black Magic' Quote." *Crypt of Cthulhu* No. 48 (St. John's Eve 1987): 9–13.

Schweitzer, Darell. "Lovecraft and Lord Dunsany." In Darrell Schweitzer, ed. *Discovering H. P. Lovecraft*. Holicong, PA: Wildside Press, 2001. 72–87.

Scott–Elliot, W. *The Story of Atlantis and The Lost Lemuria*. London: Theosophical Publishing House, 1925.

Sederholm, Carl H., and Jeffrey Andrew Weinstock, ed. *The Age of Lovecraft*. Minneapolis: University of Minnesota Press, 2016.

Sharer, Robert J., and Loa P. Traxler. *The Ancient Maya*. 6th ed. Stanford, CA: Stanford University Press, 2006.

Smail, Daniel Lord. *On Deep History and the Brain*. Berkeley: University of California Press, 2008.

Sumathi, Ramaswamy. *The Lost Land of Lemuria: Fabulous Geographies, Catastrophic Histories*. Berkeley: University of California Press, 2004.

Tribble, Scott, *A Colossal Hoax: The Giant from Cardiff that Fooled America*. Lanham, MA: Rowman & Littlefield, 2009.

Tierney, Richard, L. "The Derleth Mythos." 1972. In Darrell Schweitzer, ed. *Discovering Lovecraft*. Holicong, PA: Wildside Press, 2001. 52–53.

Tyson, Donald. *The Dream World of H. P. Lovecraft*. Woodbury, MN: Llewellyn Publications, 2010.

Wessely, Christina, *Welteis: Eine wahre Geschichte*. Berlin: Matthes & Seitz, 2013.

Worth, Aaron. "Arthur Machen and the Horrors of Deep History." *Victorian Literature and Culture* 40 (2012): 215–27.

Zalasiewicz, Jan. *The Earth After Us: What Legacy Will Humans Leave in the Rocks*. Oxford: Oxford University Press, 2008.

The Sound out of the Unknown

Silence and the Unsayable in the Fiction of H. P. Lovecraft

James Goho

In his *Tractatus Logico-Philosophicus* (1921), Ludwig Wittgenstein proposed that "*The limits of my language* mean the limits of my world" (68). He affirmed this with his final proposition: "What we cannot speak about we must pass over in silence" (89). These statements suggest that what is beyond the reach of words remains in the silent unknown. Bruce Aune argues that we experience the world through our conceptual scheme, which is our language. That means language determines how we characterize and experience the world. But Wittgenstein's propositions suggest there is something outside of our current language, the unsayable. The unsayable cannot be denoted or have a signifier that links to what is unsignifiable. Wittgenstein recognized the vast unsayable and argued that we must be silent even though there may be an unknowable world beyond our current powers of expression. He argued for the inadequacy of language and the irrationality of going beyond it. At least this is true for Wittgenstein's philosophy of the *Tractatus*. What, then, lies beyond language? Perhaps, it is only through the creative arts that one can hazard that unknown country as H. P. Lovecraft did in his fiction. His staunch and inventive devotion to what we cannot speak about powered his dark writings. Silence haunts his fiction.

"Silence" derives from the Latin neuter noun *silentium* ("being silent"), which comes from *silens,* the present participle of *silere* ("be quiet or still"). The definitions[1] of "silence" include:

---

1. All etymologies and definitions are from the *New Shorter Oxford English Dictionary* (Oxford: Clarendon Press, 1993).

the absence of sound, complete quietness or stillness, abstaining from or renouncing speech, and making no noise. Kristina Grob sorts these into three categories. The first is the unsaid—the "forbearance of speech." The second is the aspect of silence that arises from narrative gaps and omissions. The final quality of silence is a gesture "toward the realm of phenomena that cannot be measured" (3). This last sense is "silence" as the unsayable. The unsayable is akin to the ineffable, that which cannot be put into language. "Ineffability" comes from the Latin *ineffabilis* (*in-* "not, opposite of" and *effabilis* "speakable"; from *effari* "speak out"). It is what cannot be expressed or described in language. It is too unknown for words and transcends expression. Patricia Ondek Laurence, in *The Reading of Silence* (1991), explores Virginia Woolf's lifelong focus on silence and the barrier between "the sayable and the unsayable" (1). Laurence organizes Woolf's silence into three categories somewhat similar to Grob's. There is the "unsaid," something that one might have said but did not; the "unspoken," something not yet expressed in voiced words; and the "unsayable," either because of social taboos or because it is something about life that is ineffable. Laurence says this last form of the unsayable expresses "the inadequacy of language" (7).

Annika J. Lindskog suggests that this sense of silence relates to "experiences of life and self that are not necessarily unintelligible, but rather ineffable or non-verbal by their very nature" (18)—non-verbal because they do not fit into the categories of our current language. Such experiences go beyond the unsaid. The unsayable refers to something that escapes words because it is ineffable, ungraspable, or unknowable. At least part of the point seems to be that whatever the unsayable is, it is impossible to describe it or place it in a category familiar to human experience. Knowing, in part, is denoting, naming things. In a sense, it is grasping the world through categories of language. But the unnamable is unknown. The unsayable is not simply misrepresentation; it is the mute idiom of the unknown.

In this essay I will identify how silence, as the unsayable, is shown in a selection of Lovecraft's texts. In addition, I will attempt to understand what these signs of silence mean in Lovecraft, that is, their purpose in his work. Lovecraft was challenging the sense and sound limits of language. And this challenge reinforces his notion of the core of supernatural literature. Generally, his silences are means of approaching or conveying the unsayable, or perhaps more precisely for Lovecraft, the unknown and the unknowable. He was challenging the traditional use of language in supernatural literature. Sound in Lovecraft is often strange and foreign. His soundscapes are discordant, terrifying, chilling, and unbearable. But the silence is the most terrible. On the other side of silence waits that which we all fear, that everlasting unknown, the silent darkness of Louise Glück's "kingdom of death" (5). Carter experienced that silence in the cemetery in "The Statement of Randolph Carter" (1919). Moreover, this sophisticated use of silence represents one of Lovecraft's connections with the modernist movement in literature.

Lovecraft expressed the unsayable through stated silences, negations, language fragments, and neologisms. More specifically, he represented the unsayable through:

1. The use of stated silences to evoke the proximity of the unknown.
2. Apophasis, that is, defining things in terms of what they are not, rather than what they are. This is a traditional method of reaching beyond language into ineffability. It signals the inability of language to convey an experience.
3. The use of fragmented language, excessive language, or narrative discontinuity to allude to what cannot be directly represented.
4. The creation of neologisms to stand for that which is outside our current language capacity.

Expressions of Silence in Lovecraft

Lovecraft deployed stated silences in many of his stories. In "Dagon" (1917), for example, the unnamed narrator writes that he could "not hope to convey in mere words the unutterable hideousness that can dwell in absolute silence" when he awakened to find himself on a vast expanse of black mire (CF 1.53).

Similar statements of silence are part of Lovecraft's unknown landscapes. In addition, the silence in Lovecraft's fiction does not seem to be anything that is missing or not there; rather, it feels as if it is there.

"The Statement of Randolph Carter" contains four instances of the word "silence." The first occurs when Carter and Harley Warren enter the ancient cemetery. Carter thinks he and Warren were "the first living creatures to invade a lethal silence of centuries" (CF 1.134). The second use happens when Warren enters the "indescribable ossuary" and proceeds down the stone stairs underground, that is, into the unknown. On the surface, Carter waits in the "lone silence of the cemetery" (CF 1.136). After a time, Warren's voice sounds from the depths. He screams at Carter to flee. But "[a]fter that was silence" (CF 1.139). Warren is trapped in the unknown. Carter repeatedly calls for Warren but only his voice "broke the hideous silence," which is the fourth and final use of the term (CF 1.139). These stated silences reflect the characters' perceptions of and experiences in their environment. And they indicate that their full experiences cannot be expressed in words. It is noteworthy that the story states that Carter knows many languages, and Warren knows even more. But Warren cries that what he sees below the ground is *"unbelievable"*—a negative word, suggesting something that cannot be described (CF 1.137).

In "The Call of Cthulhu" (1926) there are four uses of "silence" or "silent." I will look at three of them. The first appears early when Francis Wayland Thurston says that Professor Angell "intended to keep silent" on what he knew (CF 2.22). He would have destroyed his papers, if he had not died suddenly. He wanted it all left unsaid. Another is the "moment of really awed silence" when Inspector Legrasse and Professor Webb agreed on the commonality of the phrase, *"Ph'nglui mglw'nafh Cthulhu R'lyeh wgah'nagl fhtagn,"* heard at rituals on continents far apart (CF 2.33). That commonality seemed inconceivable, beyond the range of probability. Lovecraft fashions an unknown language to represent the unsayable. That string of odd consonant combinations seems unpronounceable. This feature of Lovecraft's language of the unsayable will be discussed fully in the section on his neologisms. The incident of the impossible commonality suggests something beyond our understanding. The final use of the word describes twenty police officers who "for miles splashed on in silence through the terrible cypress woods where day never came" (CF 2.34). The silence refers to the inability of the police to express their experience in that unknown environment.

William Dyer opens *At the Mountains of* Madness (1931) saying he is forced into speech. In part, the novel surveys the problem of the unsaid, which refers to something that could have been stated or spoken but is not (Lindskog 18). Dyer writes that he wants to say something about his and others' experiences in the Antarctic. Yet he doubts that he will be heeded in his warning against another expedition to Antarctica. That is because his narration is all about silence: "the unfathomed silences" of the ice fields, the "vast silent pinnacles," and the terror of the continuing "stony silence" (CF 3.21, 29–30, 48). Everywhere "silence continued to answer all calls" (CF 3.49). Silence is a conspicuous presence throughout the novel. On their exploration of the lost city of the Old Ones, Dyer and Danforth are amazed at the "aeon-silent maze of unhuman masonry" combining silence with a negation to signal their utter disorientation and inability to correlate their "moods, memories, and impressions" (CF 3.90). The entire novel seems imbued with an eerie quiet in the vast snow fields and on the high unforgiving mountains in Lovecraft's Antarctica. *At the Mountains of Madness* evokes a feeling of existential despair and loneliness. Reading the story is like experiencing a deep loss. Lovecraft explored the depths of an awful silence in the novel. The characters Dyer and Danforth feel that loss in the "silence of the great dead city" of the Old Ones (CF 3.133).

That is the silence that Randolph Carter confronted in "Through the Gates of the Silver Key" (1932–33), written in collaboration with E. Hoffmann Price. Up against the "masses of towering stone," Carter suffers how terrifying and incomprehensible "utter silence, mental and physical" could be. He nears the unsayable, expressed by Lovecraft as the "hush of the abyss" falling upon him (CF 3.296). And in that region of the unknown, only a sort of anti-language makes sense, one "not of physical sounds or articulate words" (CF 3.296). It is an anti-soundscape that Lovecraft presents in this story, where he portrayed the experience of the unsayable. It is a "chilling and awesome silence full of the spirit of desolation" that pervades the story, where Lovecraft forces readers to feel "the illimitable vastness of the void" (CF 3.302). In this story and others, Lovecraft's forms of silence take readers close to the unsayable.

Apophasis or the Negation of Language

In "Hypnos" (1922), the narrator writes of "that chief of torments—inarticulateness" (CF 1.327). He finds it impossible to express his and his friend's experiences because of the lack of any symbols or words to be found in his language. For the narrator, this is the essence of his anguish.

"Apophasis" comes from the Greek *apophatikos* (negative). Aristotle used it to express the denial of a proposition or the negation of a term (Horn and Wansing). But William Franke argues that the word's etymology suggests a more negative meaning. Because it comes from the combination of *apo-* (off, away, from) and *phanai* (speak), "apophasis" means an "unsaying." "Apophasis" or negative language arises in the face of what cannot be said. It signals where language fails because there are no words for what one has experienced. It is the experience of the unknown or the unknowable. In *At the Mountains of Madness*, Lovecraft used "unknown" twenty-eight times, by my count. Faced with an unfathomable experience, one can only say what it is not, because, as Franke writes, "whatever *can* be said is *not* it" (1). The unsayable troubles language, which means it troubles readers. Lovecraft wrote about the failure of language to express certain experiences. Rosemary Jackson argues that Lovecraft's fictions stress the impossibility of naming an unnamable presence. His negations show that "the endeavor to visualize and verbalize the unseen and unsayable is one which inevitably falls short, except by drawing attention to exactly this difficulty of utterance" (39).

Lovecraft often used negations like "unspeakable" and "unnamable" to signal experiences beyond our human ability to comprehend and express in language. The negation, "unspeakable," appears in many stories, for example: "an unspeakable horror" (CF 1.47) in "The Tomb" (1917); "some fear unspeakable" (CF 1.124) in "The Doom That Came to Sarnath" (1919); "an unspeakable quality that chilled me" (CF 1.271) in "The Outsider" (1921); "some unspeakable beast" (CF 1.342) in "The Hound" (1922); and "the unspeakable straggling object" (CF 1.373) in "The Lurking Fear" (1922).

Lovecraft used "unnamable," "unnamed," and "nameless" to indicate his concern with the failure of language to designate or describe some things and experiences. The negation "unnamable" appeared in many of Lovecraft's stories throughout his writing career. Indeed, "The Unnamable" (1923) is the title of a Lovecraft story. The word is embedded in his lexicon. The "unnamable" represents something beyond the human ability to describe and understand. For example, in *The Case of Charles Dexter Ward* (1927) Marinus Bicknell Willett descends below Joseph Curwen's old Pawtuxet bungalow. In that underground area, he experiences "unnamable realities behind the protective illusions of common vision" (CF 2.336). In some stories, "unnamable" is paired with "unnamed," which may seem redundant, but the two words do differ in meaning. Together the words emphasize the impossibility of using our language to express an irrational experience. For example, in "The Colour out of Space" (1927), the presence of a member of the Gardner family in a house "was a breath from regions unnamed and unnamable" (CF 2.383). In "The Hound," St. John seeks "refuge from the unnamed and unnamable" (CF 1.348).

The term *"unaussprechlichen"* (inexpressible, unutterable) appears as *Unaussprechlichen Kulten* in "The Dreams in the Witch House" (1932), "The Thing on the Doorstep" (1933), "The Shadow out of Time" (1934–35), and "The Haunter of the Dark" (1935). It is a forbidden book invented by Robert Howard as Von Juntz's *Nameless Cults*. S. T. Joshi reveals and clarifies the complexities and problems involved with this title (*IAP*

803). Another negation, "inexplicable," appears in many of Lovecraft's stories across his career such as "Beyond the Wall of Sleep" (1919), "The Nameless City" (1921), "The Shunned House" (1924), "The Colour out of Space," "The Whisperer in Darkness" (1930), and "The Haunter of the Dark." "Inexplicable" is also found multiple times in *The Case of Charles Dexter Ward* and "The Shadow out of Time."

Lovecraft deployed keywords to signal where our language fails and our current epistemology ends. John P. Langan expresses a similar observation in "Naming the Nameless: Lovecraft's Grammatology" (1999). He calls it Lovecraft's "approximate language" (26), which conveys a sense of the limits of our language in describing reality. Supernatural literature, at its best, reveals a fissure in our customary view of or discourse about the world. The inexplicable or ineffable represents the instability of our grasp of the world through ordinary language.

The negation, "ineffable," appears in such stories as "The Thing on the Doorstep," "The Dreams in the Witch House," and "The Dunwich Horror" (1928). In *At the Mountains of Madness*, Lovecraft suggests the unsayable through several negations when Dyer looks out on the cloud-shrouded mountains that emitted: "ineffable suggestions of a vague, ethereal *beyondness* far more than terrestrially spatial; and gave appalling reminders of the utter remoteness, separateness, desolation, and aeon-long death of this untrodden and unfathomed austral world" (CF 3.50).

Another negation, "indescribable," occurs in at least nineteen stories. Lovecraft routinely deployed negations to signal the problem of expressing the supernatural encounters of his characters. Whatever the thing, experience, or event is in many of Lovecraft's stories, it is not part of our understanding of the world. It is inexpressible, indefinable, or "infandous" (CF 3.265). That last word appears in "The Dreams in the Witch House" (1932). "Infandous" (unspeakable) is an archaic term that comes from the Latin *infandus*, the combination of *in-* (to express negation) and *fandus* the gerundive of *fari* (speak). Roger B. Salomon argues that horror literature's essential aim is to "remind us of the unspeakable" (15). Lovecraft does more than remind us. He takes us onto the ledge over that void. He wrote myths in the old sense of the term. *Mûthos* originally meant "utterance" or what one says. G. S. Kirk explained that it came to mean what one says in the form of a tale. *Mûthoi* are stories. Lovecraft wanted readers to experience his stories as if they were journeys into the unknown, about which nothing could be explained coherently. Commenting on the ancient Greek Mysteries, Aristotle wrote that those "being initiated into the mysteries are to be expected not to learn anything but to suffer some change, to be put into a certain condition" (87). The experience of the unsayable is similar. The frequency of Lovecraft's use of negations illustrates one method in his strategy to force readers to experience the unsayable.

Fragmented Language

Many of Lovecraft's stories feature disjointed language and structures. He designed such techniques to give readers a sense of the chaotic experiences of the characters in the stories. For example, at the end of "The Unnamable" Manton struggles to describe what he encountered in the graveyard. But he cannot. Lovecraft used broken phrases, askew words, and incoherent stammers to show language as powerless. At times his character's language capability is incommensurate with their experiences. Manton babbles: "'It was everywhere—a gelatin—a slime—yet it had shapes, a thousand shapes of horror beyond all memory. There were eyes—and a blemish. It was the pit—the maelstrom—the ultimate abomination. Carter, *it was the unnamable!*'" (CF 1.405). This torrent of words exhibits the often purposeful indeterminacy of Lovecraft's language in his stories.

With its extravagance of adjectives and rhetorical devices, "The Hound" seems overwritten and absurd. It typifies a baroque horror style, where the language seems exaggerated and the images overdone. But I think Lovecraft's purpose was to show that language cannot protect us from the intrusions of the unknown. Even a flamboyant language cannot express the truly unsayable, that is, to domesticate it, to make it known. Words fail in the story because they cannot describe the experienced phenomena. Instead, the story mentions things of which one "must not speak" (CF 1.341), "less explicable things" (CF 1.342), and that which is "utterly impossible to describe" (CF 1.345). The odd sentence "Bizarre manifestations were now too frequent to count" (CF 1.345) signals the crumbling and breakdown of language. By the last paragraph, language becomes confused, inarticulate, and chaotic. The story ends in fragments: "Madness rides the star-wind . . . claws and teeth sharpened on centuries of corpses . . . dripping death astride a Bacchanale of bats from night-black ruins of buried temples of Belial" (CF 1.348). In "The Hound," Lovecraft deploys a baroque style and multiple adjectives to hint at what evades direct expression. As in other stories, he aims to give readers an experience of the unknown, a sense of what is unsayable through his fractured sentences and exaggerated verbal styles.

At the Mountains of Madness also ends with fragmented language to express a close encounter with the unsayable. The survivors of the Antarctic expedition, Danforth and Dyer, are fleeing away in a plane. They traverse sinister jutting peaks where Dyer takes the controls from the hysterical Danforth. Looking out at the receding city of the Old Ones, the "wormily honeycombed mountains of madness," and the bizarrely clouded sky, Danforth shrieks madly (CF 3.156). He has no words to describe what he sees. Danforth has been claimed by the unsayable. What Danforth expresses about his experience comes out in fragments, or perhaps as a stream-of-horrorstruck-consciousness: "'The black pit,' 'the carven rim,' 'the proto-shoggoths,' 'the windowless solids with five dimensions,' 'the nameless cylinder,' 'the elder pharos,' 'Yog-Sothoth,' 'the primal white jelly,' 'the colour out of space,' 'the wings,' 'the eyes in darkness,' 'the moon-ladder,' 'the original, the eternal, the undying'" (CF 3.157). Language fails Danforth. Lovecraft used fractured language to have his characters convey their encounter with the unsayable.

Lovecraft's masterwork of fragmentation is "The Call of Cthulhu." The story opens with his renowned paragraph about the danger of knowing too much. Wittgenstein hinted at this in the Tractatus. Lovecraft's paragraph suggests that in experiencing the unsayable directly, one will necessarily go mad or mute. An encounter with the ineffable for Lovecraft's characters was not wonderful, but one of abject horror, dread, and muteness.

The story is constructed of fragments set in a complicated documentary structure of notebooks, letters, newspaper reports, dreams, and personal testimony presented as the "Papers of the Late Francis Wayland Thurston, of Boston" (CF 2.21) yet told through a multitude of voices. As S. T. Joshi points out in *I Am Providence*, Lovecraft deftly uses a narrative-within-a-narrative technique style in the story, yet controlled by the narration of Thurston. He frames the entire text as a found manuscript, which is a traditional (for example, Horace Walpole's *The Castle of Otranto* [1764]) and new (the found footage film *The Blair Witch Project* [1999]) supernatural story technique. This frame gives a sense of authenticity to the story due to the multiple testimonies of "witnesses."

Thurston's testimony is the primary organizing thread through the story. He assembled accounts of strange reports from around the world related to unusual events on a ship in the Pacific Ocean. The papers of George Gammell Angell (Thurston's grand-uncle) provided a rich source of information, and Thurston conducted his investigations. The story includes Angell's notes and discoveries, newspaper accounts of bizarre events, descriptions of artwork by an artist who dreamed of a gigantic entity, accounts of cultish activities in the Louisiana bayou, and Gustaf Johansen's diary recounting a sea event. Thurston's narration becomes increasingly disorienting (reflecting his increasing bafflement) for readers, as they try to weave together the various threads of evidence. The latter sections of the story near a hysterical confusion as Thurston struggles to fathom and communicate Johansen and his shipmates' experience in the Pacific Ocean and how that connects (or not) with odd events across the world. At times, the story stammers with confused voices striving to describe their experience. Moreover, the varying texts give readers an experience of puzzlement as they strive to put the fragments together.

Overall, the fragmented nature of the text suggests the presence of that which cannot be expressed fully in language. The story includes several negations such as unbelievable, indescribable, beyond description, inexplicable, and uninscribable. As the story progresses, language can only give "broad impressions" (CF 2.51). Of course, "The Thing [Cthulhu] cannot be described" (CF 2.53). But through a staggering display of verbal audacity, Lovecraft conveys an experience of it rather than a description, because there was "no language for such abysms of shrieking and immemorial lunacy, such eldritch contradictions of all matter, force, and cosmic order. A mountain walked or stumbled" (CF 2.53). Lovecraft continues Johansen's experience of the unsayable:

> There is a sense of spectral whirling through liquid gulfs of infinity, of dizzying rides through reeling universes on a comet's tail, and of hysterical plunges from the pit to the moon and from the moon back again to the pit, all livened by a cachinnating chorus of the distorted, hilarious elder gods and the green, bat-winged mocking imps of Tartarus. (CF 2.55)

One can only marvel at how Lovecraft uses language fragments (or a stream-of-consciousness style) to convey what cannot be said, the unsayable, and thus, to mark the limits of our linguistic framework of the world.

Lovecraft's Neologisms

Lovecraft's fiction exposes the impossibility of using words to denote certain aspects of reality. Often, his stories suggest an experience that escapes our language. That is why he invented many neologisms in his fiction. This demonstrates his conviction that our natural language fails to express some experiences. In "Self, Other, and the Evolution of Lovecraft's Treatment of Outsideness," Massimo Berruti contends Lovecraft's concept of "Outsideness" stands for that which language is insufficient to describe. It is the unsayable. In another essay, "The Unnamable in Lovecraft and the Limits of Rationality," Berruti writes that it is difficult to explain Lovecraft's concept of Outsideness. That Outsideness is "an 'alterity' irreducible to rational, linguistic canons of interpretation" (6). I think that alterity or outsideness is the unsayable, a complete otherness, where language fails. In a letter of 9 November 1936 to Fritz Leiber, Lovecraft wrote that he wanted to capture "the mystery & terror clinging around the eternal presence & pressure of the outside" in his stories. He tried to express the sense or feeling of "mentally & materially inaccessible gulfs . . . [which] can never be known to us" (*CLM* 268). In his stories, a character's inability to describe the other, the "beyond" or the "outside" is the result of a language collapse. Lovecraft invented neologisms to suggest what was unsayable, that is, the cosmic unknown or that "brooding & intrusive Outsideness," which he noted in a letter to Leiber of 19 December 1936 (*CLM* 293).

Dan Clore's *Weird Words: A Lovecraftian Lexicon* (2009) identifies many Lovecraftian neologisms. "Glibber" is used at least twenty times in *The Dream-Quest of Unknown Kadath* (1926–27). It seems to mean the language, or the means of expression, of ghouls and night-gaunts (another neologism). "Meep" is another neologism in that novel, suggesting the way ghouls communicate. "Gug" (a hairy and gigantic creature of Dreamland) also appears extensively in *The Dream-Quest of Unknown Kadath,* wherein Lovecraft invented many new words. Ghasts, bholes, shantaks, vooniths, zoogs, and buopoths are other horrid creatures of Dreamland. In the novel, "thagweed" is a substance smoked to lessen the horrid odors of black galleys. Lovecraft's "cacodaemoniacal" is derived from the sixteenth-century "cacodemon," which comes from the Greek *kakodaímôn,* that is, *kakos* (bad) and *daimōn* (spirit, genius), meaning evil genius. For Lovecraft, it might mean nightmarish. It is found in "The Nameless City" and "The Hound." In "The Lurking Fear," Lovecraft used "Charonian" as an adjective to characterize shadows. It comes from Charon, the ferryman on the river Styx. Clore found two previous uses but notes that Lovecraft used it differently to suggest something hellish or dark.

But there is much more to Lovecraft's crafting of new words. Christopher L. Robinson argues that linguistic invention performs a key role in Lovecraft's works. I agree, and that role in my mind is to suggest what is unsayable. Robinson focuses on

Lovecraft's invented terminology to label monsters and their abodes. He documents how Lovecraft's "onomastic" (relating to names or naming) constructions are themselves "monstrous in sound, form, and sense" (128). These monstrous names contrast strongly and purposely to his human characters' names, which reflect a traditional New England heritage. This establishes a clear and distinct difference between ordinary experience and the experience of the unknown, the unsayable. Robinson notes that Lovecraft invented some names based on sounds from foreign and ancient languages, for example, "Yaddith, Azathoth, Buzrael, Yog-Sothoth, Shub-Niggurath, Nug-Soth, Yig, Yogash, Shaggai, and shoggoth" (131). Lovecraft was precise with his invented names like Azathoth, Yog-Sothoth, and Shub-Niggurath, setting an underpinning of unearthliness, but with an "outwardly Arabic aspect" because the words were to have come from the *Necronomicon* (*Letters to F. Lee Baldwin* 141).

Lovecraft also invented names using forms that appear not to be associated with human language in sound or sense. Robinson postulates three types of neologisms that display an increasing estrangement from ordinary language forms and sounds (132). He suggests many words but does not note where they all can be found in Lovecraft's works. For the first type, Lovecraft invented words with odd consonant clusters such as Mtal (a place by a sea) in "The Doom That Came to Sarnath" and Pnath in the same story, where it seems to refer to a conquered city. It is also found as the "Vale of Pnath" in *The Dream-Quest of Unknown Kadath* and "The Haunter of the Dark." The invented word "Mthura" (a world) is in "Through the Gates of the Silver Key." Another odd consonant cluster is Pnakotic (Manuscripts) found in "Polaris" (1918) and many other stories. The neologism Gnoph-Keh (hairy, long-armed tribesmen) appears in "Polaris" and *The Dream-Quest of Unknown Kadath*. The "land of Mnar" (CF 1.122) and the Bnazic Desert are in "The Doom That Came to Sarnath." Two others, "Dho-Hna" and "Nhhngr," are found in a diary entry by Wilbur Whateley in "The Dunwich Horror" (CF 2.450).

Robinson's second type consists of words that seem entirely

foreign to English patterns, such as S'ngac (a violet gas in *The Dream-Quest of Unknown Kadath*) and K'n-yan (a subterranean world in "The Mound" [1929–30], ghostwritten for Zealia Brown Reed Bishop). It also appears in "The Whisperer in Darkness" (1930): "blue-litten K'n-yan, red-litten Yoth, and black, lightless N'kai" (CF 2.519). That final word (also in "The Mound") is another neologism. Others of this type include R'lyeh found in "The Call of Cthulhu" and other stories, L'mur-Kathulos in "The Whisperer in Darkness," the mountain Ngranek, which first appears in "The Other Gods" (1921), and Gnai-Kah in "The Doom That Came to Sarnath." Lovecraft created a plethora of neologisms, many of which Anthony Pearsall notes in *The Lovecraft Lexicon* (2005).

The third type of Lovecraft's created words and phrases includes constructions that sound alien to English. Robinson suggests "Ghatanothoa, Kynarth, Kamog, daroh, Athok, Tcho-Tcho sifi-cligh, skorah, tukah, ugrat" (132). Additional strange-sounding words are "Kythanil, the double planet" (CF 3.306) and the "primal tongue of Tsath-yo" (CF 3.317) in "Through the Gates of the Silver Key," and "the peak of Hatheg-Kla" (CF 2.93) in "The Strange High House in the Mist" (1926).

Moreover, Robinson points out that word constructions such as S'gg'ha (in "The Shadow out of Time"), Pth'thya-l'yi, and Y'ha-nthlei (both found in "The Shadow over Innsmouth") employ bizarre spellings, atypical hyphenation schemes, and other typographical peculiarities that reinforce the strangeness (133). These and other created words and phrases are found in various forms and combinations throughout Lovecraft's texts. For example, in "The Call of Cthulhu" one finds the "unpronounceable jumble of letters, '*Cthulhu fhtagn*'" (CF 2.26). In his letter to Duane W. Rimel of 23 July 1934, Lovecraft suggests some ways of attempting to say "Cthulhu," but he writes that such names should be formed against "human vocalism & language" (*Letters to F. Lee Baldwin* 195). That is because they represent the failure of our language to express the unsayable. Lovecraft crafted them to be inexpressible.

In several works, Lovecraft takes this exploration of sound

distortion to a more complex level. In *The Case of Charles Dexter Ward*, Ward's mother hears him chanting: "Yi-nash-Yog-Sothoth-he-lgeb-fi-throdog" (CF 2.292). In the novella "The Dunwich Horror," Wilbur Whateley breaks into the Miskatonic University Library and is attacked by the guard dog. Before he dies, he cries out "something like '*N'gai, n'gha'ghaa, bugg-shoggog, y'hah; Yog-Sothoth, Yog-Sothoth . . .*'" (CF 2.440). Near the end of the story, Wilbur's more monstrous twin brother is trapped on a peak by Henry Armitage and two colleagues. They chant an incantation that will remove the beast. Below a crowd is stunned by what they hear from that peak. It was nearly "erroneous to call them sounds." They were "acoustic perversions" yet they seemed "half-articulate *words*" (CF 2.463). Lovecraft showed the limits of language, yet the need to use words to give an experience of the unsayable: "'*Ygnaiih . . . ygnaiih . . . thflthkh'ngha . . . Yog-Sothoth . . .*' rang the hideous croaking out of space. '*Y'bthnk . . . h'ehye—n'grkdl'lh . . .*'" (CF 2.464). And then the final frenzy sounded from the hill: "*Eh-ya-ya-ya-yahaah—e'yayayayaaaa . . . ngh'aaaaa . . . ngh'aaaa . . . h'yuh*" (CF 2.464). These neologisms are calls from the unknown, similar to Edgar Allan Poe's "eternal Tekeli-li!" (239) in *The Narrative of Arthur Gordon Pym* (1838), where "Tekeli-li!" is a neologism to express the unknown. Lovecraft reused that term as the sound haunting Dyer and Danforth during their searches in the Antarctic. When Danforth witnesses the ultimate abomination when he and Dyer are fleeing, he screams "Tekeli-li! Tekeli-li!" (CF 3.157). Danforth becomes incoherent. He has been taken by the Antarctic, the unknown. As Lynne Jamneck concluded, that sound "signifies the breakdown of language in the face of the unknown" (150).

Lovecraft's neologisms mark the failure of language. He invented unusual utterances to convey to readers a sense of the experience of what is unsayable. This is particularly true if one reads his stories aloud. It is challenging because of the bizarre sounds of the neologisms, but a reader hears the strange soundscape of many of Lovecraft's stories. It seems an unknown soundscape. Moreover, these invented word forms suggest that Lovecraft knew the limits of language and the limits of storytelling, especially storytelling within the supernatural tradition that Lovecraft was reshaping.

Soundscapes in Lovecraft's Works

Silence and the unsayable pervade the works of Lovecraft. But in some situations, there is an actual soundscape of discord that also suggests the failure of language. That sound out of the unknown is expressed in various ways. The prominent way is through silence, but there are instances in Lovecraft where the unknown can be heard, incoherently of course. Lovecraft wrote that he wanted to evoke in readers "a profound sense of dread, and of contact with unknown spheres and powers, a subtle attitude of awed listening, as if for the beating of black wings or the scratching of outside shapes and entities on the known universe's utmost rim" (*SHL* 28). I will select examples from a few stories to provide a sampling of how his soundscape reinforces that sense of that great unknown. It is similar to that "great roar which lies on the other side of silence" (173) in George Eliot's *Middlemarch* (1871–72).

In *At the Mountains of Madness*, the cold silence of Antarctica dominates, but a strange, eerie "piping" haunts Dyer and Danforth throughout the novel. The word appears nineteen times. It sounds early when the Antarctic wind carried "wild and half-sentient musical piping" which seemed "disquieting and even dimly terrible" (*CF* 3.17). From their plane over the white expanse, the expedition hears a "bizarre musical whistling or piping," which seemed a "conscious malignity" and to evoke "repulsion" (*CF* 3.69). Later, Danforth thinks he hears "faint musical piping" coming from "unknown depths below" (*CF* 3.122). Deep down in the caverns they hear "wind-pipings" (*CF* 3.144) and flee from a white mist that sounded an "insidious musical piping" (*CF* 3.145). That piping noise occurs frequently over the closing pages of the novel.

The word "piping" suggests the nearness of the unsayable in several other stories by Lovecraft, for example, "Nyarlathotep" (1920) and "The Moon-Bog" (1921). In the closing pages of "The Rats in the Walls" (1923), Delapore descends into caverns "where Nyarlathotep, the mad faceless god, howls blindly in the darkness to the piping" (CF 1.395). In those unknown depths, Delapore's language fails as it descends into grunts. In "The Shadow out of Time," Nathaniel Wingate Peaslee, a professor of political economy at Miskatonic University, cannot bear the "damnable alien sound piping up from the open, unguarded door of limitless nether" (CF 3.445). He also tries to retell his inexplicable experiences, but they all seem "fragmentary delusions," including a fall through "sentient darkness, and a babel of noises utterly alien" obscured by that "eldritch, damnable whistling shrieked fiendishly above all the alternations of babel and silence in the whirlpools of darkness" (CF 3.447). Peaslee's account at the end appears in fragments of memory, illusion, despair, dreams, terror, and loss.

Another recurrent sound out of the unknown is "baying," used more than a dozen times in "The Hound." This repeating sound of "daemoniac baying" gets louder and louder, and closer and closer as the story progresses, suggesting the ever-increasing approach of something unknown (CF 1.345). The story gives readers an experience of awed listening, as Lovecraft uses sound throughout to increase the tension, not only with the incessant baying. Another part of the soundscape is "the stealthy whirring and flapping of those accursed web-wings circles closer and closer" (CF 1.348) from which there is no escape, as St. John learns. It is a suffocating, smothering soundscape. The heavy beating of reptilian wings, the unrelenting baying, and a "queer combination of rustling, tittering, and articulate chatter" deafen readers (CF 1.345). The story clanks with "dissonances of exquisite morbidity and cacodaemoniacal ghastliness" (CF 1.341). And it is useless to "gibber out insane pleas" (CF 1.347) to escape the "baying of that dead, fleshless monstrosity" (CF 1.348). Language breaks down entirely at the end of the story.

"The Music of Erich Zann" (1921) creates a mood of age, gloom, and despair, grounded in growing alarm expressed through the manic playing of a viol in a garret by the elderly Erich Zann. It is a story where linguistic meaning collapses. A young, poor student moves into a boarding house on the Rue d'Auseil where all the inhabitants are silent and reticent as if it were best to keep quiet, lest the dreadful void notice them. Zann is mute, emphasizing the loss of language. The student becomes "haunted by the weirdness of [Zann's] music" (CF 1.282). That music swells "into a chaotic babel of sound" one late night while the student listens at Zann's room (CF 1.286). But the music stops. The student knocks at the door and Zann lets him enter. At that point Zann starts to write feverishly. He stops when a sound comes through the curtained window, an "infinitely distant musical note" (CF 1.287). Zann plays wildly as if trying frantically to ward off the sound of the unknown. Repeatedly he glances warily at the window. That sound from the "blackness of space illimitable," an "unimagined space," is incoherent chaos (CF 1.289). The student feels trapped in the darkness between that chaos and the "night-baying viol" with its "unutterable music" (CF 1.289). He is surrounded by a linguistic void or babel that crashes through the window and carries off Zann's explanatory manuscript to illustrate that language fails in the soundscape of the unknown.

Modernism and H. P. Lovecraft

Norman R. Gayford, Steven J. Mariconda, and Sean Elliot Martin suggest that Lovecraft's fiction exhibits commonalities with modernist literature. Gayford argues that Lovecraft's work experiments with such modernist methods as discontinuity between texts and reality, the distortion of temporal time, and the use of unreliable narrators (291). He claims that Lovecraft is a "moderated modernist" (289) restrained by his intense hold on traditional literature. Mariconda says Lovecraft was an ambivalent American modernist. He shows where Lovecraft shared literary tendencies with the modernists, such as a distain for the Victorian style, a focus on "subjective states of consciousness" (120), and experimentation with literary "form in his longer stories" (122). Mariconda also points out that Lovecraft attacked modernists especially for their non-representational works. Martin maintains that Lovecraft combined modernism and the modern grotesque in his weird fiction to intensify his sense of

human insignificance in an indifferent universe (110). He suggests Lovecraft's "cosmic absurdity" texts exhibit the limitations
of human perception and knowledge, which is a theme in some
modernist writing (111). Martin sees this expressed directly by
Crawford Tillinghast in the early tale, written in 1920, "From
Beyond":

> "What do we know," he had said, "of the world and the uni-
> verse about us? Our means of receiving impressions are absurdly
> few, and our notions of surrounding objects infinitely narrow.
> We see things only as we are constructed to see them, and can
> gain no idea of their absolute nature." (CF 1.193)

Lovecraft became much more sophisticated in his presentation
of the unknown in later works.

In *I Am Providence,* S. T. Joshi counters that Lovecraft was a
confirmed traditionalist and that he found most modernist
works to be overly disruptive of the European classical tradition.
In "Lord Dunsany and His Work" (1922), Lovecraft excoriates
the "bizarre, tasteless, defiant, and chaotic literature of that terrible newer generation" (CE 2.60). And in "Rudis Indigestaque
Moles" (1923), Lovecraft called T. S. Eliot's *The Waste Land*
(1922) "incoherent and disjointed" (CE 2.64). In 1931, Lovecraft declared James Joyce was "hardly worth reading" and Ger-
trude Stein's work was a "total loss so far as real art is concerned"
(JVS 27). In that letter, he argued for the importance of Marcel
Proust, who inherited "many qualities from the main tradition of
the French novel" (*Letters to Elizabeth Toldridge* 27). Lovecraft's
foremost contemporary novelist was Proust, who, as Joshi writes,
"occupied the middle ground between stodgy Victorianism and
freakish modernism" (IAP 924). Lovecraft wrote that Proust was
"the one real novelist of the last decade or two" (*Letters to Maurice W. Moe* 286). In his letter to J. Vernon Shea of 25 September 1933, Lovecraft contended nothing in the "20th century has
so far produced anything to eclipse the Proustian cycle as a
whole" (JVS 167). Lovecraft was aware of modernist works and
criticized many but noted the importance of some. In his "Suggestions for a Reading Guide," he notes the "essential poems of

[. . .] T. S. Eliot" and that James Joyce's "*Ulysses* is important but difficult" (CE 2.190). And in a letter to J. Vernon Shea of 5 February 1932, Lovecraft claimed that "there was no more powerful or penetrant writer living than Joyce when he is not pursuing his theory to these ultimate extremes" (*JVS* 89). Lovecraft mentioned "Anna Livia Plurabelle," of which he said he had seen extracts.

I think Lovecraft's fiction shares a common element with modernist writing. This is not surprising, as Lovecraft experienced similar cultural, economic, literary, and political changes. Fiction writers responded to the disruptive effects of the beginning decades of the twentieth century in varying ways. Lindskog, Laurence, and others have demonstrated the focus on silence in the modernist novel, which generally stressed a highly subjective perspective, the chaotic flux of experience, and the personal in the period from 1900 to 1940. They also claim an emphasis on silence, the unsaid, and the unsayable as distinguishing features of modernist writing. These emphases resulted from the inadequacies of language to convey the internal experiences of characters, the felt need to explore the silencing of some segments of society, and the desire to express, in some fashion, what goes beyond normal experience, what is ineffable. Lovecraft's expressions of the unsayable are not comparable to a silent time of transcendence, such as Woolf's "moments of being" or Joyce's "epiphanies."

Lovecraft's silence is more like Joseph Conrad's, whose silence conveys a sense of terror. According to Joshi, Lovecraft was impressed by Joseph Conrad's *Lord Jim* (1900) as evidenced in a letter from Lovecraft to his aunt Lillian D. Clark of 25 May 1925 (*IAP* 923). Conrad is an early modernist. In *Lord Jim*, a deadly silence "became intolerably oppressive" (62). It seems an awful presence. There was a "silence of the sea, of the sky, merged into one indefinite immensity still as death" (83), followed by "[o]nly a night; only a silence" (84). The word "silence" appears at least sixty times in the novel. In *Heart of Darkness* (1899), Marlow senses a "great silence around and above" (21). As he travels "deeper and deeper into the heart of darkness" he finds it "very quiet there" (37). Deep into the bush, "the wood [. . .] looked with their air of hidden knowledge, of patient expectation, of unapproachable silence" (61). Marlow confronts the horror of darkness at the edge of the unknown, embodied in Kurtz's "inconceivable ceremonies," "unspeakable rites" (53), and his "vast grave of unspeakable secrets" (67). Lindskog shows how Conrad struggled with the insufficiency of language. Akin to Conrad, Lovecraft's silent moments are terrifying because they signal what is beyond human comprehension.

Silence is more than an absence of sound. Silence calls to mind the presence of something behind or beyond language. The silences, fragments, negations, and neologisms of Lovecraft's texts express human experiences outside language. Some of his expressions of these experiences are akin to a stream-of-consciousness, which was deployed especially by Joyce, but by other modernists as well. Lovecraft wrote that the extreme use of this narrative technique went beyond real art. Yet he recognized the importance of the technique in unveiling the inner life of characters. In a letter from 1928, he conceded the method would impact the progress of the literary arts, but he believed it needed to be used judiciously by artists to "leave the main current of Western-European literature undisturbed" (*Letters to Woodburn Harris* 388). Lovecraft was a literary traditionalist. His use of stream-of-consciousness was not extensive. In a way, he settled with modernism but wrote in a traditional manner that he thought best allowed him to express his dark aesthetic vision.

Lovecraft was a modern in the sense that he reshaped supernatural literature for modern times. By including silence in his fiction, akin to the modernists, he suggested the presence of the unsayable, an uncanny and horrific presence, which varies from that expressed by most mainstream modernists. Lindskog writes that modernists "wrote texts that moved closer to reality as experienced by an individual human being" (336). Such texts showed how characters attempted to make sense of the world where language was inadequate to tell all, where there was something beyond our current discourse. And the silence in modernist novels signaled "'something' that is unsayable" (340).

More closely, it reveals an aspect of the human experience beyond words. Silence then, however it is manifested, draws attention to what escapes the net of words. It shows that language is inadequate for a complete understanding of our experiences in the world. This is true for much of Lovecraft's fiction. For him, silence was the failure of language to tell of the beyond, the unknown. And the unknown is our deepest fear. It is the phantom we hide from in our science, epistemology, and ontology. It overthrows "those fixed laws of Nature which are our only safeguard against the assaults of chaos and the daemons of unplumbed space" (*SHL* 28). Lovecraft used silence to portray what a person's experience might be like when faced with an experience of the unknown, where one was struck silent by physical and psychological realities that overwhelmed the senses. In Lovecraft's works, silence is the palpable presence of fear.

Conclusion

Silence reigns through much of Lovecraft's oeuvre. That is because silence, in one sense, means the unsayable, which was what Lovecraft wanted readers to experience. His unwavering and imaginative focus on the unsayable powered his dark fiction. In this essay I argue, with many selections from his works, that Lovecraft expressed the unsayable in at least four ways: through stated silences, the use of negations, employing fragmentary language, and creating neologisms. He marked several stories with the word "silence" to signal the closeness of the unknown. In many of his stories, he defined things and experiences in terms of what they are not because language cannot convey an ineffable experience. He deployed fragmented language, extravagant phrasing, and narrative discontinuity to suggest that which cannot be denoted. Lovecraft also created neologisms to express what cannot be signified in language. This sophisticated use of silence connects him to the modernist movement in literature. Several scholars have argued that modernist writers emphasized silence in their fiction. Although Lovecraft cannot be said to be a modernist, since he was a traditionalist, he does share at least this aspect of modernism. He strove to convey the sense of an inexpressible or unthinkable contact with something unnamable. His form of silence suggests that which is unsayable, that is, experiences or states of mind that cannot be represented linguistically. They evade the net of words. His silences convey horrific experiences of life and self that are non-verbal by their unknown nature.

Works Cited

Aristotle. *The Works of Aristotle, Volume XII: Selected Fragments.* Tr. Sir David Ross. Oxford: Oxford University Press, 1952.

Aune, Bruce. *Knowledge, Mind, and Nature.* New York: Random House, 1967.

Berruti, Massimo. "H. P. Lovecraft and the Anatomy of Nothingness: The Cthulhu Mythos." *Semiotica* 150 (2004): 363–418.

———. "Self, Other, and the Evolution of Lovecraft's Treatment of Outsideness." *Lovecraft Annual* No. 3 (2009): 109–46.

———. "The Unnameable in Lovecraft and the Limits of Rationality." Paper presented at Research Seminar, University of Helsinki, 2005. www.helsinki.fi/filosofia/tutkijaseminaari/berrutti.pdf Accessed February 27, 2009.

Clore, Dan. *Weird Words: A Lovecraftian Lexicon.* New York: Hippocampus Press, 2009.

Conrad, Joseph. *Heart of Darkness.* 1899. Ed. Owen Knowles and Allan H. Simmons. Cambridge: Cambridge University Press, 2018.

———. *Lord Jim.* 1900. Ed. Jacques Berthoud. Oxford: Oxford University Press, 2012.

Eliot, George. *Middlemarch.* 1871–72. London: Folio Society, 1999.

Franke, William. *On What Cannot Be Said: Apophatic Discourses in Philosophy, Religion, Literature, and the Arts. Volume 2: Modern and Contemporary Transformations.* Notre Dame, IN: University of Notre Dame Press, 2007.

Gayford, Norman R. "The Artist as Antaeus: Lovecraft and Modernism." In David E. Schultz and S. T. Joshi, ed. *An Epicure in the Terrible: A Centennial Anthology of Essays in Honor of H.P. Lovecraft.* Rutherford, NJ: Fairleigh Dickinson University Press, 1991. 273–97.

Glück, Louise. *Faithful and Virtuous Night*. New York: Farrar, Straus & Giroux, 2015.

Grob, Kristina. "Moral Philosophy and the Art of Silence." Ph.D. diss.: Loyola University, 2014. ecommons.luc.edu/luc_diss/1263 Accessed 24 February 2022.

Horn, Laurence R. and Heinrich Wansing. "Negation." *The Stanford Encyclopedia of Philosophy* (Winter 2022 Edition). Ed. Edward N. Zalta and Uri Nodelman. plato.stanford.edu/archives/win2022/entries/negation.

Jackson, Rosemary. *Fantasy: The Literature of Subversion*. London: Routledge, 1981.

Jamneck, Lynne. "Tekeli-li!: Disturbing Language in Edgar Allan Poe and H. P. Lovecraft." *Lovecraft Annual* No. 6 (2012): 126–51.

Kirk, G. S. *Myth: Its Meaning and Function in Ancient and Other Cultures*. Berkeley: University of California Press, 1970.

Langan, John P. "Naming the Nameless: Lovecraft's Grammatology." *Lovecraft Studies* No. 41 (1999): 25–30.

Lovecraft, H. P. *The Annotated Supernatural Horror in Literature*. Ed. S. T. Joshi. New York: Hippocampus Press, 2nd ed. 2012. [Abbreviated in text as *SHL*.]

———. *Letters to C. L. Moore and Others*. Ed. David E. Schultz and S. T. Joshi. New York: Hippocampus Press, 2017. [Abbreviated in the text as *CLM*.]

———. *Letters to Elizabeth Toldridge and Anne Tillery Renshaw*. Ed. David E. Schultz and S. T. Joshi. New York: Hippocampus Press, 2014.

———. *Letters to F. Lee Baldwin, Duane W. Rimel, and Nils Frome*. Ed. David E. Schultz and S. T. Joshi. New York: Hippocampus Press, 2016.

———. *Letters to J. Vernon Shea, Carl F. Strauch, and Lee McBride White*. Ed. S. T. Joshi and David E. Schultz. New York: Hippocampus Press, 2016. [Abbreviated in the text as *JVS*.]

———. *Letters to Maurice W. Moe and Others*. Ed. David E. Schultz and S. T. Joshi. New York: Hippocampus Press, 2018.

———. *Letters to Woodburn Harris and Others*. Ed. S. T. Joshi and David E. Schultz. New York: Hippocampus Press, 2022.

Laurence, Patricia Ondek. *The Reading of Silence: Virginia Woolf in the English Tradition*. Stanford: Stanford University Press, 1991.

Lindskog, Annika J. *Silent Modernism: Soundscapes and the Unsayable in Richardson, Joyce, and Woolf*. (Lund Studies in English, Vol. 118.) Lund, Sweden: Lund University, 2017.

Mariconda, Steven J. *H. P. Lovecraft: Art, Artifact, and Reality*. New York: Hippocampus Press, 2013.

Martin, Sean Elliot. "Lovecraft, Absurdity, and the Modernist Grotesque." *Lovecraft Annual* No. 6 (2012): 82–12.

Pearsall, Anthony. *The Lovecraft Lexicon*. Tempe, AZ: New Falcon Publications, 2005.

Poe, Edgar Alan. *The Narrative of Arthur Pym of Nantucket*. Ed. Harold Beaver. New York: Penguin, 1975.

Robinson, Christopher L. "Teratonymy: The Weird and Monstrous Names of H P Lovecraft." *Names* 58, No. 3 (September 2010): 127–38.

Salomon, Roger B. *Mazes of the Serpent: An Anatomy of Horror Narrative*. Ithaca, NY: Cornell University Press, 2002.

Wittgenstein, Ludwig. *Tractatus Logico-Philosophicus*. Tr. D. F. Pears and B. F. McGuiness. London: Routledge Classics, 2001.

Briefly Noted

S. T. Joshi's *I Am Providence* continues to appear in translations around the world. A Spanish translation, as *Yo soy Providence*, by Carlos M. Pla, was published in Spain in 2022 in one enormous volume (Valencia: Aurora Dorada, 2022). The first volume of a Russian translation also appeared in 2022. These join the translation of the work in German (*H. P. Lovecraft: Leben und Werk*, tr. Andreas Fliedner [Munich: Golkonda Verlag, 2017–20; 2 vols.]), French (*Je suis Providence*, ed. Christophe Thill, tr. Thomas Bauduret et al. [Paris: ActuSF, 2019; 2 vols.]), and Italian (*Io sono Providence*, ed. Giacomo Ortolani; tr. Elena Cervi, Lara Baldini, and Gianfranco Calvitti [n.p.: Providence Press, 2019–21; 3 vols.]).

"A Kind of Sophisticated Astarte": On the Nature of Shub-Niggurath

> . . . procul a mea tuos sit furor omnis, era, domo:
> alios age incitatos, alios age rabidos.
> —Catullus 63

> And as she lay upon the durtie ground,
> Her huge long taile her den all overspred,
> Yet was in knots and many boughtes upwound,
> Pointed with mortall sting. Of her there bred
> A thousand yong ones, which she dayly fed,
> Sucking upon her poisnous dugs, each one
> Of sundry shapes, yet all ill favored:
> Soone as that uncouth light upon them shone,
> Into her mouth they crept, and suddain all were gone.
> —Edmund Spenser, *The Faerie Queene* 1.15

1. A Foreplay

For an entity mentioned by name as often as Shub-Niggurath is in the Lovecraft Mythos, the only physical description Lovecraft gives of this enigmatic power is in a letter to Willis Conover as "Yog-Sothoth's wife is the hellish cloud-like entity Shub-Niggurath, in whose honor nameless cults hold the rite of the Goat with a Thousand Young. By her he has two monstrous off-spring—the evil twins Nug and Yeb. He has also begotten hell-ish hybrids upon the females of various organic species throughout the universes of space-time" (*Letters to Robert Bloch* 391). Excluding the inventions of other authors, the rest must be inferred from tantalizing hints. The reference to "the Goat with a Thousand Young" tends to suggest to most people unrestrained fertility and procreation, and the wildness of nature à la the Greek god Pan and satyrs.

The name itself appears to derive from an obscure and abandoned jungle god, Sheol-Nugganoth, invented by Lord Dunsany for his story "Idle Days on the Yann" (1910). "Sheol" is attractively suggestive as also being the name of the Israelite underworld, and the Hebrew/Arabic phoneme "oth" probably inspired Lovecraft in contriving the names Yog-Sothoth, Yuggoth, Azathoth, and shoggoth (cf. FLB 141). Lovecraft merely blunted the Sheol to Shub, and potentially added the probably unconscious suggestion of a racial slur in reference to the color of the goat. At least that's one reading. An equally valid reading is that it derives from the Latin root for black in reference to the color of the "goat."

In a letter to Robert E. Howard dated 14 August 1930, Lovecraft writes, "Regarding the solemnly cited myth-cycle of Cthulhu, Yog-Sothoth, R'lyeh, Nyarlathotep, Nug, Yeb, Shub-Niggurath, etc., etc.—let me confess that this is all a synthetic concoction of my own" (A Means to Freedom 40). Shub-Niggurath is right there in the canonical mythos pantheon. As Will Murray rightly observes of the genealogy of Azathoth outlined in Lovecraft's well-known letter to James F. Morton, dated 27 April 1933 (JFM 317), the family tree is clearly modeled on Hesiod's Theogony of the Greek gods (Murray 55). In Hesiod, primordial Chaos gives birth to Gaia (Earth), Tartarus (the Abyss), Eros (Desire/Attraction/Action/Procreation), Night, and Erebus (Darkness). In the letter Azathoth (Chaos) gives birth to Nyarlathotep (Action), The Nameless Mist, and Darkness. In Hesiod, Night and Erebus mate and give birth to Aether (Air) and Day. Gaia and Tartarus mate and give birth to the monster Typhon, whom even the gods fear, while Gaia spontaneously gives birth to several other primordial, often monstrous deities. By contrast, in the Lovecraft chart, The Nameless Mist sires Yog-Sothoth, and Darkness births Shub-Niggurath. Shub-Niggurath seems to combine aspects of both Gaia as mother of monsters and primeval Eros as the power of procreation. Conceptually there are hints of this perversion of the Earth Mother as early as

1919 in the final couplet of Lovecraft's poem "Mother Earth": "I AM THE VOICE OF MOTHER EARTH, / FROM WHENCE ALL HORRORS HAVE THEIR BIRTH" (*AT* 61, ll. 39–40). Compare this with the poet John Milton's description of the goddess Cybele in his masque *Arcades* (1645): "Or the towred *Cybele*, / Mother of a hunderd [*sic*] gods" (44).

In the only sexual union in the chart, Yog-Sothoth and Shub-Niggurath mate to produce Nug and Yeb, who Murray suggests are inspired by the Egyptian Nut (Heaven) and Geb (Earth) (56), implying a connection between Yog-Sothoth and Shub-Niggurath, and the parents of Nut and Geb—the primordial deities of the Egyptian ennead Shu (god of the air) and Tefnut (goddess of moisture). Nug and Yeb find their parallels in Hesiod with two of the offspring of Gaia, Ouranus (god of the sky) and Ourea (goddess of the mountains). Lovecraft himself said that he chose the names Nug and Yeb to "suggest the dark and mysterious tone of Tartar or Thibetan folklore" (*FLB* 141).

In Lovecraft's writings the name Shub-Niggurath often appears in the context of certain formulae and epithets, implying that at least on some level Lovecraft had formed a consistent picture of Shub-Niggurath in his own mind. In "The Dunwich Horror" (1928), the first mention of Shub-Niggurath under Lovecraft's name exclusively, the *Necronomicon* is quoted: "Iä! Shub-Niggurath!" (*CF* 2.434). The "Whisperer in Darkness" (1930), in the context of a ceremony involving the Mi-Go we find: "Ever Their praises, and abundance to the Black Goat of the Woods. *Iä! Shub-Niggurath! Iä! Shub-Niggurath! The Black Goat of the Woods with a Thousand Young!*" (*CF* 2.486–87; emphasis in original). Similar references occur in "The Dreams in the Witch House" (1932) and "The Thing on the Doorstep" (1933). No doubt Lovecraft found it convenient to pepper these mysterious utterances in his fiction for effect, but they are certainly suggestive of his grounding in the Greek and Latin classics. "Iä" seems a warped echo of both the ritual Greek funerary lament "Ai" or "Oi" (cf. Nagy) and the "*Io Hymen Hymenaee! Io Hymen!*" of Roman weddings invoking the marriage god Hymen and found in Plautus, Catullus, and Ovid. Robert M. Price claims that "Iä!" is associated with the Greek Bacchantes ("Artificial Mythology" 264), but there is little evidence for this in classical literature, and Lovecraft uses it indiscriminately, applying it in the invocation of, for example, the Aztec deity Tloquenahuaque in the revision story for Adolphe de Castro, "The Electric Executioner" (1930; CF 4.196).

The latter invocation of fertility and consummated union seems particularly relevant here, given the consensus that Shub-Niggurath is a deity of miscegenation of the human and ab-human and an unconscious indication of Lovecraft's xenophobia. And yet, there is very little evidence from Lovecraft that this is what Shub-Niggurath represented to him. One of the more interesting arguments that this is what he had in mind is advanced by Mitch Fry, noting that in the same decade Lothrop Stoddard published *The Rising Tide of Color against White World-Supremacy* (1920), Lovecraft had written "into existence two evil gods with eugenic subtexts"—Yog-Sothoth, "an alien deity who desired to mate with white New Englanders," and Shub-Niggurath, "whose derogative name and title (Black Goat of a Thousand Young) both echo Stoddard's fear that Caucasian power would be threatened by high birth rates in African nations" (86). Yet this seems doubtful: Lovecraft was primarily interested in race as it applied to the United States, which was largely an urban phenomenon—no "woods" to speak of. More to the point, the mythology and folklore that best fit are those of the Northern Europeans and the Mediterranean. There is nothing in "The Dunwich Horror" to suggest Yog-Sothoth has an ethnic preference in the mother of its offspring. While this assertion is debatable and perhaps suggests more embroidering by Fry than close reading of the text, he is perfectly accurate when he observes:

> Lovecraft's terrible gods interact logically with their historical setting, as those of the Greeks and Romans did in their own times. Beings in the Cthulhu pantheon are, appropriately, troubling fictional deities for a troubling real world. An air of classical mythology surrounds these characters, even though it is intermittently dispersed by sharp bursts of modernity. (86)

This is insightful, though I would add a caveat. HPL's prejudice was less "modern" in the Jim Crow sense than infused with a classist nostalgia for a half-imagined aristocratic colonial lifestyle supported by slavery and hierarchy, finding expression in poems written in childhood such as "C.S.A.: 1861–1865" and "De Triumpho Naturae"—the latter dedicated to William Benjamin Smith, author of the appalling 1905 tract *The Color Line: A Brief in Behalf of the Unborn* (AT 33).

Returning to the most frequent invocation of Shub-Niggurath in Lovecraft's oeuvre, we find in "Medusa's Coil" (1930; a revision tale for Zealia Bishop) the cod Swahili variant chant *"Iä! Iä! Shub-Niggurath! Ya-R'lyeh! N'gagi n'bulu bwana n'lolo!"*[1] uttered in an excruciating minstrel patois by Sophonisba, an elderly Black servant with ties to witchcraft and ancient African magic, devotee to the story's villain (depending on your point of view), the seductive and lamia-like Marceline:

> "Ya, yo, pore Missy Tanit, pore Missy Isis! Marse Clooloo, come up outen de water an' git yo chile—she done daid! She done daid! De hair ain' got no missus no mo', Marse Clooloo. Ol' Sophy, she know! Ol' Sophy, she done got de black stone outen Big Zimbabwe in ol' Affriky! Ol' Sophy, she done dance in de moonshine roun' de crocodile-stone befo' de N'bangus cotch her and sell her to de ship folks! No mo' Tanit! No mo' Isis! No mo' witch-woman to keep de fire a-goin' in de big stone place! Ya, yo! N'gagi n'bulu bwana n'lolo! Iä! Shub-Niggurath! She daid! Ol' Sophy know!" (CF 4.329–30)

Even by the standards of Lovecraft's xenophobia, the racist caricature in "Medusa's Coil" is outlandish to the point of self-parody, the protagonist less horrified at the revelation that Marceline is an eldritch abomination than at the other revelation that she is a mulatto who has been passing as white.[2] It is inter-

---

1. Speculatively, the phrase "N'gagi n'bulu bwana n'lolo" may simply reiterate in faux African, Tanit, Isis, and "Master Clooloo."

2. A similar gilding of the lily occurs in the revision story "The Disinterment" (1935; written with Duane W. Rimel), in which the protagonist appears more horrified that his head has been transplanted onto the body of a Black Haitian than the fact of the transplantation in the first place.

esting to see Shub-Niggurath invoked again in the context of miscegenation between human and ab-human, and racial mixing, but also in connection with two other ancient African fertility goddesses that Marceline apparently embodies, the Carthaginian Tanit and the Egyptian (latterly Egypto-Hellenic and Egypto-Roman) Isis.

Lovecraft's description of Shub-Niggurath as an "evil cloud-like entity" may also have been suggested by the story of Nephele from various sources—Pindar, Apollodorus, Diodorus Siculus, Hyginus, and Cicero—a nymph fashioned from a cloud in the shape of Juno by Jupiter as a decoy for lustful Ixion, upon whom Ixion fathered the archetypal miscegenetic race of the Centaurs.[3] The redolent phrase "the Black Goat of the Woods with a Thousand Young" is rich and multivalent with classical and Christian allusions—Pan, the satyrs, and Goya's lurid depictions of the devil as a humanoid goat in attendance at witches' sabbats. Lovecraft's interest in Goya is attested to in several instances of allusive ekphrasis in "Pickman's Model" (1926) and in a letter to William Lumley dated 21 December 1931 (*Letters to Woodburn Harris* 446). One may also detect the palpable influence of Arthur Machen's *The Great God Pan* (1894) with its themes of witchcraft and human-eldritch hybrids.

2. A Sophisticated Astarte

But of course, Shub-Niggurath predates the events on the Whateley farm, first being named in one of the "revision tales," "The Last Test" (1927) with Adolphe de Castro. Given the plot—the cultivation and spread of a preternatural plague—this seems rather appropriate. In his introduction to *The Shub-Niggurath Cycle* (1994), Robert M. Price notes that the name occurs among others created by Lovecraft for these ghostwritten "collaborations" at a remove from his own mythos (xv). It is also in these "revision tales" that we glean the greatest detail about how Shub-Niggurath operated in Lovecraft's imagination, though it should

---

3. Lucretius in Book 4 of the *De Rerum Natura* singles out Centaurs as his primary example of creatures that could not exist in nature because of their conflicting parts.

be remembered that it is not necessarily the same entity in his own stories as it is in the revisions and vice versa. In the novella "The Mound" (1929–30), written with/for Zealia Bishop, a Spanish Conquistador protagonist in the subterranean realm of K'n-yan describes a temple of Clark Ashton Smith's Tsathoggua there that "had been turned into a shrine of Shub-Niggurath, the All-Mother and wife of the Not-to-Be-Named-One. This deity was a kind of sophisticated Astarte, and her worship struck the pious Catholic as supremely obnoxious" (CF 4.266). Astarte was the great goddess of the Phoenician port cities Tyre, Sidon, and Elat, a goddess of the heavens, war, and fertility.

In many respects "The Mound" appears to draw heavily on Edward Bulwer-Lytton's *The Coming Race* (1871) for inspiration for some plot and setting elements, particularly the subterranean civilization of psychic supermen. It is not unlikely that the reactionary tone of the Bulwer-Lytton novel would chime with Lovecraft, though Lovecraft inverts Bulwer-Lytton's barely sublimated eugenicist enthusiasm into a standard pulp horror/speculative fiction tale.

Lovecraft no doubt understood that a pious Catholic Conquistador would know his Vulgate Bible and be aware that King Solomon, under the influence of his foreign wives, "went after Ashtoreth the goddess of the Sidonians" (1 Kings 11:5), and that the cult places of worship of the goddess were destroyed by Josiah (2 Kings 23). Astarte is also the Queen of Heaven to whom the Canaanites burned offerings (Jeremiah 44). It is also very likely that Lovecraft would been thinking of Poe's poem, "Ulalume: A Ballad":

> Out of which a miraculous crescent
>   Arose with a duplicate horn—
> Astarte's bediamonded crescent
>   Distinct with its duplicate horn.
> And I said—"She is warmer than Dian:
>   She rolls through an ether of sighs—
>   She revels in a region of sighs . . . (128)

As a classicist, Lovecraft may also have had in mind texts like Lucian of Samosata's *De Dea Syria* with its descriptions of castration and ritual sex that went on in the temple precinct at Hierapolis Bambyce (now Manbij) in Syria, and similar descriptions in Herodotus and Pausanias. Astarte/Ashteroth is cognate with other goddesses of love and fertility around the Levant and Mediterranean—Ishtar, Isis, Aphrodite, Venus. One suspects the entry on Phoenicia in the ninth edition of the *Encyclopaedia Britannica,* owned and much mined by Lovecraft (and the real *Necronomicon* in my opinion), is relevant here:

> In other places we find as spouse of the highest god the moon goddess Astarte with the cow's horns, who in Tyre was worshipped under the symbol of a star as queen of heaven. With her worship as with that of Baaltis were associated with wild orgies; and traces of the like are not lacking, even at Carthage (Aug. *Civ. Dei.* ii.4), where theology had given a more earnest and gloomy character to the goddess. (18.803)

The same passage draws explicit parallels with the Egyptian myth of Osiris, and therefore Isis, and Adonis, and thus Venus.

The "Not-to-Be-Named-One" supplied in "The Mound" as the spouse of Shub-Niggurath is intriguing. While this may simply be intended epithet of Yog-Sothoth, it seems far more likely to be cognate with the *"Magnum Innominandum"* that Lovecraft included in the grammatically questionable neo-Latin invocation he composed for Robert Bloch. This snippet, *"Tibi, magnum Innominandum, signa stellarum nigrarum et bufaniformis Sadoquae sigillum,"*[4] appears in Bloch's fictional grimoire and is trotted out in various stories, notably "The Shambler from the Stars" (1935). The mention of *"stellarum nigrarum"* (black stars) echoes the black stars of Robert W. Chambers's Carcosa, and in conjunction with the Chambers references in the following quotation from "The Whisperer in Darkness" has led to the somewhat strained suggestion that this *Magnum Innominandum* is Hastur, given the epithet "The Unspeakable" by later writers, notably Derleth in "The Return of Hastur" (1939), in which that author introduces his controversial quasi-Paracelsian system

---

4. "To you, the great Not-to-Be-Named, signs of the black stars, and the seal of the toad-shaped Tsathoggua."

of elemental categories and cosmic black hats and white hats.

> I found myself faced by names and terms that I had heard else-
> where in the most hideous of connections—Yuggoth, Great
> Cthulhu, Tsathoggua, Yog-Sothoth, R'lyeh, Nyarlathotep, Aza-
> thoth, Hastur, Yian, Leng, the Lake of Hali, Bethmoora, the
> Yellow Sign, L'mur-Kathulos, Bran and the Magnum Innomi-
> nandum . . . . There is a whole secret cult of evil men (a man of
> your mystical erudition will understand me when I link them
> with Hastur and the Yellow Sign) devoted to the purpose of
> tracking them down and injuring them on behalf of the mon-
> strous powers from other dimensions. (CF 2.483)

As Price points out, though, "all we have are mere references,
not incorporations: these items do not form part of the Mythos"
("H. P. Lovecraft and the Cthulhu Mythos" 8). Clark Ashton
Smith similarly warned Derleth about losing sight of the wood
for the goats when he cautioned the latter in 1937: "The intent
here, it would seem, is to suggest a *common* immemorial background for mythic beings and places created by *various* modern
writers" (12). The only other entity Lovecraft mentions in his
oeuvre as being unnamable is the Nameless Mist of the aforementioned genealogy of Azathoth (JFM 317), which is the identification taken up by Lin Carter.[5] Perhaps the key, however, is
in Lovecraft's short story "The Unnamable" (1923), which reads
like a parody of spiritualism and supernatural literature: "It was
everywhere—a gelatin—a slime—yet it had shapes, a thousand
shapes of horror beyond all memory. There were eyes—and a
blemish. It was the pit—the maelstrom—the ultimate abomination. Carter, *it was the unnamable!*" (CF 1.405).

3. Venus Stygia

In "Out of the Æons" (1933), another "revision tale" written
with Hazel Heald, the character T'yog of the lost continent Mu
is described as the "High Priest of Shub-Niggurath and guardian
of the copper temple of the Goat with a Thousand Young" (CF

---

5. "The Madness out of Time," *Crypt of Cthulhu* No. 39 (Roodmas 1986).

4.462). Elsewhere I have made the case that although Lovecraft was scornful of astrology, he understood its lore in detail and this, in turn, may have influenced his conception of the core pantheon of mythos deities. In "The Rings of Cthulhu" I argued that Cthulhu may be partly inspired by astrological, mythological, and humoral associations of Saturn. In that context it is worth observing that the metal copper falls under the astrological influence of Venus, and it would be logical that copper would feature in a temple associated with Venus.

In the story, T'yog claims that "the gods friendly to man could be arrayed against the hostile gods, and . . . that Shub-Niggurath, Nug, and Yeb, as well as Yig the Serpent-god, were ready to take sides with man" (CF 4.462). This is baffling, as Lovecraftian deities are inevitably amoral and uninterested in human insects. We may, of course, make allowances for this being a "revision tale" rather than mythos proper, but Shub-Niggurath undeniably is also canonical in the purely Lovecraftian mythos. The only deity in the mythos proper that has a benign attitude—Derlethian revisionism aside—is Nodens in "The Strange High House in the Mist" (1926) and *The Dream-Quest of Unknown Kadath* (1926–27). In "A Note on Nodens" I make comparisons between that deity and Neptune/Poseidon and other minor classical gods. In terms of the classical astrological planets, however, Nodens appears more like Neptune's brother Jupiter, being rather more Jovial in aspect. Of the Jovian temperament, C. S. Lewis says:

> We may say it is *Kingly*, but we must think of a King at peace, enthroned, taking his leisure, serene. The Jovial character is cheerful, festive, yet temperate, tranquil, magnanimous. When this planet dominates we may expect halcyon days and prosperity. In Dante wise and just princes go to his sphere when they die. He is the best planet and it is called The Greater Fortune, *Fortuna Major*. (*Discarded Image* 105–6; emphasis in original)

In many ways, though by no means perfect, this would fit Nodens more precisely than comparisons to the planet Neptune in post-classical astrology; but what is interesting is that in similar terms, the Lesser Fortune, *Fortuna Minor*, is Venus. As Lewis observes:

In beneficence Venus stands second only to Jupiter; she is *Fortuna Minor*. Her metal is copper. The connection is not clear till we observe that Cyprus was once famed for its copper mines; that copper is *cyprium*, the Cyprian metal; and that Venus, or Aphrodite, especially worshipped in that island, was κύπρις, the Lady of Cyprus. In mortals she produces beauty and amorousness; in history, fortunate events. (*Discarded Image* 107)

Indeed, Nodens's shell chariot would be equally apt for Aphrodite Urania, born from the waves as so burned into the imagination by Botticelli. But I digress.

If it seems difficult to imagine equating Shub-Niggurath with Venus Aphrodite, goddess of beauty and love, it must be recalled that Venus, too, had her terrifying aspects in classical literature. These range from the personal cruelty directed at Psyche in Books 4–6 of Apuleius' *Metamorphoses* or *The Golden Ass* to inspiring the bloody mass androcide by the women of Lemnos in Book 2 of Valerius Flaccus' *Argonautica,* though neither author makes an appearance in Lovecraft's essay "The Literature of Rome." Flaccus in the *Argonautica* in particular elides *eros* (love) and *eris* (strife) by making Venus, surrounded by the forces of hell, essentially a Fury—Venus Stygia, *"virginibus Stygiis . . . simillima"* (*Arg.* 2.106). We may also observe that Cloacina,[6] goddess of the sewers of Rome, is an aspect of Venus, as testified by several ancient sources, but particularly Pliny the Elder (*Nat. Hist.* 15.119). We might also consider the post-pagan "Venus Infernal" identified by Lewis in in the work of Edmund Spenser (*Allegory of Love* 332).[7] Nor should we neglect the more obvious fact, of which keen amateur astronomer Lovecraft was no doubt aware, that Venus is also the morning star Lucifer with all the cultural baggage that entails.

As an interesting aside, while Lovecraft mentions the planet Venus several times in his fiction, his most Clark Ashton Smith-

---

6. Thomas Ligotti has adapted Cloacina as his entity Cynothoglys the Mortician God in his stories, notably "The Prodigy of Dreams" (1994).

7. Clark Ashton Smith deploys this trope successfully in his story "The Disinterment of Venus" (*Weird Tales*, July 1934).

esque and only planetary romance, "In the Walls of Eryx" (1936; co-written with Kenneth Sterling), is set there. Venus, in this story, contrary to the barren reality we now know, is lushly verdant with unrestrained fecundity and rife with unpleasant creatures named in parody of various acquaintances: "wriggling akmans" and "efjeh-weeds" (Forrest J Ackerman, with whom Lovecraft feuded over Smith's writing), "farnoth flies" (Farnsworth Wright, editor of *Weird Tales*), and "ugrats" (from Lovecraft's sobriquet "Hugo the Rat" for Hugo Gernsback, editor of *Wonder Stories*). For all that Venus as primeval jungle planet is a common enough trope in pulp writing of the period, that too is an astrological-mythological inheritance, as is the contrasting arid austerity and stoicism of Mars.

4. Cybele, Magna Mater, the Moon, and Others

We are, of course, now entering dangerous waters, as one could sophomorically point at anything vaguely resembling a fertility goddess in Lovecraft and claim it as a manifestation of Shub-Niggurath. This is, of course, unlikely, as is the notion that Lovecraft had any deep, analytical schema in mind when it came to his pantheon; but he does repeatedly return to the archetype of the fertility deity as eldritch abomination to suit his purposes. If he indeed had a more fleshed-out idea of Shub-Niggurath in mind, the only female-ish Old One,[8] it is in these references, largely cribbed by Lovecraft from the 9th edition of the *Encyclopedia Britannica*, that we shall find hints of it.

Price asserts that the connection with Astarte links Shub-Niggurath to another fertility goddess, Cybele, the *Magna Mater* mentioned in "The Rats in the Walls" (1923), suggesting that the "great mother worshipped by the hereditary cannibal cult of Exham Priory had to be none other than Shub-Niggurath" (*Shub-Niggurath Cycle* xiv). This is not an unreasonable suggestion; both Cybele and Astarte were at times depicted with lions and wearing a turreted mural coronet (Layard 456). The Elder Pliny

---

8. Although Lovecraft fleetingly mentions "Mother Hydra" in "The Shadow over Innsmouth" (1931), it is not clear if she and Father Dagon are some kind of lesser Old Ones or a superior kind of Deep One.

in the *Naturalis Historia* says that the planet Venus was called Juno, Isis, and Cybele (*Nat. Hist.* 2.6.37). Cybele was a Phrygian mother goddess whose cult was adopted by the Greek colonies in Asia Minor, eventually spreading to the Greek peninsula by the sixth century B.C.E., where she was regarded as an exotic mystery goddess combining aspects of Gaia and Demeter and attended by an ecstatic and disorderly retinue of mendicant eunuch priests.

It was in Rome that Cybele acquired the soubriquet Magna Mater, becoming an official Roman cult in 205 B.C.E. when the Sibylline oracle recommended her evocation in the defeat of Carthage in the Second Punic War.[9] This was an unusual case, as Cybele was not a Carthaginian goddess; but the Romans may have run out of options, having previously lured away the Carthaginian goddess Tanit to Rome during the First Punic War in the guise of Juno Caelestis. But as Fred Blosser notes, Lovecraft doesn't make the unpleasant practices of the cult of Cybele an explicit part of the horror of the story; rather, the focus is on the cannibalistic aspects of the indigenous cult the priests of Cybele end up merging with (Blosser 26).

Valentina Sirangelo argues cogently for a lunar aspect to Shub-Niggurath, which is later taken up by Ramsey Campbell in his story "The Moon-Lens." Sirangelo's argument is based on the apparent fluidity of the entity's gender (usually identified as a mother but referred to at least once by Lovecraft as "Lord of the Woods" (CF 2.486),[10] the association with fertility, Lovecraft's explicit reference in "The Mound" to Astarte, whom the Poe poem categorically defines as a moon goddess, and who is

9. Livy, *Ab Urbe Condita* 29.14.15. *Evocatio* was the magico-religious practice during the Roman Republic era of "calling forth" a deity, usually of a foreign enemy (though not in this case) with the promise of a superior temple and cult in Rome.

10. On the other hand, both Murray (58n9) and Ferraresi (18, 22) argue that two distinct entities with different ontologies are implied, though Ferraresi suggests that the caprine Lord of the Woods is the form Shub-Niggurath adopts to copulate with its followers at their sabbats, i.e., the medieval Pan-Satan, noting that Astarte was sometimes worshipped in the male form Athtar. A similar ambiguity can be found in the male demon Ashteroth.

frequently depicted as horned—a connection to both goats and the moon. Astrologically the moon represents mutability in its changing phases and rules over damp and swampy places—making Lovecraft's "The Moon-Bog" (1921) most apropos—and causes madness.

While Lovecraft doesn't mention Shub-Niggurath explicitly in "The Horror at Red Hook" (1925), the Semitic demoness Lilith substitutes with callouts to Hecate, the Magna Mater, and Ashtaroth (a variant on Astarte that somehow becomes male at the hands of medieval demonologists):

> Avenues of limitless night seemed to radiate in every direction, till one might fancy that here lay the root of a contagion destined to sicken and swallow cities, and engulf nations in the foetor of hybrid pestilence. Here cosmic sin had entered, and festered by unhallowed rites had commenced the grinning march of death that was to rot us all to fungous abnormalities too hideous for the grave's holding. Satan here held his Babylonish court, and in the blood of stainless childhood the leprous limbs of phosphorescent Lilith were laved. Incubi and succubae howled praise to Hecate, and headless moon-calves bleated to the Magna Mater. Goats leaped to the sound of thin accursed flutes, and aegipans chased endlessly after misshapen fauns over rocks twisted like swollen toads. Moloch and Ashtaroth were not absent; for in this quintessence of all damnation the bounds of consciousness were let down, and man's fancy lay open to vistas of every realm of horror and every forbidden dimension that evil had power to mould. (CF 1.499)

The worship of all the above-mentioned goddesses is discussed in detail in Margaret Murray's controversial *The Witch-Cult in Western Europe* (1921), a book Lovecraft namedrops in "The Rats in the Walls" and "The Call of Cthulhu." Murray also extensively references accounts of the devil appearing at witches' sabbats in the form of a great black goat. Confusingly, this role is also fulfilled by Nyarlathotep in "The Dreams in the Witch House" (1932). We may draw parallels between this scene and the ekphrasis of the diabolical portrait of Marceline in "Medusa's Coil":

> And God! The shapes of nightmare that float around in that perpetual daemon twilight! The blasphemies that lurk and leer and hold a Witches' Sabbat with that woman as a high-priestess! The black shaggy entities that are not quite goats—the crocodile-headed beast with three legs and a dorsal row of tentacles[11]—and the flat-nosed Ægipans dancing in a pattern that Egypt's priests knew and called accursed! (CF 4.334–35)

The "black shaggy entities that are not quite goats" and the "flat-nosed aegipans" remind one irresistibly of that other infamous goat, the Black Goat of the Woods with a thousand young. Returning to Red Hook, the purported Greek inscription, lifted wholesale from the 9th edition of the *Encyclopedia Britannica*'s entry on magic,[12] is also replete with intriguing references: "O friend and companion of night, thou who rejoicest in the baying of dogs and spilt blood, who wanderest in the midst of shades among the tombs, who longest for blood and bringest terror to mortals, Gorgo, Mormo, thousand-faced moon, look favourably on our sacrifices!" (CF 1.505). Gorgo, Mormo, and the thousand faced moon (with a faint echo of the thousand young?) are all epithets of Hecate, the Greco-Roman goddess of night, witchcraft, and in some sources, she is identified with Artemis/Selene (the moon) and Persephone (the goddess of the underworld) as part of a triple goddess.

5. A Note on Lovecraft's Sexuality and Attitudes to Gender

Without getting too deeply into the fraught territory of Lovecraft's sexuality, it is probably not too controversial to acknowledge that if not outright asexual he was distinctly prudish in matters of sexuality, as attested to in his letters. One may conjure with allusions to succubae, the vampiric anima, and

---

11. One wonders if this description might have inspired Zoth-Ommog from Lin Carter's Xothic stories, though Zoth-Ommog has four legs.

12. As Dirk W. Mosig has noted, this in turn can be traced back to the *Philosophumena*, or *The Refutation of All Heresies*, by the third century C.E. theologian Hippolytus of Rome, quoting Porphyry of Tyre.

Freudian *vagina dentata;* and the connection of Shub-Niggurath with goddesses such as Astarte, Cybele, and Venus and their associations with castration is decidedly suggestive. My own view is that Lovecraft was, in the modern parlance, "demisexual"—which is to say, only interested in sexual consummation with people he felt particularly emotionally close to, vis-à-vis Sonia Greene's testimony about his prowess (Everts, "Howard Phillips Lovecraft and Sex").

The only occasion that Lovecraft can be said to have written a tale specifically about sexuality, not merely implied some ab-human or bestial miscegenation in the past, is the revision story "The Loved Dead" (1924) with C. M. Eddy, Jr. This tale of necrophilia seems to be Lovecraft's self-parodic "The Hound"–like rewriting of Eddy's original 1919 plot with morbid Poe-esque flourishes; it is highly unlikely he would have chosen the topic of his own volition. Unironic or positive literary depictions of sexuality seem only to have aroused disgust in him: note his negative comments to Frank Belknap Long on the subject of Henry Fielding's 1749 picaresque *Bildungsroman* romp *Tom Jones* (cited Houellebecq 58).

There have been many attempts to interpret Lovecraft's few female characters being either incidental or ab-humanly malevolent as an expression of hostile misogyny. Certainly, they are inevitably associated with themes of domination, corruption, incest, and miscegenation: Keziah, Lavinia, Marceline, and Asenath being the obvious examples (see Pighetti). SF author Ruthanna Emrys even goes so far as to make the ludicrous assertion that the Lilith of "Red Hook" is an anti-Semitic expression of Lovecraft's resentment at her taking him to New York. This is a risible given that all the evidence points to Lovecraft and Greene remaining cordial at the conclusion of their brief marriage, and while most certainly an old-fashioned chauvinist, Lovecraft was first and foremost an old-fashioned gentleman for whom such behavior would be unconscionable (Everts, "Mrs. Howard Phillips Lovecraft").

It is far more likely Lovecraft had in mind George MacDonald's Victorian fantasy novel *Lilith* (1895), in which the titular creature is a beautiful sorceress who takes the form of a monstrous leech to feed on the living. Lovecraft owned a copy of *Lilith* (*LL* 611), and he mentions it in his essay "Supernatural Horror in Literature" (1927). Its surreal quality and central picaresque dream-quest as allegory for death make it a likely influence on Lovecraft's Dreamlands as well. In that sense Lovecraft is a kind of anti–C. S. Lewis, who likewise drew on MacDonald (and quite possibly Dunsany as well) to create Narnia—a kind of fantasy world-cum-afterlife.

If we must tiptoe into the foggy minefield of psychoanalyzing Lovecraft, Federica Pighetti makes some interesting Jungian observations on the role of Lovecraft's mother, being the dominant figure in his development following the demise of his father, while being both simultaneously distant and controlling (cf. also Faig). This is within the broader context of analyzing the multiple occurrences of the "Terrible Mother" Jungian archetype in Lovecraft's oeuvre. Curiously, Pighetti sees this strongly in the conception of Cthulhu and barely mentions Shub-Niggurath at all. Such post-mortems of the psyche can be taken or left as the reader sees fit, as there is a tendency to drift into something akin to reading tea leaves, appealing as it is to imagine the maternal relationship as a drive to Lovecraft's creative urge transmogrifying into an eldritch abomination.

6. *Algernon Blackwood and Conclusion*

If, indeed, Lovecraft had a more concrete notion of Shub-Niggurath in mind, I suspect it wasn't any more substantial than the abstract consciousness of the Earth that Algernon Blackwood infuses throughout his 1911 novel *The Centaur,* though with the malignity of Blackwood's 1907 story "The Willows." Blackwood, whom Lovecraft regarded as the greatest living author of the weird tale (see Ashley), had a knack for conjuring sublime horror from Nature. The weird nature stories collected in Blackwood's collection *Pan's Garden* (1912) cumulatively transform Nature into a supernatural animistic presence that is both seductively inviting and alienatingly terrifying—"ecogothic" in contemporary discourse (see Poland).

Indeed, I would go so far as to suggest that Shub-Niggurath, at least in part, is a nod to Blackwood. Lovecraft's circle of correspondents frequently indulged in pseudo-fantastical nicknames that occasionally made their way into each other's fictions. One of the more obvious examples is the Atlantean priest "Klarkash-Ton" in "The Whisperer in Darkness" (*CF* 2.519), being a hat tip to Clark Ashton Smith. While Blackwood and Lovecraft were not personally acquainted, there is a hint in the epithet *Black* Goat of the *Woods* with a Thousand Young. The "Thousand Young" part could easily apply to one of the most prolific authors of horror and weird fiction of the period. In "Supernatural Horror in Literature," Lovecraft mentions the "well-nigh endless array of Mr. Blackwood's fiction" and writes:

> Another amazingly potent though less artistically finished tale [than Blackwood's "The Willows"] is "The Wendigo", where we are confronted by horrible evidences of a vast forest daemon about which North Woods lumber men whisper at evening. The manner in which certain footprints tell certain unbelievable things is really a marked triumph in craftsmanship. (CE 2.121–22)

"The Wendigo" (1910) describes a group of moose hunters in northwestern Ontario who have an encounter with a vast, unseen presence in the forest. When one of their number disappears into the trees in the night, they track his footprints in the snow, only to find them in the presence of much larger, monstrous tracks; the missing man's tracks gradually morph into a smaller version of the giant ones. Later one of the hunters briefly encounters a hideous parody of the missing man. Eventually the missing hunter returns to camp and dies from exposure and frostbite. The giant being is intimated to be a Wendigo from Native American folklore, but it could easily fill the role of Shub-Niggurath as well. Curiously, Derleth based his short story "Ithaqua" (1941) on this tale, and in his earlier Wendigo-inspired story "The Thing That Walked on the Wind" (1933) he namechecks Blackwood, describing "The Wendigo" as a story of "air elementals" (Price, *Ithaqua Cycle* xi).

One might easily imagine Lovecraft forming a kind of synthesis with Arthur Machen's *The Great God Pan*, perhaps inspired by the god being namechecked in both "The Dunwich Horror" and "The Whisperer in Darkness." Shub-Niggurath as a primal abstract personification of the beauty and terror in Nature makes considerably more sense to me, given Lovecraft's complete lack of interest in writing about sex, than the idea of some kind of monstrous mother. There is also the possibility of some allusion to the New England Transcendentalists of the nineteenth century. Lovecraft owned editions of the critical writings of Ralph Waldo Emerson, and there is a distinctly Emersonian tinge to both Lovecraft's early romanticism and later cosmicism (see Wood, "A Note on Nodens" 139). Lovecraft held similar holistic views about nature and skepticism regarding industrial capitalism as expressed by Emerson in his 1836 collection of essays *Nature*. Lovecraft, in his own (not revision) stories rarely invoked Shub-Niggurath in urban settings, but more often in places like rural hinterland of Massachusetts and Vermont. Who can forget his masterly descriptions of landscape in "The Dunwich Horror" and "The Whisperer in Darkness" with their use of the pathetic fallacy?

Ultimately the pleasure and utility of Shub-Niggurath in the Mythos is the exotic name, the sinister contexts in which it is invoked, and an absolute lack of detail that might otherwise constrain its use. The embroidered Shub-Niggurath as a monstrous earth mother found in the fiction of others almost inevitably can be traced to Derlethian innovations rather than anything written by Lovecraft himself. As David E. Schultz states, Lovecraft had no immutable plan for his pantheon beyond hinting at an unimaginable past and arbitrary cosmic happenings far beyond mere human comprehension.

Works Cited

Ashley, Mike. "Lovecraft and Blackwood: A Surveillance," *Crypt of Cthulhu* No. 51 (Hallowmas 1987): 3–8, 14.

Blosser, Fred. "The Sign of the Magna Mater." *Crypt of Cthulhu* No. 97 (Hallowmas 1997): 25–27.

Derleth, August. "The Return of Hastur." In Robert M. Price, ed. *The Hastur Cycle*. Oakland, CA: Chaosium, 1997. 262–83.

Emrys, Ruthanna, and Anne M. Pillsworth. "Lovecraft's Most Bigoted Story, No Really: 'The Horror at Red Hook.'" 2015, www.tor.com/2015/03/03/lovecrafts-most-bigoted-story-no-really-the-horror-at-red-hook/

Encyclopaedia Britannica. 9th ed. Edinburgh: A & C. Black, 1898.

Everts, R. Alain. "Howard Phillips Lovecraft and Sex; or, The Sex Life of a Gentleman." *Nyctalops* 2, No. 2 (July 1974): 19.

———. "Mrs. Howard Phillips Lovecraft." *Nyctalops* 2, No.1 (April 1973): 45.

Faig, Kenneth W., Jr. *The Parents of Howard Phillips Lovecraft*. West Warwick, RI: Necronomicon Press, 1990.

Ferraresi, Rodolfo A. "The Question of Shub-Niggurath." *Crypt of Cthulhu* No. 35 (Hallowmas 1985): 17–18, 22.

Fry, Mitch. "*Astonishing Stories*: Eudora Welty and the Weird Tale." *Eudora Welty Review* 5 (Spring 2013): 75–93.

Houellebecq, Michel. *H. P. Lovecraft: Against the World, Against Life*. Tr. Dorna Khazeni. London: Gollancz, 2008.

Layard, Austen Henry. *Nineveh and Its Remains, with an Account of a Visit to the Chaldaean Christians of Kurdistan, and the Yezidis, or Devil-Worshippers*. Volume 2. Cambridge: Cambridge University Press, 1849.

Lewis, C. S. *The Allegory of Love: A Study in Medieval Tradition*. Oxford: Oxford University Press, 1953.

———. *The Discarded Image*. Cambridge: Cambridge University Press, 1964.

Lovecraft, H. P. *Letters to F. Lee Baldwin, Duane W. Rimel, and Nils Frome*. Ed. David E. Schultz and S. T. Joshi. New York: Hippocampus Press, 2016. [Abbreviated in the text as *FLB*.]

———. *Letters to James F. Morton*. Ed. David E. Schultz and S. T. Joshi. New York: Hippocampus Press, 2011. [Abbreviated in the text as *JFM*.]

———. *Letters to Robert Bloch and Others*. Ed. David E. Schultz and S. T. Joshi. New York: Hippocampus Press, 2015.

———. *Letters to Woodburn Harris and Others*. Ed. David E. Schultz and S. T. Joshi. New York: Hippocampus Press, 2022.

———. *A Means to Freedom: The Letters of H. P. Lovecraft and Robert E. Howard.* Ed. S. T. Joshi, David E. Schultz, and Rusty Burke. New York: Hippocampus Press, 2009.

Milton, John. *Comus and Other Poems.* Cambridge: Cambridge University Press, 1906

Mosig, Dirk W. "A Note on *The Occult Lovecraft.*" *The Miskatonic: The Lovecraft Centenary Edition.* Glenview, IL: Moshassuck Press, 1991.

Murray, Will. "On the Natures of Nug and Yeb." *Lovecraft Studies* No. 9 (Fall 1984): 52–59.

Nagy, Gregory. "Ancient Greek Elegy." In Karen Weisman, ed. *The Oxford Handbook of the Elegy.* Oxford: Oxford University Press, 2010. 13–45.

Pighetti, Federica. "La madre terribile nell'opera di H. P. Lovecraft." 2016, www.academia.edu/38559109/LA_MADRE_TERRIBILE_NELLOPERA_DI_H_P_LOVECRAFT

Poe, Edgar Allan. *Collected Poems.* Ann Arbor: Lowe & B. Hould, 1998.

Poland, Michelle. "Walking with the Goat-God: Gothic Ecology in Algernon Blackwood's *Pan's Garden: A Volume of Nature Stories.*" *Critical Survey* 29, No. 1 (2017): 53–69.

Price, Robert M. "H. P. Lovecraft and the Cthulhu Mythos." *Crypt of Cthulhu* No. 35 (Hallowmas 1985): 3–11.

———. "Lovecraft's 'Artificial Mythology.'" In David E. Schultz and S. T. Joshi, ed. *An Epicure in the Terrible: A Centennial Anthology of Essays in Honor of H. P. Lovecraft.* 1991. New York: Hippocampus Press, 2011. 259–68.

———, ed. *The Ithaqua Cycle: The Wind-Walker of the Icy Wastes,* Oakland, CA: Chaosium, 2006.

———, ed. *The Shub-Niggurath Cycle: Tales of the Black Goat with a Thousand Young.* Oakland, CA: Chaosium, 1994.

Schultz, David E. "Who Needs the Cthulhu Mythos?" *Lovecraft Studies* No. 13 (Fall 1986): 43–53.

Sirangelo, Valentina. "Sulla natura lunare di Shub-Niggurath: dalla mythopoeia di Howard Phillips Lovecraft a 'The Moon-Lens' di Ramsey Campbell." *Caietele Echinox* 35 (2008): 48–68.

Smith, Clark Ashton. "CAS to AWD." *Crypt of Cthulhu* No. 35
    (Hallowmas 1985): 12–16.
Wood, Andrew Paul. "A Note on Nodens in Lovecraft's My-
    thos." *Lovecraft Annual* No. 16 (2022): 128–44.
———. "The Rings of Cthulhu: Lovecraft, Dürer, Saturn, and
    Melancholy." *Lovecraft Annual* No. 13 (2019): 53–68.

H. P. Lovecraft, Jules Verne, and the Future City

Edward Guimont

Introduction

When one thinks of sinister cities in the works of H. P. Lovecraft, there is no shortage of candidates: the Nameless City, the Old Ones' Antarctic citadel, the Great Race's bibliopolis, to say nothing of gambrel-roofed Arkham or squamous Innsmouth. However, it would be remiss not to include one of his most commonly described urban locales: Providence itself. But my focus here is not the cult-infested Providence of "The Call of Cthulhu" or the necromantic haunt of *The Case of Charles Dexter Ward*, but an even more unrecognizable version of the Storied City: Providence in 2000 A.D.

An anti-immigrant satire, "Providence in 2000 A.D." (*AT* 201–2), was Lovecraft's first published poem, printed in the 4 March 1912 issue of the *Providence Evening Bulletin*. Despite its early position in his public output, it is not widely discussed now, considered only a minor example of young Lovecraft's xenophobia, albeit one that demonstrates his humorous side, even if it is a type of humor that would not be accepted today (*IAP* 137; Faig 39). Lovecraft himself did not widely discuss the poem in his letters (Joshi, *Recognition* 11). However, despite the quiet reception of "Providence in 2000 A.D.," both at the time and since, this article argues that the poem is worth deeper investigation on several grounds, which all reveal an importance to the work that has not yet been demonstrated in existing scholarship.

First, through a comparison not only of themes but of plot, "Providence in 2000 A.D." will be shown to relate not only to

several other early Lovecraft works, particularly his 1912 poem
"New-England Fallen" and World War I–era polemics, but also
to be a prototype for one of his classic pieces of fiction, the novella "The Shadow over Innsmouth" (1931). Second, in its exploration of a future cityscape and its society, "Providence in
2000 A.D." serves as a way of comparing Lovecraft's fiction to
that of one of his youthful influences, the French science fiction
master Jules Verne (1828–1905), particularly his lesser-known
novels *Paris in the Twentieth Century, The Begum's Fortune, Propeller Island,* and the short story "In the Year 2889," co-written
with his son Michel (1861–1925). Finally, given the explicit positioning of "Providence in 2000 A.D." as being set eighty-eight
years into the future of its writing, the poem serves as a notable
example of what might be called Lovecraft's futurism, itself an
overlooked category of his fictional output.

By looking at "Providence in 2000 A.D." through these three
categories, it will be shown that the poem serves as an important
lens to look at the development of Lovecraft's fiction and of his
political and social views, and to interpret his influences. However, before analyzing the poem, it would be useful to begin by
reviewing the poem itself.

Providence in 2000 A.D. in 2023 A.D.

A good description of "Providence in 2000 A.D." was provided
by Lovecraft in his 16 November 1916 letter to Rheinhart
Kleiner, one of the few times he actually discussed the poem:

> In 1912 my first bit of published *verse* appeared in *The Evening
> Bulletin.* It is a 62-line satire in the usual heroic couplet, ridicul-
> ing a popular movement on the part of the Italians of the Fed-
> eral Hill slums to change the name of their main street from
> "Atwells' [*sic*] Avenue" to "Columbus Avenue". I pictured
> Providence in 2000 A.D., with *all* the English names changed to
> foreign appellations. This piece received considerable notice of
> a minor sort, I am told, though I doubt if it had much effect in
> silencing the Italians' clamour. The idea was so foolish that it
> probably died of its own weakness. (*RK* 74)

Notably, for a scenario that inspired one of Lovecraft's first pub-
lished works of fiction, Atwells Avenue has a role in one of
Lovecraft's last stories as well. The Free-Will/Starry Wisdom
Church from "The Haunter of the Dark" (1935) was based on
St. John's Catholic Church, which was located on Atwells Avenue before its 1992 demolition; the site is now St. John's Park
(*IAP* 961). In his 30 December 1935 letter to Natalie H.
Wooley, Lovecraft refers to the church as "Irish, though the district has since become Italian" (*Letters to Robert Bloch* 207)—
ironically, a recognition by Lovecraft that the boundaries of
Providence's ethnic neighborhoods can shift over time. As this
was a shift that had no impact on the borders of what Lovecraft
would consider the "American" residents, it seems not to have
concerned him as much as the 1912 proposal by the Federal Hill
Italians. Another piece of irony is that St. John's Park now contains a memorial to Giovanni da Verrazzano (1485–1528), the
Florentine sailor who gave Rhode Island its name in 1524. The
demolition of an Irish Catholic church and its replacement with
a monument to a sixteenth-century Italian navigator well fits
the themes of the poem.

The poem begins with a prose text stating how "It is announced in the *Providence Journal* that the Italians desire to alter
the name of Atwell's Avenue to 'Columbus Avenue'." The poem proper begins with the nameless narrator describing his
background. His ancestors were British-descended Rhode Is-
landers who emigrated to England under the pressure of "foreign
immigrations" in their home state. After years of saving his mea-
ger salary, the narrator can afford to take a trip to Providence,
crossing the Atlantic by boat in a single day. Disembarking in the
city, he finds it changed greatly from the city of his ancestors.

The narrator's ship arrives in the region of Providence once
known as Fox Point. In reality, Lovecraft would become well acquainted with the area; his friends C. M. and Muriel Eddy moved
there in the early 1920s, and Lovecraft visited them often (Eddy
9). But at some point in the seventy-plus years since the Eddys'
move, Fox Point had been renamed Sao Miguel's Cape by "negro
Bravas." The term "Brava" is a now-archaic term for immigrants

from the Cape Verde islands. Uninhabited before their discovery by Portuguese sailors in 1456, the islands' population is an ethnic and cultural mix of Portuguese and West Africans. In the early nineteenth century, as the transatlantic slave trade and its prosperity declined, whaling crews from Providence and New Bedford, Massachusetts, began to recruit large numbers of Cape Verdeans, who settled in the region of those cities with their families. The majority of those Cape Verdeans came from the island of Brava and more often identified themselves as Bravas than Cape Verdeans, a categorization that only changed after the islands' 1975 independence from Portugal (Halter 36–38). However, for the historical accuracy of the term Brava alone, Phillip A. Ellis has noted that "With the phrase 'negro Bravas' . . . we have an association of blacks specifically with mixed races. It is as if the latter drag themselves down to the former's level by virtue of their 'innate' impurity and degeneration" (132).

"Bravas" are mentioned in two later works by Lovecraft. In "The Call of Cthulhu" (1926), the Cthulhu cultists arrested by Legrasse in New Orleans included "seamen, and a sprinkling of negroes and mulattoes, largely West Indians or Brava Portuguese from the Cape Verde Islands" (CF 2.37). Cape Verdean sailors in New Orleans would be far less likely than Fox Point, given that as of the 2000 census, 87 percent of Cape Verdeans in the United States live in the New England states of Massachusetts, Rhode Island, and Connecticut, a ratio that would probably have been even higher in 1908 (Halter 38–39). More accurately, *The Case of Charles Dexter Ward* (1927) features the minor character Tony Gomes, the manservant of the incognito Joseph Curwen in his Pawtuxet bungalow, described as both a Brava and an "evil Portuguese mulatto" (CF 2.310, 355).

Moving on from Fox Point/Sao Miguel's Cape, the narrator finds that the Irish have renamed South Main Street to O'Murphy's Avenue, which is traversed with a "shaky streetcar" indicating the decline of infrastructure. Lovecraft was somewhat prescient in his association of the Irish with South Main Street: in 2007, the city erected a memorial to the 1845–52 Irish Potato Famine across the Providence River from South

Main Street, followed in 2016 by a memorial to the 1916 Easter Rising, a revolution that Lovecraft would condemn along with Irish nationalism more broadly (Brown 22–23). In Lovecraft's Providence of 2000, the Irish have also renamed the neighboring city of Pawtucket to New Dublin Town, and the city of Woonsocket has become Nouvelle Paris thanks to the Quebecois. Back in Providence, the Swedes have renamed Westminster Street[1] to Svenson's Lane, and the Polish have turned the Olneyville neighborhood into "Wsjzxypq$?&%$ ladislaw" [*sic*]. For their part, the Italians have not only achieved their goal of transforming Atwells Avenue to Il Passagio di Colombo, but Federal Hill in general has become La Collina Federale. As with the public transit of O'Murphy's Avenue, the streetcars of La Collina Federale pass along "rusty rails."

However, the largest recipients of Lovecraft's ire in the poem are Jews (Bolden). They have renamed an unspecified area in the northern part of the city, possibly North Providence, to New Jerusalem, where great wealth has been amassed. In the city proper, Jews have not only renamed Market Square to Goldstein's Court, but torn down the 1775 Market House used by the Providence Board of Trade. In reality, the Board of Trade—which became the Chamber of Commerce the year after Lovecraft wrote the poem—occupied the Market House until being forced to leave in 1938 due to dangerous conditions in the building. The city renovated it, and in 1948 it was given to the Rhode Island School of Design, which still occupies the building as of 2023 (Cady 111–15). Given Lovecraft's love of Georgian architecture and dislike of urban renewal, his having the Jews destroy a colonial building in the heart of the city, especially one associated with (presumably rival) commercial interests, marks them as major villains; they are the only ethnic group in the poem who destroy aspects of the "American" Providence, rather than just renaming them.

---

1. Along which is Arcade Providence, which currently contains Lovecraft Arts & Sciences, organizers of NecronomiCon Providence. In the world of the poem, perhaps it would instead be home to a Swedenborgian church or a group promoting John Ajvide Lindqvist.

On those lines, the narrator finds that Jews have also re-named the corner of Turk's Head to Finklestein's Cross-ways and decided to sell off the "stone Post Office." At the time the building was new, having been completed in 1908. In reality, it continued to be used as a post office until 1961, when it became the Providence Federal Building and Courthouse, which is still in use today. As the Post Office was (and is) a federal building, neither the Providence city government nor neighborhood or-ganizations would be able to sell it. Undoubtedly this fact was simply overlooked by young Lovecraft, but it can also perhaps be read as an indication that in his conception of Providence in 2000 A.D. there has been a further devolution of federal powers to state and local governments. This might be in line with Love-craft's youthful support of the Confederacy and the states' rights claims of the Lost Cause narrative, as in his 1902 poem "C.S.A.: 1861–1865" (*AT* 33) and 1905 "De Triumpho Naturae" (*AT* 33–34). Outside of matters of legal jurisdiction, it is hard to see Lovecraft lamenting the loss of a recently built building on aes-thetic grounds as with the Market House. Instead, his criticism seems to be on the wastefulness of selling off a new building that had cost $1.3 million (more than $40 million in 2023).

For the region itself, the Turk's Head intersection dates back to the mid-eighteenth century, when the settler Jacob Whitman mounted a ship's figurehead of an Ottoman warrior on his shop there. By 1912, the location of Whitman's shop was the site of the construction of a skyscraper that would be completed the next year, becoming (for nine years) the tallest building in downtown Providence. In honor of Whitman's effigy, the sky-scraper became known as the Turk's Head Building and in-cludes a sculpted re-creation of the Ottoman figurehead in the façade above the entrance. Lovecraft's writing a poem where Jews rename an area that was named after an Ottoman warrior, at a time when the Ottomans still controlled the Holy Land, might come across as unintentionally Zionist.

However much perfidy Lovecraft might have attributed to the Jewish population in destroying and selling off Providence's heritage, he saves the most shocking twist for last. "With terror struck" from all that he had seen, the narrator returns to the wharf to board the steamship back to England. However, a "shrivell'd form, half crouching 'twixt the freight" grabs the narrator's arm, halting him. Asked who he is, the figure responds, "A monstrous prodigy . . . / Last of my kind, a lone unhappy man, / My name is Smith! I'm an American!"

Although the poem ends with that striking revelation, from the point of view of more than a century later there are three absences in Lovecraft's future Providence that are of note. The first is that he lacks a Black neighborhood in contrast to the various immigrant white communities (although he may have considered the Bravas to functionally be Black). One assumes that if Lovecraft had written the poem after his first visit to Harlem a decade later, he would have remedied this. The second is the similar absence of an Asian enclave. This is especially surprising given that not only did Providence have a small Chinatown, but Lovecraft actually visited it during the 1920s, being an occasional patron of a chow mein restaurant (Derie). The lack of Chinese in "Providence in 2000 A.D." may be an indication either that their numbers were very small or that, as with Blacks, Lovecraft considered Asians to be necessary as a pool for menial labor, and that their living in a concentrated enclave was preferable to their settling in white-dominated neighborhoods. The Providence Chinatown was located at the intersection of Empire and Westminster Streets, which in the world of "2000" would place it roughly in between Svenson's Lane and La Collina Federale.

The third absence is that of a cultural group that began to settle in Providence en masse in the 1980s: Latinos, particularly the Guatemalans in the southwestern part of the city. As of the 2010 census, the Providence metropolitan area has the eleventh largest population of Guatemalans in the country in terms of total numbers; in terms of percentage of the population, it is the largest, and the only one where the Guatemalan percentage is in double digits (Uriarte 125–48). No doubt this would have interested R. H. Barlow, whose interest in the Maya of Guatemala included leaving a "do not disturb" message on his door written in Mayan glyphs when he committed suicide in 1951 (*Eyes of the God* 544).

"New-England Fallen" and "The Shadow over Innsmouth"

Doug Bolden has noted that "Providence in 2000 A.D." has a parallel in Lovecraft's poem "On an Accomplished Young Linguist" (c. 1915; AT 266), pointing out that it "has a sort of similar vibe, as a young polyglot [named Paul] who can speak many languages, including classical ones, is chided for not knowing proper English" (Bolden). Similarly, Lovecraft's 1916 essay "Old England and the "Hyphen"" (CE 5.21–23) and 1919 essay "Americanism" (CE 5.33–35) establish English ancestry as the core of American identity and reject more recent waves of immigrants who see themselves as "hyphenated-Americans"—Irish-Americans, Polish-Americans, and the other groups who form the villains of "Providence in 2000 A.D." And obviously, his 1925 short story "The Horror at Red Hook," with its negative focus on "the polyglot abyss of New York's underworld" (CF 1.482), forms a sort of spiritual sequel to the poem from thirteen years earlier—although it is worth pointing out that there are no supernatural tomes, cults to eldritch gods, or other such later stock tropes among the ethnic minorities of "Providence in 2000 A.D.," the explicit horror being the minorities themselves. That the textual theme of the poem became subtext in "The Horror at Red Hook" points to an evolution of technique, if not an enlightening of views.

However, among Lovecraft's early output, the closest and most obviously connected work to "Providence in 2000 A.D." is "New-England Fallen" (AT 385–88). Although written in April 1912, less than a month after "Providence in 2000 A.D.," it was not published until the 1943 Arkham House volume *Beyond the Wall of Sleep* (AT 527). S. T. Joshi has argued that Lovecraft's 1919 story "The Street" (CF 1.113–21) is essentially a prose adaptation of "New-England Fallen" (IAP 341). The poem was received even poorer than "Providence in 2000 A.D."; Joshi has called it "wretched" and "close to the nadir of Lovecraft's poetic output," not only for its racism but for its triteness and hypocritical appeal to Christianity (IAP 137–38).

"New-England Fallen" also has a nameless narrator, who lives in present-day New England and compares the region to the time of his grandfather, John. John was a yeoman farmer of British descent who spent his days farming on his idyllic plot of land by a hillside and evenings reading scripture to his wife and son. On weekends, Farmer John would buy horses from the bucolic village trader or take his family to church. This is in contrast to the New England of his grandson the narrator's day. The hills are less green and the air less clear, thanks to the new industrial mills. The tottering houses "crumble from neglect," much like the streetcars of O'Murphy's Avenue and La Collina Federale, "[t]ho' in a few some wretched aliens dwell." The church that Farmer John loved so much lies empty and decaying, the priest dead.

Along the coast, "Once prosp'rous ports are sunk in poverty. / The rotting wharves as ruins tell the tale / Of days when Yankees mann'd the swelling sail." Schools are empty and reduced to ruins; farmland is no longer tilled; the streets are overgrown. Thanks to immigration, New England has changed from agrarian Christianity to godless industrialism. As the poem ends, "The Saxon yeoman made New-England great, / And when he leaves, he leaves it to foul fate. / . . . This pow'r lies lock'd within the noble BRITISH race!"

Besides the general themes of rejecting immigration and decline of infrastructure, "New-England Fallen" contains a passage that seems intentionally inspired by the earlier poem. After describing the silence of the abandoned church in its overgrown yard (shades of St. John's Catholic Church), Lovecraft's narrator notes that "The village rings with ribald foreign cries; / Around the wine-shops loaf with bleary eyes / A vicious crew, that mocks the name of 'man', / Yet dare to call themselves 'American'." In associating drinking with immigrants, Lovecraft finds a way to combine his xenophobia with his teetotaling, just as his comments against the Jews earlier blend his anti-Semitism with his financial abstemiousness and love of colonial architecture.[2] But more than that thematic link, that line from "New-England

---

2. In "The Street," by associating "the squalid Rifkin School of Modern Economics" (*CF* 1.118) to the list of seditious institutions established by non-Anglo-Saxon immigrants, Lovecraft further weds anti-Semitism to anti-intellectualism, and seemingly anti-communism.

Fallen" is clearly evocative of the ending lines of "Providence in 2000 A.D." with the "shrivell'd form" of Smith, the last American of Providence.

Phillip A. Ellis has noted that Smith's proclamation "leads us to consider the other, non-Anglophonic races as, by extension, non-American, 'foreign'" just as the phrase "freaks of alien blood" in the later poem "allows us to see that he regarded white Anglo-Saxon Americans and British as the norm, and as 'natural'" (132). However, there are some conceptual differences. Smith is closer to Jones's grandson than he is to the narrator of his own poem, as both Smith and Jones's grandson are the last remnants of Anglo-Saxons living in their immigrant-overrun New England. But just as the immigrants of "New-England Fallen" are coded as barely human, "mock[ing] the name of 'man',", Smith himself is deformed, far from the ideal humanity both poems ascribe to Anglo-Saxons.

The implication in "New-England Fallen" that immigrants are barely human is carried over into "The Shadow over Innsmouth," with the standard interpretation that the Deep One hybrids are a stand-in for the same immigrant groups denounced in "Providence in 2000 A.D." However, there are more direct comparisons between the novella and the earlier poem than just xenophobia. Most obviously but also at the most surface level is that "Innsmouth" also features a nameless narrator, though Lovecraft elsewhere identified him as Robert Olmstead. At the end of the novella, Olmstead learns that his great-grandmother was from Innsmouth, and his trip to the city in question was in a way an (initially) disappointing homecoming (CF 3.224–30). In this, Olmstead mirrors the narrator of "Providence in 2000 A.D.," whose ancestors similarly were from Providence, and which he returns to, is frightened by, and escapes from. The ending of "Innsmouth," with the Deep Ones' apocalyptic planning to unleash a shoggoth (CF 3.200), echoes another early Lovecraft work, the 1920 prose poem "Nyarlathotep," in which—tinged with similar Yellow Peril tropes over and fears of urban crime—the arrival of the titular character from Egypt triggers a collapse of urban (if not global) civilization (CF 1.202–5).

Another prominent theme linking "Innsmouth" to the earlier poems is that of the decline of infrastructure. This is apparent to Olmstead from the start, when he boards the bus to Innsmouth and finds it to be "a small motor-coach of extreme decrepitude and dirty grey colour [with a] half-illegible sign on the wind-shield" (*CF* 3.169). This combines the decline of infrastructure and the English language from both "Providence in 2000 A.D." and "On an Accomplished Young Linguist."

When Olmstead actually reaches Innsmouth, he finds

> the rusted, grass-grown line of the abandoned railway, with leaning telegraph-poles now devoid of wires, and the half-obscured lines of the old carriage roads to Rowley and Ipswich. The decay was worst close to the waterfront, though in its very midst I could spy the white belfry of a fairly well-preserved brick structure which looked like a small factory. The harbour, long clogged with sand, was enclosed by an ancient stone breakwa-ter. . . . Here and there the ruins of wharves jutted out from the shore to end in indeterminate rottenness, those farthest south seeming the most decayed. (*CF* 3.173)

Beyond the mere fact of transportation infrastructure decline from "Providence in 2000 A.D.," there are also the specific mention of overgrown transportation routes and the emphasis on the rise of industrial factories and decline of sea trade, both of which were also present among the laments of Farmer Jones's grandson in "New-England Fallen." Likewise, the ending of "Nyarlatho-tep" notes the failure of electric lights, the seeming collapse of skyscrapers, and "a line of rusted metal to shew where the tram-ways had run [with] a tram-car, lone, windowless, dilapidated, and almost on its side" (*CF* 1.204). Nearby, Olmstead "now faced a new zone of former industry and commerce; noting the ruins of a factory ahead, and seeing others, with the traces of an old railway station and covered railway bridge beyond" (*CF* 3.173). Ironically, this specific aspect of infrastructure decline enables the escape of Olmstead—the ostensible remnant of pure New England stock—near the end of the novella, as he finds that the "rails were rusty but mainly intact, and not more than half the ties had rotted away. Walking or running on such a surface was very difficult; but I did my best, and on the whole made very fair time" (CF 3.218).

The final major plot point connecting "Providence in 2000 A.D." and "Innsmouth" is, as mentioned before, Smith the American from the poem and his similarities to "This hoary character, Zadok Allen, [who] was ninety-six years old and somewhat touched in the head, besides being the town drunkard. He was a strange, furtive creature who constantly looked over his shoulder as if afraid of something, and when sober could not be persuaded to talk at all with strangers" (CF 3.179). When Olmstead first finds Zadok, he "saw the tumbledown fire station on my left, and noticed the red-faced, bushy-bearded, watery-eyed old man in nondescript rags who sat on a bench in front of it. . . . This, of course, must be Zadok Allen, the half-crazed, liquorish nonagenarian whose tales of old Innsmouth and its shadow were so hideous and incredible" (CF 3.184). From his introduction, therefore, Zadok is paired not only with the theme of infrastructure decline, but also the anti-alcoholism of "New-England Fallen." As alcohol consumption and "bleary eyes" are linked with immigration in that poem, Zadok's habits—albeit whiskey, and not the wine of the poem—is a way of illustrating that he is not of pure New England stock himself. Of course, Smith with his "shrivell'd form" is also impacted by his residence among so many non-Americans, and from his "half crouching 'twixt the freight" on the docks of Sao Miguel's Cape, he also seems to be hiding from the authorities of the future Providence. Just as Smith is nervous, Zadok of course has reason to be afraid as he talks to Olmstead on an abandoned wharf, with Deep Ones seemingly emerging from "the incoming tide"— itself a metaphor, along with 'waves,' for immigrant arrival—to seize him as punishment for speaking to Olmstead (CF 3.200–201). The shoreline, whether the Cape Verdean–staffed docks of future Providence or the Deep One–infested wharves of Innsmouth, serve as a liminal space of both potential escape and potential capture for Smith and Zadok.[3]

---

3. Conversely, in "The Street" it is the "men of hidden badges" who "linger and listen" among immigrant haunts on behalf of the Anglo-Saxon authorities

There are, of course, key differences in the narrator of "Providence in 2000 A.D." and Olmstead's fates. The narrator of the former is of pure English stock, while Olmstead eventually not only discovers, but embraces, the fact that he has Deep One ancestry. Perhaps after the events of the poem, the narrator returns to England to find that he has a distant Irish ancestor? There would even be some parallel examples of this in the Lovecraftian canon: in "The Rats in the Walls" (1923), Delapore is an American of British ancestry who returns to England, only to discover the shocking secret about his distant ancestors' backgrounds, the same secret that caused them to emigrate to Virginia (CF 1.374–75). A parallel with "Rats" would especially be apt considering that while "Providence in 2000 A.D." was Lovecraft's first published poem, "Rats" was arguably the first story he published as a professional author (IAP 459–60).[4]

One of the likely influences of "The Rats in the Walls" was Edgar Allan Poe's 1840 horror classic, "The Fall of the House of Usher" (IAP 460). However, when it comes to "Providence in 2000 A.D.," one of the more instructive connections to be made is not Poe, but an author who, like Lovecraft, also drew inspiration from Poe: Jules Verne.

The Immortal Jules

As a child, Jules Verne was one of the first authors I could consider myself a fan of. I read through my grandfather's early 1900s edition of From the Earth to the Moon (1865) along with young readers' versions of Journey to the Center of the Earth (1864) and Twenty Thousand Leagues under the Seas (1869). The latter was particularly relevant to me given that I grew up in Connecticut, whose state ship is the nuclear submarine USS Nautilus, named after Captain Nemo's vessel. When visiting the actual Nautilus, I saw that the museum contained a wall reproducing an illustration from Verne's novel, and a model of the Nautilus from the

---

(CF 1.118), a role essentially filled by Detective Thomas Malone in "The Horror at Red Hook," despite his own Irishness (Brown 29).

4. Before both of these is the similar twist of Lovecraft's 1920 story "Facts concerning the Late Arthur Jermyn and His Family."

1954 Disney film adaptation hanging overhead. As such, when I later became a fan of Lovecraft, I was heartened to discover that he had also been a fan of Verne as a young man.

Lovecraft wrote of his enjoyment of Verne in several letters. In a letter to the *All-Story Weekly* dated 7 March 1914, he praised the magazine for remaining "under the imaginative school of Poe and Verne" (*IAP* 140). In his 20 January 1916 letter to Rheinhart Kleiner, he recalled how "When I was about twelve [1902] I became greatly interested in science, specialising in geography, (later to be displaced by astronomy), & being a Verne enthusiast. In those days I used to write fiction, & many of my tales showed the literary influence of the immortal Jules" (*RK* 49). As late as his letter to Richard F. Searight of 10 September 1933, Lovecraft argued that when it came to science fiction, "Verne & Wells really worked the vein out, leaving little save colourless imitation for others" (*Letters to E. Hoffmann Price* 289). And in his letter to Barlow of 13 January 1934, Lovecraft added to a description of his literary tastes, "I also liked Verne & Wells—principally the former, whose stuff I know best" (*OFF* 101). Indeed, in Lovecraft's correspondence to Barlow can be found an indirect connection between the authors. In his 3 September 1933 postcard to Barlow from a vacation to Quebec City, Lovecraft mentions that he had "just met an odd character here—a blind French doctor & soldier of fortune ... [who] knew Jules Verne personally" (*OFF* 77). After returning to Providence, he expounded on the French expatriate in a letter that same month: "As for that doctor & soldier of fortune in Quebec—I don't think he has any tangible Verne reliquiae. He seems to have met Verne rather casually, though he always remembered him" (*OFF* 81).

As to what works of Verne's Lovecraft read, only a few are specifically known. He possessed both an English version of *From the Earth to the Moon* (presumably owned from an early age) and a French edition given to him by Richard Ely Morse in 1935, as well as a copy of *Twenty Thousand Leagues under the Seas*; it is not known which specific editions of those he had (*LL* 160). He also owned magazine reprints of other Verne works; for example, *Off on a Comet* (1877) was reprinted in the first two issues of *Amazing Stories* in 1926. However, some of Lovecraft's works offer hints of Verne. Atlantis—a fantastic city of a different sort from Providence of the year 2000—is in *Twenty Thousand Leagues* (Verne, *Leagues* 239–41), which could conceivably be a distant influence on R'lyeh. Lovecraft's short story "The Mysterious Ship" (CF 3.488–93), written at the age of twelve, has clear stylistic influences from Verne's main body of novels, the *Extraordinary Voyages*. Lovecraft's 1906 article "Can the Moon be Reached by Man?" (CE 3.31–32) also shows the obvious influence of *From the Earth to the Moon* and its 1870 sequel *Around the Moon*, among other works of science fiction.[5]

But what was the appeal of Verne to Lovecraft? To some degree, this can be answered with the simple retort: why wouldn't young Lovecraft enjoy Verne? In the decades on either side of the fin de siècle, Verne was so widely read in the United States that he even had an influence on Americans' interest in maps, charting the Earth, and collapsing the world into a more easily traversable place (Brückner 346–49), sentiments that incidentally would have obvious ramifications for immigration. But beyond the literary merits that have drawn millions of youths to Verne, his lifestyle offers some interesting similarities to Lovecraft. Verne was very abstemious, although through choice rather than necessity (Dehs x). After Verne's death, his son Michel published ten unreleased works of his father from 1905 to 1919, in some cases making extensive changes to, or even completely rewriting, them (Dehs x). This predates by decades August Derleth's "posthumous collaborations" with Lovecraft.

Verne lived in Paris during both the 1848 republican revolution and 1871 communist revolution but was unaffected by both, remaining a staunch royalist throughout his life, long after it had become apparent that France would remain a republic—even citing Poe to argue that monarchies gave the greatest chance for individual freedoms against the mob rule of democ-

5. The influences Lovecraft took from Verne's two lunar novels, as well as *Off on a Comet*, are explored more in depth in the book *When the Stars Are Right: H. P. Lovecraft and Astronomy*, by Horace A. Smith and myself (Hippocampus Press, 2023).

racy (Dehs vii, x, xviii). The similarities to Lovecraft's early roy-alist Anglophilia are obvious. Verne's use of Poe to defend his politics did not emerge from nowhere; like Lovecraft, Verne was a lifelong fan of Poe and even wrote his own sequel to Poe's *Narrative of Arthur Gordon Pym of Nantucket* (1838), the 1897 novel *The Sphinx of the Ice-Fields* (Dehs x–xii; Unwin 13). Out-side of his monarchism, after 1890—coincidentally the year of Lovecraft's birth—Verne's outlook on the United States dimmed considerably, largely due to his negative view of Ameri-can capitalism and the sense that it had captured the national spirit, lessening the earlier promise of the country (Dehs xiii–xiv; Chesneaux 122–26; Unwin 10). These critiques of capital-ism, for differing reasons, can be found in both the early and lat-er writings of Lovecraft.

However, Verne's view of just what the earlier promise of the United States was illustrates some differences with Lovecraft. Most prominently, Verne had always supported the North, not only during the Civil War but to the extent that, as one scholar wrote, the "positive aspects of American society—the great in-dustrial works, the mastery of nature, the sense of personal initi-ative and enterprise, the economic activity—are inseparable from a kind of Yankee national character . . . the United States [to Verne] means above all the Northern States" (Chesneaux 117). Connected to this was the fact that Verne had been a staunch abolitionist and had a positive view of American Blacks—although a less positive one of native Africans, some-thing that again might have united him and Lovecraft (Verne, *Paris* 84–85; Aberger 201–4; Dehs xiii). However, many early English translations changed his depictions of Blacks to be more racist while generally leaving Verne's anti-Semitic references in-tact, which may have appealed to especially the younger Love-craft (Evans, "Translations" 95–96).

For decades, Verne's works were guided by his publisher, Pierre-Jules Hetzel (1814–1886). After Hetzel's death, Verne's output began to better reflect his own unfiltered views, which tended to be more pessimistic of progress—and consequently, much less popular. However, despite the decrease in sales,

Verne remained popular in the public mind due to his earlier stories (Dehs x; Evans and Miller 93–94). It is to several of those works we turn, perhaps counterintuitively at first. As one critic has noted, "It is often hastily deduced that, because Jules Verne depicts a changing world, it is also by definition futuristic; but the two notions are far from being synonymous" (Unwin 6). However, the four works mentioned in the opening of this article—*Paris in the Twentieth Century, The Begum's Fortune, Propeller Island,* and "In the Year 2889"—are exceptions to this, being works of Verne largely written outside of the influence of Hetzel at various points of time throughout his career, which focus on speculative cities. For various reasons, it is extremely unlikely (and in some cases impossible) that Lovecraft would have read them, particularly during his youth.[6] However, this makes their comparison to "Providence in 2000 A.D." and related works all the more illustrative of the ways in which Verne and Lovecraft viewed ideas of social and political development, helping to explain not only why Lovecraft may have been drawn to Verne, but the ways in which the Old Gentleman serves as a successor to the Father of Science Fiction, a lineage not often considered.

As these four works are obscure even among Verne's fans, it will be useful to provide a general overview of them before discussing their connection to Lovecraft's early work. *Paris in the Twentieth Century* was written as Verne's second novel after *Five Weeks in a Balloon* (1863), but when Hetzel rejected it as too pessimistic a take on the future, Verne locked the manuscript away. Discovered by a descendent in 1989, it was first published in 1994 and translated into English in 1996. Conceivably, if this and not *Journey to the Center of the Earth* had gone on to be Verne's second published novel, it could have started him down an earlier, darker, more satirical path, well ahead of his actual turn in the late 1890s. A quasi-dystopian novel that has been

---

6. Though outside the scope of this article, extensive studies are available describing both errors in early translation efforts (Evans, "Translations" 80–104) and when Verne's works were first translated into English (Evans, "Bibliography" 105–41) which illustrate the unlikeliness that a young Lovecraft would have read these four works.

equated to Orwell's *1984* (Dehs ix; Evans and Miller 92), *Paris in the Twentieth Century* is set in the year 1960, in a city that has experienced enormous technological advancements, but also several cultural decline due to the focus on technical education.

The Begum's Fortune (1879), probably the most widely read of these four works, was written in the aftermath of France's defeat in the Franco-Prussian War (1870–71), a conflict that is reflected in the novel (Unwin 9–10). In this way, Verne's anti-German sentiment reflects the anti-German sentiment in much of Lovecraft's World War I–era poems (Ellis 125–34), such as "The Teuton's Battle-Song" (1914; *AT* 390–92), "1914" (1915; *AT* 392–94), "The Crime of Crimes" (1915; *AT* 394–96), and "Ad Britannos—1918" (1918; *AT* 409–12). In the novel, two characters, one French and one German, inherit the titular fortune, and both use it to build city-states in the Pacific Northwest of the United States. The Frenchman builds the peaceful Ville-France and the German builds Stahlstadt, which becomes a major arms manufacturer and whose leader decides to dedicate its weapons to the destruction of Ville-France. Despite being written before Hetzel's death, *The Begum's Fortune* was the novel that marked a change in Verne's work toward scientific pessimism; perhaps relatedly, it also sold less than half of his usual novels, although this was also due to a notably bad English translation (Evans and Miller 96–97).

Propeller Island (1895) marked the height of Verne's criticism of how post–Civil War American society had become dominated by the desire to make and keep money (Chesneaux 122–24; Unwin 10). Set at some point in the (then) near future, the novel almost entirely takes place on Standard Island, an enormous artificial island miles in circumference, upon which has been built Milliard City. This city is home to ten thousand of the richest Americans from both North and South, engaged on a perpetual pleasure cruise around the Pacific. However, the combination of the jealous British, perfidious island natives, and tension between the Northern and Southern settlers ultimately dooms the utopian dreams of Standard Island as a getaway for the mega-rich.

"In the Year 2889" (1889) is included last, despite the fact that it was written six years before *Propeller Island,* because it was almost certainly co-written (if not almost entirely written) with his son Michel and published under the elder Verne's name for publicity (Unwin 6). However, "2889" still fits in well with the themes of (Jules) Verne's later works, especially *Propeller Island.* In the words of one critic, the story "goes to show that Capital has become the master of politics and culture" in the America of the 1880s, as reflected by the saga of a journalist in Centropolis, the capitol of the United States of the year 2889 (Chesneaux 125–26). Like *Paris in the Twentieth Century* and *Propeller Island,* there is a large emphasis on the technological developments of the future city.

From these Verne works, we have the Paris of 1960, Ville-France, Stahlstadt, Milliard City, and the Centropolis of 2889 to contrast with the Providence of 2000. What comparisons are there to be drawn between Lovecraft and Verne's views for the future of urban life?

Most prominent as a theme, given Lovecraft's poem, is anti-immigration sentiment. In *The Begum's Fortune,* the commercial center of San Francisco is described as having a

> cosmopolitan character, which is one of its most remarkable features. Beneath its handsome red granite porticoes, the tall, fair Saxon jostles the slight, active dark-haired Celt. The negro meets the Finlander and the Hindoo. The Polynesian gazes with astonishment at the Greenlander. The Chinaman, with oblique eyes and long plaited pigtail, endeavours to outdo in trade his historic enemy, the Japanese. Every tongue, every dialect, every jargon mingles there as in a modern Babel. (189–90)

This description of a multicultural city would seem to fit Lovecraft's worst fears for the future of Providence, although there are two key differences. One, while Lovecraft's Providence of 2000 is divided into ethnic enclaves, Verne's San Francisco brings its ethnicities together in a central district. Second, the racial intermixing is not given a negative connotation; what competition exists is limited to commercial efforts. However, this apparent endorsement of multiculturalism comes only after Verne describes the process by which Ville-France was built:

> By January 1872, the territory was already surveyed, measured, laid out, and an army of twenty thousand Chinese coolies, under the direction of five hundred over seers and European engineers, were hard at work. Placards posted up all over the State of California, an advertisement van permanently attached to the rapid train, which starts every morning from San Francisco to traverse the American continent, and a daily article in the twenty-three newspapers of that town, were sufficient to ensure the recruiting of the labourers. It was not even found necessary to resort to the expedient of publishing on a grand scale, by means of gigantic letters sculptured on the peaks of the Rocky Mountains, that men were wanted. It must be said that the influx of Chinese coolies into western America had just at this time caused much perturbation in the labour market. Several States had, in the interest of their own population, actually expelled these unfortunate people en masse. The building of Frankville came just in time to save them from perishing. Their wages, fixed at a dollar a day, were not to be paid them until the works were finished, and their rations were distributed by the municipal administration. Thus all the disorder and shameful speculations, which so often attend any great displacement of population, were avoided. The wages were deposited every week, in the presence of delegates, in the great Bank at San Francisco, and every coolie was warned that when he drew it out, he was not to return. This precaution was absolutely necessary to get rid of a yellow population, which would otherwise have infallibly lowered the tone and standard of the new city. The founders having, besides, reserved the right of granting or refusing permission to live there, the application of this measure was comparatively easy. (145–47)

The cheap labor of expelled Chinese laborers is therefore required for the construction of Verne's city, whose utopian characteristics are defended by ensuring the Chinese are not allowed to settle in the city they built. Of course, it is not only Verne's heroic French who rely on Chinese labor; so too do the German designers of Stahlstadt (*Begum* 184).

Anti-immigrant sentiment can be found throughout *Propeller Island* as well. First and foremost, no Germans are welcome there; the only Black person is the servant of the only French resident (*Island* 76–77, 84). Milliard City has no poor, no workers, no merchants; all these are associated with immigrants. As the character Calistus Munbar, a P. T. Barnum analogue, tells the four French musicians who serve as central characters: "When we need workmen, we bring them from outside, gentlemen, and when their work is done, they go home. . . . We ask [criminals] to stay in the old and the new continents, where they can practice their vocation under more advantageous conditions" (29–30). No foreign residents are allowed, and bars are banned in order to prevent drunkenness, a combination that is reflected in "New-England Fallen" (*Island* 51).

Lest the Milliardites be seen as only discriminating against Europeans, the description given to the New Hebrides island chain reveals a racist streak, albeit potentially satirical on the part of Verne: "Kanakas, Papuans, and Malays mingled there with Australian Blacks, all treacherous and cowardly people who resisted any attempts at civilization" (180). These views are supported by the fact that the climax of the novel is an attack on Standard Island by Kanakas, saved only by the arrival of French colonial military forces from Sandwich Island (277–88). One wonders whether these were the same "Kanakys" from whom the tenets of the Esoteric Order of Dagon were taught to the Innsmouth sailors (CF 3.188–92). Indeed, Zadok Allen specifically mentions the "stone ruins older'n anybody knew anything about" of Tahiti as relics of the Deep Ones, and Verne spends two full chapters on an extensively described and laudatory layover at Tahiti (CF 3.187; Verne, *Island* 139–63). Following the Kanaka attack on Standard Island, anti-immigration sentiment swells in Milliard City, with Munbar stating, "Those Malays who seemed so helpful and that [pirate captain], no one would have suspected them . . . ! For sure, this is the last time that Standard Island will ever give shelter to strangers. . . . I don't believe in shipwrecks or shipwrecked people anymore!" (*Island* 289).

In line with the anti-immigrant sentiments of *Propeller Island*,

its political themes—though scant, and the only one of the four
listed Verne works in which the political process is addressed to
any degree—also show some parallels to Lovecraft's political
thought. The governor of the island is Cyrus Bikerstaff, named
after Jonathan Swift's satirical pseudonym Isaac Bickerstaff
(Dehs xvii; Verne, *Island* 68). In a series of letters to the editor
of the *Providence Evening News* in 1914, Lovecraft also took on
the persona of "Isaac Bickerstaffe, Jr.," in his epistolary duel with
a local astrologer (CE 3.11). Instead of an elected council, the
island's governor is aided by a council of notables chosen based
on intelligence and wealth (Verne, *Island* 82–83). This is more
line with Lovecraft's later technocratic view of politics, which
would become embodied by the Great Race (Joshi, "Civilizations" 10–11; CF 3.404–5). When Bikerstaff is killed by Kanaka
pirates during the attack, the election for his replacement—
which incidentally is held on 15 March, a date that would become important to Lovecraft's life—becomes stalemated between the island's Northern and Southern populations (295).
Besides reflecting Verne's own critiques of democracy, the disso-
lution of the body politic based on the geographic origins of the
different factions also reflects the anti-populist element of Lovecraft's Providence (as well as the fallen New England), where
the city's cohesion is lost due to its giving in to the demands of
the various ethnic enclaves. In both authors, political cohesion
is connected to cultural cohesion.

That decline of culture is another theme that crosses both
Verne and Lovecraft's future cities. *Propeller Island* is set at an
unknown time, "give or take thirty years," in which "the United
States has doubled the number of stars on its federal flag" by an-
nexing Canada, Mexico, and the Central American republics
down to the Panama Canal. In this new imperial United States,
a taste for fine arts, visual as well as musical, has developed,
even though the production of said arts in the country itself remains limited, requiring the import of art and musicians from
Europe (*Island* 5–6). At this time as well, the French musician
protagonists are glad that the "Wagnerian craze" has gone in
decline, and the decadent arts of futurism and impressionism

prominent on the mainland are not allowed into the art galleries of Milliard City (65, 73). These themes, slight as they are, are clearly part of the carryover from *Paris in the Twentieth Century* and the geopolitics of *The Begum's Fortune*. They are taken to their extreme in the America of "2889," in which the art of painting has vanished due to color photography (presaging twenty-first-century concerns over the impact of artificial intelligence–generated imagery on art) and in which "our greatest maestros" broadcast out "to subscribers their delightful successions of accords determined by recondite algebraic formulas."

To Lovecraft, with his concerns over the "mechanical age," the notion of culture reduced to production via "algebraic formulas" would no doubt seem dystopian—especially if they were produced by machines themselves. But to what extent does technology, or at least its prediction, fit into these views of future cityscapes?

The Poem as Lovecraftian Futurism

The algebraic formulas of Verne's 2889 were presumably created by human hands, as that future America apparently lacked any equivalent development of the computer—although given Verne's interest in Swift, he may have been inspired by 'the Engine' from *Gulliver's Travels* (1726), considered to be the first depiction of a proto-computer, in this case a word generator (Weiss 164–65). Indeed, many of the technological developments envisioned by Verne in *Paris in the Twentieth Century* and his other works were already under development in the mid-nineteenth century (Unwin 6). Like Verne, Lovecraft's futures—when depicted—are analog ones, with seemingly little adoption of the early robots and computers from the pulp science fiction magazines of the time, although he himself owned *Gulliver's Travels* and would have also been exposed to the Engine (*LL* 152).

Lovecraft rarely set works in the future, and when his stories touched in the future, he rarely gave dates (Cannon 6–7). The few examples include the reign of "the cruel empire of Tsan-Chan which is to come three thousand years hence" in "Beyond the Wall of Sleep" (1919; CF 1.83); the mention of a Mongolian invasion of Australia in 2169 in "Through the Gates of the Silver Key" (1932–33; CF 3.306); and several dates in "The Shadow out of Time" (1934–35), including another reference to Tsan-Chan and its Yiang-Li from 5000, and "dark conquerors" of the year 16,000 (CF 3.399). A recurring theme is the belief in a coming race war between Asians and whites, which Lovecraft discusses in various personal letters over the years. Other future-set works, such as his Barlow collaborations "'Till A' the Seas'" and "Collapsing Cosmoses" (both 1935) and Kenneth Sterling collaboration "In the Walls of Eryx" (1936), are set in undated distant futures.[7]

Perhaps the closest connection to "Providence in 2000 A.D." is another Barlow collaboration, their 1934 short story comedy "The Battle That Ended the Century." Taking place on 31 December 2000, the story depicts a boxing match "amidst the romantic ruins of Cohen's Garage, on the former site of New York" (CF 4.470). The story is primarily an excuse to make a number of puns and jokes based on the names of the wider Lovecraft circle—interestingly, an element also present in his subsequent future-set story "Eryx."[8] Although it is almost certainly unintentional, the references to both a 'fallen' New York City and the presence of a Jewish place name demonstrate a continuity of themes from "Providence in 2000 A.D.," appropriately linking one of Lovecraft's earliest works to one of his last. If this liberal interpretation to continuity is permitted to be indulged, then there are some aspects of the wider world of the "Providence/Battle cycle" that can be gleaned. The presence of the "Thibetan Lama Bill Lum Li" (William Lumley) and three Chi-

---

7. As the space opera parody "Collapsing Cosmoses" contains no human characters or reference to Earth, it is possible that it could also be set in the distant past, in some other part of the universe—a long time ago, in a galaxy far, far away, one might say.

8. Although "Eryx" is undated (Cannon 7), it is set 72 years after the first landing on Venus; from his letters, Lovecraft (optimistically) believed that that event would likely be at least a century in his future, making "Eryx" set in the early twenty-second century at the earliest.

nese at the fight, along with the cream-puff vendor Wladislaw Brenryk (H. Warner Munn), suggests that this future New York is not as ethnically divided as Providence (although one wonders whether Brenryk has relatives in Wsjzxypq$?&%$ ladislaw). Also present is the Effjay of Akkamin (Forrest J Ackerman), "a potentate from a neighbouring kingdom." The kingdom neighboring New York could be Canada, or it could indicate that the United States has splintered and at least part of it has become a monarchy. Such a collapse of the federal government could indicate how the Providence post office was sold off by the denizens of Finklestein's Cross-ways. In contrast to the apparent collapse of the American federal republic, the Soviet Union apparently still exists, given the presence of Robertieff Essovitch Karovsky (Robert S. Carr), the Marxist ambassador from Moscow.

Besides the humorous byline connecting "Battle" with the later "Eryx," there is one other connection to a science fiction story. The song played for the funeral of the boxing match's loser is "Messrs. De Silva, Brown, and Henderson's celebrated aria, 'Never Swat a Fly', from the old cantata *Just Imagine*" (CF 4.473). This refers to the fames 1920s songwriting trio Buddy G. DeSylva, Lew Brown, and Ray Henderson, and the 1930 film written by them, *Just Imagine*. A science fiction musical, *Just Imagine* is set in a futuristic New York City of the year 1980 and involves such plot elements as a man from 1930 being revived and a space voyage to see the ruling monarchs of Mars. Notably, the electrical props used to revive the 1930 man would be reused the next year in *Frankenstein*—which Lovecraft saw and disliked (*Dawnward Spire* 344)—and *Just Imagine* was the first science fiction film to be nominated for an Academy Award, in Best Art Direction (Miller 18–25). The reference to *Just Imagine* is a rare, and potentially unique, reference to a contemporary work of popular culture in one of Lovecraft's stories.

Just Imagine is something of a satire of the fast-paced city life of New York, so it is especially noteworthy that Lovecraft referenced it, given that in his 1934 essay "Some Notes on Interplanetary Fiction" he states that "Social and political satire are always undesirable, since such intellectual and ulterior objects detract from the story's power as a crystallization of a mood" (CE 2.181). He also adds that such works should have "no stereotyped Armageddons with ray-guns and space-ships" (CE 2.181). This advice seemingly was only intended for space operas and not general future-set science fiction, given that from at least a cultural perspective, "Providence in 2000 A.D.," "New-England Fallen," and even "Innsmouth" and "Battle" would seemingly qualify as Armageddons from both the narrators' and Lovecraft's viewpoints. Indeed, while "Providence" does not feature a spaceship, it does feature a futuristic regular ship:

> When on my trip I ventur'd to embark,
> I stepp'd aboard a swift and pond'rous ark
> Which swimm'd the waves, and in a single day
> Attain'd its port in Narragansett Bay.

This enormous liner that can cross the Atlantic in a single day is one of the most prominent examples of 'future technology' in one of Lovecraft's stories. For example, in his 1924 story "The Shunned House," the narrator is equipped with "large and specially fitted Crookes tube operated by powerful storage batteries and provided with peculiar screens and reflectors, in case [the entity] proved intangible and opposable only by vigorously destructive ether radiations" (CF 1.470). While seemingly futuristic technology, it is actually outdated; the use of a Crookes tube to hunt ghosts relates to the Victorian spiritualist belief of British physicist and spiritualist William Crookes, who had died in 1919 (Noakes 185–237).[9] In line with Lovecraft's space opera injunction, even the Venusian air mask in "Eryx" was based on contemporary breathing apparatus for miners (CF 4.550; Lubnow 12–13).

From these examples, whether through the technology or the examination of the evolution of society into the future, there is at least an argument to be made that "Providence in 2000 A.D."

---

9. See also Lovecraft's 1918 essay "Merlinus Redivivus" (CE 5.31–32) against the spiritualist revival that accompanied World War I; the general sense of the paranormal that Lovecraft parodies in "The Shunned House" was already receding from its immediate postwar high.

is one of the most proper works of science fiction that Lovecraft wrote—well positioning the early Lovecraft as an inheritor of the tradition established by the late Verne.

Conclusion

Given Lovecraft's self-image of a Georgian squire, living in then-modern Providence was almost like living in a future city, a disconnect even greater than someone of 1912 being transported into the actual year 2000. One can well see why the 1933 time-displacement film *Berkeley Square* so fascinated him (*IAP* 898). But as noted in the letters mentioned at the start of this essay, Verne was not the only early science fiction pioneer whom Lovecraft admired: he paired Verne with H. G. Wells (1866–1946), the British counterpart (*CE* 2.190). After all, as Wells scholar Bernard Loing noted, "the exhaustive topology of the Vernean universe, with its circles and ellipses, its meridians and parallels, remains within the Euclidian framework, a three-dimensional world. . . . This strict geometry of travel is paralleled by a no less strict narrative structure, which also proves to be Euclidian and three-dimensional" (7). The thematic parallel to Lovecraft seemingly favored Wells over Verne. It was Wells who invented the notion of the time machine, helping launch the genre of time travel that Lovecraft himself would delve into in "The Shadow out of Time." And as Loing noted, "While Jules Verne had tried to become a 'universal geographer'. . . Wells tried to become a 'universal historian' with the publication of *The Outline of History* (1920)," a work Lovecraft owned and endorsed (Loing 11; *LL* 164–65).

The influence of Wells and his strain of science fiction on Lovecraft has been commented upon, if not widely, then at least to the degree where it is generally accepted. With this essay I hope to demonstrate that Verne also had an appreciable influence on Lovecraft—not through the stories analyzed above, which Lovecraft almost certainly did not read, but through earlier works that contributed to Lovecraft's own early development of a strand parallel to Verne's own later evolution. Those early, largely poetic works of Lovecraft in turn exhibit strains of futurist, if not outright science fictional, themes in their depictions of urban development, and also foreshadow some of Lovecraft's better-known later works of prose fiction. While I certainly do not challenge either the low literary quality of "Providence in 2000 A.D." or "New-England Fallen," let alone their racism, hopefully they can be better appreciated as ciphers in helping to illuminate several aspects of Lovecraft's early evolution as a writer of genre fiction.

Works Cited

Aberger, Peter. "The Portrayal of Blacks in Jules Verne's *Voyages extraordinaires*." *French Review* 53, No. 2 (December 1979): 199–206.

Barlow, R. H. *Eyes of the God: Selected Writings of R. H. Barlow*. Ed. S. T. Joshi, David E. Schultz, and Douglas A. Anderson. Rev. ed. New York: Hippocampus Press, 2023.

Bolden, Doug. "Lovecraft's 1912 poem, his first published, 'Providence in 2000 A.D.'" *Dickens of a Blog* (4 April 2015), www.wyrmis.com/blots/2015/13/blot60940-providence-2000.html.

Brown, Rob. "Hybrids and Hyphenates: H. P. Lovecraft and the Irish." *Green Book* 3 (Bealtaine 2014): 13–33.

Brückner, Martin. "Popular Map Genres in American Literature." In Anders Engberg-Pedersen, ed. *Literature and Cartography: Theories, Histories, Genres*. Cambridge, MA: MIT Press, 2017. 325–60.

Cady, John Hutchins. "The Providence Market House and Its Neighborhood." *Rhode Island History* 11, No. 4 (October 1952): 97–116.

Cannon, Peter. *The Chronology out of Time: Dates in the Fiction of H. P. Lovecraft*. 1986. West Warwick, RI: Necronomicon Press, 2019.

Chesneaux, Jean. "Jules Verne's Image of the United States." Tr. Frances Chew. *Yale French Studies* 43 (1969): 111–27.

Dehs, Volker. "Introduction." In *The Self-Propelled Island*. Tr. Marie-Thérèse Noiset. Lincoln: University of Nebraska Press, 2015. vii–xx.

Derie, Bobby. "Deeper Cut: Lovecraft in Chinatown." *Deep Cuts in a Lovecraftian Vein* (5 October 2022), deepcuts.blog/2022/10/05/deeper-cut-lovecraft-in-chinatown/.

Eddy, Muriel E. "The Gentleman from Angell Street." 1961. In *The Gentleman from Angell Street: Memories of H. P. Lovecraft.* Ed. Jim Dyer. Narragansett, RI: Fenham Publishing, 2001. 3–28.

Ellis, Phillip A. "The Construction of Race in the Early Poetry of H. P. Lovecraft." *Lovecraft Annual* No. 4 (2010): 124–35.

Evans, Arthur B. "A Bibliography of Jules Verne's English Translations." *Science Fiction Studies* 32 (March 2005): 105–41.

———. "Jules Verne's English Translations." *Science Fiction Studies* 32 (March 2005): 80–104.

———, and Ron Miller. "Jules Verne, Misunderstood Visionary." *Scientific American* 276 (April 1997): 92–97.

Faig, Kenneth W., Jr. *Lovecraftian Voyages.* New York: Hippocampus Press, 2017.

Halter, Marilyn. "Cape Verdeans in the U.S." In Luís Batalha and Jørgen Carling, ed. *Transnational Archipelago: Perspectives on Cape Verdean Migration and Diaspora.* Amsterdam: Amsterdam University Press, 2008. 35–46.

Joshi, S. T. "Lovecraft's Alien Civilizations: A Political Interpretation." *Crypt of Cthulhu*, No. 32 (St. John's Eve 1985): 8–24, 31.

———. *The Recognition of H. P. Lovecraft.* New York: Hippocampus Press, 2021.

Loing, Bernard. "Space and Time in Wells and Jules Verne." *The Wellsian: The Journal of the H. G. Wells Society* 27 (2004): 3–13.

Lovecraft, H. P. *Letters to E. Hoffmann Price and Richard F. Searight.* Ed. David E. Schultz and S. T. Joshi. New York: Hippocampus Press, 2021.

———. *Letters to Rheinhart Kleiner and Others.* Ed. S. T. Joshi and David E. Schultz. New York: Hippocampus Press, 2020. [Abbreviated in the text as *RK.*]

———. *Letters to Robert Bloch and Others.* Ed. David E. Schultz and S. T. Joshi. New York: Hippocampus Press, 2015.

———. *O Fortunate Floridian: H. P. Lovecraft's Letters to R. H. Barlow.* Ed. S. T. Joshi and David E. Schultz. Tampa: University of Tampa Press, 2007. [Abbreviated in the text as *OFF.*]

————, and Clark Ashton Smith. *Dawnward Spire, Lonely Hill: The Letters of H. P. Lovecraft and Clark Ashton Smith.* Ed. David E. Schultz and S. T. Joshi. New York: Hippocampus Press, 2017.

Lubnow, Fred S. "The Lovecraftian Solar System." *Lovecraft Annual* No. 13 (2019): 3–26.

Miller, Thomas Kent. *Mars in the Movies: A History.* Jefferson, NC: McFarland, 2016.

Noakes, Richard. *Physics and Psychics: The Occult and the Sciences in Modern Britain.* Cambridge: Cambridge University Press, 2019.

"Turk's Head Building." *Providence Architecture* (2002), www.brown.edu/cis/sta/dev/providence_architecture/locations/downtown/turks_head_building/.

Unwin, Timothy. "Jules Verne: Negotiating Change in the Nineteenth Century." *Science Fiction Studies* 32 (March 2005): 5–17.

Uriarte, Miren. "Growing into Power in Rhode Island." In Andrés Torres, ed. *Latinos in New England.* Philadelphia: Temple University Press, 2006. 125–48.

Verne, Jules. *The Begum's Fortune.* Tr. W. H. G. Kingston. Philadelphia: J. B. Lippincott & Co., 1879. [Abbreviated in the text as *Begum.*]

————. *Paris in the Twentieth Century.* 1863. Tr. Richard Howard. New York: Random House, 1996. [Abbreviated in the text as *Paris.*]

————. *The Self-Propelled Island.* 1895. Tr. Marie-Thérèse Noiset. Lincoln: University of Nebraska Press, 2015. [Abbreviated in the text as *Island.*]

————. *Twenty Thousand Leagues under the Seas.* 1869. [No translator given.] Chicago: M. A. Donohue, 1895. [Abbreviated in the text as *Leagues.*]

————, and Michel Verne. "In the Year 2889." 1889. *Project Gutenberg* (7 February 2018. www.gutenberg.org/files/19362/19362-h/19362-h.htm.

Weiss, Eric A. "Jonathan Swift's Computing Invention." *Annals of the History of Computing* 7, No. 2 (April–June 1985): 164–65.

Briefly Noted

The Netflix series *Guillermo del Toro's Cabinet of Curiosities* featured two adaptations of Lovecraft stories, but both are highly unsatisfactory. *Pickman's Model* (directed by Keith Thomas; teleplay by Lee Patterson) makes several errors right off the bat. First, the setting has been transferred to Arkham—and, specifically, to Miskatonic University—rather than Boston. Anyone who has read the story should be aware that the ambiance and, particularly, the history of Boston is the very essence of the tale. Instead, we see Pickman as a somewhat elderly student in an art class at Miskatonic—and, curiously, the focus of nearly the entire episode is on William Thurber, another student who becomes fascinated with Pickman's paintings. But in this meandering broadcast there is not the slightest attempt to focus on the core elements of the story: the horrors that emerge out of the remote past (counteracted strikingly by the story's conclusion, where a modern phenomenon—a photograph—clinches the supernatural climax). Instead, there is meaningless blather about the nature of horror—a weak attempt to mimic the story's profound discussions of "the physiology of fear." And as for the accent that the director had Pickman use—well, that is something more reminiscent of a working-class Brooklynite than of an educated Bostonian. *Dreams in the Witch House* (directed by Catherine Hardwicke; teleplay by Mika Watkins) is only marginally better. Here a setting at Miskatonic University is *not* used, even though it is central to the story. Walter Gilman, instead of being a student of mathematics, is an investigator of spiritualist phenomena. He becomes fascinated with the witch house, which he believes might allow him to re-establish contact and communication with his beloved twin sister. Keziah Mason does emerge, but she is a rotting reanimated corpse. All the science-fictional elements in the story—the updating of the witchcraft myth by means of advanced mathematics, hyperspace, etc.—is entirely dropped and a hackneyed Gothic horror scenario is put in its place. One hopes that del Toro—who is the executive producer of the series, but who apparently adopted a "hands-off" approach in regard to the work of the directors of each episode—will exercise better editorial judgment in future episodes.

Indecipherable Manuscripts, Old Families, and Bloody Murder

Three Speculations on Origins in Lovecraft Stories

Duncan Norris

Mystery attracts mystery. The opening line of "Under the Pyramids" is immediately somewhat of a truth that proves itself, given that the putative author is Harry Houdini, although the well-known reality is that it was ghostwritten on commission by H. P. Lovecraft. The twain are both figures who in modern pop cultural memory are intimately associated with mystery. The irony that the spiritualist debunker Houdini and materialist atheist Lovecraft are equally thought by many to be figures associated with genuine magic and the supernatural only underscores this element.

In this vein perhaps no single element of Lovecraft has been as much dissected as his famous invention of the *Necronomicon*. Such ranges from its origins and inspirations, usages in tales by Lovecraft, usages by others, the belief that it is a real tome, and the further belief that it is in fact a genuine work. As such it is natural that, at some point, the Voynich Manuscript would become involved in the discussion. Mystery attracts mystery. Colin Wilson's short story "The Return of the Lloigor," published in the Arkham House anthology *Tales of the Cthulhu Mythos* (1969), does exactly that. The tales posits that the Voynich Manuscript is actually a ciphered version of the *Necronomicon*; somewhat inevitably, an ill fate comes to the protagonist who uncovers this. The entire story is saturated in a bibliophilic excess and weaves in a lot of genuine booklore, as well as real persons and events, with the creations of Lovecraft, Machen, and others to create this highly metatextual work. The blending is perhaps a bit uneven in places, but is strongly convincing in others. The notable aspect for our purposes is that the initial section on the Voynich Manuscript is a highly accurate, and is worth repeating verbatim by way of an introductory historiography:

The story of the Voynich manuscript is briefly this. It was found in an old chest in an Italian castle by a rare book dealer, Wilfred M. Voynich, and brought to the United States in 1912. With the manuscript, Voynich also found a letter asserting that it had been the property of two famous scholars of the seventeenth century, and that it had been written by Roger Bacon, the Franciscan monk who died about 1294. The manuscript was 116 pages long and was apparently written in cipher. It was clearly some kind of scientific or magical document, since it contained drawings of roots or plants. But it also contained sketches that looked amazingly like illustrations from some modern biological textbook of minute cells and organisms—for example, of spermatozoa. There were also astronomical diagrams.

For nine years, professors, historians, and cryptographers tried to break the code. Then, in 1921, Newbold announced to the American Philosophical Society in Philadelphia that he had been able to decipher certain passages. The excitement was immense; it was regarded as a supreme feat of American scholarship. But the excitement increased when Newbold disclosed the contents of the manuscript. For it seemed that Bacon must have been many centuries ahead of his time. He had apparently invented the microscope some four hundred years before Leeuwenhoek, and had shown a scientific acumen that surpassed even that of his namesake Francis Bacon in the sixteenth century.

Newbold died before completing his work, but his "discoveries" were published by his friend Roland Kent. It was at this point that Professor Manly took up the study of the manuscript and decided that Newbold's enthusiasm had led him to deceive himself. When the manuscript was examined under a microscope, it was seen that the strange nature of the characters was not entirely due to a cipher. The ink had peeled off the vellum as it dried, so that the "shorthand" was actually due to ordinary wear and tear over many centuries.

There is much more known around the Voynich Manuscript today than when Wilson wrote his story, including a more accurate dating, known and likely former owners, previous medieval investigations of it, and other aspects. But the cipher itself remains unreadable, the botanical illustrations remain uncorrelated with known species, and there is nothing approaching a consensus opinion as to what the majority of the images depict.

Which brings us back to the issue of mystery attracting mystery. That Lovecraft would have been interested in such a work as the Voynich Manuscript is, I feel confident in saying, fairly certain. I am also far from the first to suggest it as a possible inspiration for the *Necronomicon*. Yet the document was in private hands until its donation to the Beinecke Rare Book and Manuscript Library at Yale in the same year as Wilson's tale,[1] and remained largely unavailable to the public until it was published online by the holding library in 2020. There is seemingly no obvious way Lovecraft could have been familiar with the codex, and to the best of my knowledge he does not mention it in any of his extant letters. Yet, as Wilson used fictionally, a connection to the *Necronomicon* is very tantalizing. The following is speculative and definitely in the realms of the possible far more than the probable, yet there are enough glimpses of this possible connection to make it worthwhile to offer for consideration that Lovecraft's conception of the *Necronomicon* may have come in part from ideas about the Voynich Manuscript.

As Wilson asserts, William Romaine Newbold of the University of Pennsylvania—where Wilson incorrectly locates the manuscript itself in the tale—addressed the American Philosophical Society in Philadelphia on 20 April 1921, offering his ideas of the decipherment of Voynich's manuscript. The disclosure was big news at the time. The following day the *New York Times* ran two and a half full columns—about a third of the page—on page 3 on Newbold's announcement under the head-

---

1. The uncertain nature of the manuscript made it oddly difficult to sell, as it was obviously going to be expensive but might ultimately prove worthless. This was probably a particular disappointment for Newbold's widow Ethel, who was to realize 10% from the sale.

line "ROGER BACON'S LORE DUG OUT OF CIPHER: Thirteenth Century Friar Shown by Prof. Newbold to Have Used Telescope. MAY HAVE HAD MICROSCOPE Wisdom Ahead of His Time Was Hid Under Sixfold Cipher Now Being Solved. DOCUMENT'S ODD STORY Believed to Have Passed From John Dee, Shakespeare's Prospero, to Emperor of Germany." This was actually the second article upon the topic the *Times* had run that year, having a much smaller piece on page 11 of the 20 February issue presaging the Newbold lecture offering "HAS FRIAR BACON'S CIPHER: Voynich Says It Shows Ancient Magic Surpassed Our Science."

Such articles appearing in such a widely read source at the *Times* meant that variants and syndication would inevitably follow. Typical—and a far from an exhaustive sampling—are the appearances in the *Alexandra Gazette* (21 February 1921), with the headline "Deciphers Code of Monk's Work on Black Magic"; the *Washington Times* (21 April 1921), with a larger piece offering "Scientific Secrets of 700 Years Ago Bared in Bacon Manuscript"; the *American Review of Reviews* (July 1921), which mentions the *New York Times* article and misspells Voynich's name, giving it phonetically as Votnitch; and a letter from Newbold himself in the *Catholic Historical Review* (October 1921), which also offers a copy of page of the manuscript itself.

Lovecraft is known to have collected an abundance of newspaper and magazine clippings upon topics that interested him, many of a fantastical nature, of which only the tiniest fraction are known. Articles on the Voynich Manuscript seem very much in line with items he was known to be interested in. As noted before, this is highly speculative as concerns Lovecraft's reading such material, as he was not as omnivorous in reading the *Times* as with other materials, although he was a frequent reader and clipper therefrom. For example, Lovecraft sent an article from that paper to Clark Ashton Smith concerning the Loch Ness Monster in early 1934, following an abundance of news upon the topic subsequent a series of alleged sighting (*Dawnward Spire* 511). There is an offhand reference to the obscure locale of the goldfields of Koolgarlie in Western Australia in a later 1934 letter to August Derleth to make an emphatic note of far-flung distance (*Essential Solitude* 669). Koolgarlie had been briefly in the news earlier in the year, including a small syndicated article page 13 of the *New York Times,* concerning races riots therein.

Yet there is a source that edges closer to Lovecraft. The June 1921 *Hearst's International*—again there is no proof Lovecraft read this issue, but he did read other of the Hearst publications of a similar nature such as the *American Weekly*—carried an article about the Voynich Manuscript entitled "A Cinderella in Parchment: The Romance of the New 600-Year Old Bacon Manuscript," which not only carried the basic details found in most of the other articles but carried two images of the codex itself showing the script, some of the botanical features, and what is commonly referred to as the balneological section. Given that Lovecraft was not overly impressed with most genuine medieval grimoires (*Letters to Robert Bloch* 377–79) and their modern ilk, which was another reason why he invented his own in the *Necronomicon,* the potential appeal of the mysterious Voynich version would probably be the greater still. This of course brings us back to the point of whether Lovecraft was even aware of this article or the Voynich manuscript generally, into which is added an extra increment of likelihood. The author of the *Hearst* article was Montrose Jonas Moses, who wrote number of compositions in a variety of fields including children's literature and in connection with the theatre along with much work in literary review. This last may in particular have caused him to come across Lovecraft's path. But more crucial is that Moses was friends with Houdini, whom Lovecraft met with several times. The roots for discovery of Voynich via this route this become enlarged.

By 1928, when Lovecraft composed "The Dunwich Horror," the *Necronomicon* was by now a paradoxical fictional reality in Lovecraft's already forming literary world. The longest quotation from it he gives in the entirety of his stories and elsewhere is in this tale, and as such what is often overshadowed is Wilbur Whateley's diary as a source of malign text. That book, in a cipher, is eventually decrypted, to reveal the deeper horror of the events unfolding in Dunwich. The sources for certain aspects seem well cemented. The connection with John Dee evolved out of Frank Belknap Long's use of such an edition of the *Necronomicon* and Machen's invention of the dark Aklo cult language to which Lovecraft will refer as such in so many words in "The Haunter of the Dark." Lovecraft was utilizing ciphers connected with black magic and hidden cult ideas in *The Case of Charles Dexter Ward*, written in 1927, but it is in "The Dunwich Horror" that he suddenly makes a more genuine attempt to discuss and convey verisimilitude upon the topic, borrowing heavily from the *Encyclopedia Britannica* entry upon the subject for his information. But there is an interplay with all these aspects and the Voynich manuscripts that is highly suggestive, especially given this year also sees the publication of Newbold's posthumous book *The Cipher of Roger Bacon*. Absent further information, this must all remain firmly in the realm of speculation, but the possibility is too intriguing not to at least consider.

From a highly speculative but at least possible correlation to another, this time with more tangible connections. The "old Crowninshield Place" in "The Thing on the Doorstep" is not a happy home. Edward Derby will be a prisoner there, both in the house itself and in the forced exchange into his wife's perhaps not entirely human body, which will eventually be buried in the house's cellar, until animated by the doomed Derby in actions that lead to the title of the story. Unhappy perhaps seems a wildly inadequate term, but it is at least uncontestable.

Like most names chosen in a Lovecraft tale, Crowninshield is one loaded with significance, and the Georgian-style Crowninshield-Bentley House built c. 1730 is a genuine locale in Salem, now a slightly relocated and restored museum owned by the Essex Peabody Museum. The Crowninshield family itself is one of those early colonial dynasties whose descendants are known today as Boston Brahmins. Showing the interesting strands of heredity, in addition to the expected military, business, and political figures who litter both New England and even broader America history—even a brief examination of them would be an article in itself—contemporaneously famous names such as Olympic swimmer Michael Phelps, late Academy Award–winning actor William Hurt, and a previous generation's pop idols of the Everly Brothers are all distant descendants.

The dynastic founder in America was Johann Casper Richter von Kronenschieldt, who arrived in America around 1688 with (seemingly) an entirely spurious claim to an armigerous heraldry whence derived his name—canting arms is the term, but that refers to a heraldic bearing in which the bearer's name is represented. The (possibly illegitimate) Johann merely creatively added the arms of the locale from his birthplace, which may itself be spurious; as the saying goes, accounts vary. Johann was certainly of a dubious but ingenuous character, at least as concerns truthfulness in such matters, eventually acting as a doctor in now new homeland despite a lack of the relevant qualifications. He was also smart enough to understand the need for blending into his adopted society, Anglicizing his name to the more familiar John Casper Richter von Crowninshield.

It would probably not have escaped Lovecraft's notice that John Crowninshield had bought the key land of Spring Pond that surrounded the community of Salem, nor that Increase and Cotton Mather were visitors to the locale, which was famed for its restorative properties. Crowninshield Island is a small island located off the coast of the town (much favored by Lovecraft) of Marblehead, but the name change from Brown's Island has been—and in fact remains—a controversial issue to some. The former title remains on some official maps and was likely so for much of Lovecraft's life. A 1929 tourist map entitled *Points of Interest in Quaint Marblehead* published by the Marblehead Craft Shop gives the island as Brown's, as does a 1940 Tourist Motoring Map. The change seems to have come in 1955 when the island was donated by Louise DuPont Crowninshield, who had purchased the locale from the Browns for $1 in 1918, for public use under the Trustees of Reservations.[2]

Marblehead proper has a Crowninshield Road, which runs

---

2. Google Maps, for the lazy traveler, has it as Crowninshield Island.

on the mainland shoreline parallel to Crowninshield Island, and Providence itself has a Crowninshield Street in the suburb of Hartford. But perhaps the most significant aspect of the choice of the Crowninshield place as a location wherein the unhappy Asenath and Edward Derby marital home was placed is that the genuine Crowninshield family was at one time at feud with the Derby family of Salem, although in the eighteenth century there was intermarriage between the two families, with Elias Hasket Derby wedding Elizabeth Crowninshield—memorably described by the New England Historical Society as "a social lioness"—at the time when his wealth was such that Nathaniel Hawthorne later wrote of him as King Derby. Debate continues about whether he was America's first millionaire, while Derby's sister Mary had previously married Capt. George Crowninshield.

Perhaps they would have been better off avoiding the mixture of the family lines. Hasket and Elizabeth's daughter, named for her mother, would create one of biggest scandals in New England at the time with her sensational 1806 divorce from her husband Nathaniel West, with whom she had unwisely eloped in 1783. The legal spectacle featured charges of paying witnesses to commit perjury, along with a parade of prostitutes who were bought into court in order for Elizabeth to prove infidelity, as she was taking advantage of changes in relation to property and divorce passed that year. Thus whether this Crowninshield/Derby connection is designed as a form of foreshadowing, a clue to the aware, or simply a deeply buried historical reference for Lovecraft's own amusement is almost impossible to ascertain, but the association is certainly not an accidental one.

A third interesting connection with a Lovecraft tale, again with the Crowninshield name, also presents itself. "The Terrible Old Man" is very much a lesser tale in the Lovecraft canon, mostly noted today for the signposting of Lovecraft's views of immigrants to New England in the ethnically patent names of the three home invaders who set out to rob a rich elderly retired sea captain who lived alone. The tale is largely given from the perspective of the third of the villains, who waits outside the house while his confederates perform the actual robbery. All of course receive a brutal justice at the hands of a supernatural aspect directed by the Terrible Old Man. Little known is that Lovecraft is probably mirroring the facts of a genuine murder case and adding his own elements to create a more fantastic narrative.

On 6 April, 1830 rich elderly retired sea captain Joseph White, who never married and lived alone save for three domestic servants comprising a niece, Mary White Beckford, Lydia Kimball, and another more distant relative, Benjamin White, was bludgeoned and stabbed to death in his bed. White was a New England captain of the old school, one who had stayed loyal during the American Revolution until a British raid upon one of his own ships caused him to discard old allegiances. He purchased another vessel from Elias Hasket Derby, which White bluntly renamed *Revenge,* and became the first of the Salem privateers of the war. Even more notoriously, both to the modern audience and his own contemporaries, White was a happy and unbothered participant in the slave trade. Local minister William Bentley—a boarder at the aforementioned Crowninshield-Bentley House that now bears his name as a result, and who bequeathed to posterity a thirty-two-volume diary of events in Salem that has proved invaluable to historians—stated in his journal that White had informed him in 1788, when Massachusetts banned the slave trade, of having "no reluctance in selling any part of the human race."

White's killer was a man of ill reputation named Richard Crowninshield. His collaborators, the instigators of the plot who hired Crowninshield to do the act of killing, were brothers John Francis (Frank) and Joseph Jenkins (Jr.) Knapp, both of whom were waiting outside the house while the actual murder was committed. The motive, as might be expected, was money. Joseph, being the grandnephew of White and married to Mary's daughter, was anticipating a large sum via inheritance following White's death, the murderer having broken in and stolen a new disinheriting will a few days previously.[3] After a public panic and

---

3. At least Joseph thought he had; in actuality he had taken an earlier document. White was a shrewd old New England sea captain and thus placed the potentially unpopular new will safely in his lawyer's office. Joseph's flawed un-

an enormous media outcry, Crowninshield and the Knapp brothers were caught in the manner ubiquitous to crime in the nineteenth century: police informants, including a counterfeiter who offered up Crowninshield's name from a jail cell for leniency and a particular dastard who attempted to blackmail the Knapps but whose threatening letter was accidentally opened by Joseph Jenkins (Sr.).

Crowninshield killed himself in confinement after learning that Joseph had confessed subsequent to the Knapps being taken into custody, and despite this confession it appeared for a while that the two Knapp siblings would escape on legal technicalities, since the judicial conviction of Crowninshield as a murderer for foundation was lacking,[4] as was the requirement of an accessory to murder being actually present at the crime scene when the act was committed. Recognizing the problem, the Commonwealth of Massachusetts appointed no less a political and judicial titan than Daniel Webster as prosecutor, and the famed lawyer created legal precedent, successfully convicting both Knapps brothers over three separate trials. Frank's first resulted in a deadlocked jury, and he was retried. Joseph was offered immunity for his testimony against his brother, but fraternal bonding proved stronger than fear of execution.[5] The jury was ultimately swayed by incorrect testimony in Frank's case that placed him in the house as an active participant with

---

derstand of per capita ["by the head'] versus per stripes ["by branch"] rules in Massachusetts's inheritance law would have deprived him of the windfall he sought in any case.

4. It has been speculated that Crowninshield committed suicide to avoid his brother George being convicted as an accessory for this reason. George was named by the jailhouse informant Hatch that led to Richard's arrest as having discussed with his brother robbing White, and was arrested an accessory along with two others present in the gambling house where this occurred before the role of the Knapps became known. The two unlucky gamblers were never prosecuted, and George was acquitted after two trials on the unusual alibi of having been in the company of two prostitutes the evening of the murder.

5. And probably guilt. It seems in truth Joseph was far more the blameworthy party.

Crowninshield,[6] and Webster's arguing the legal subtlety that "presence" was more than merely being at the location in the moment. Both brothers were subsequently hanged on the same scaffold three months apart.

The massiveness of the case, and its lingering in memory, is difficult to encompass to a twenty-first-century audience daily bombarded by the latest criminal atrocity. Public interest was so immense that reporters traveled from New York to cover it. Most unusually for the times, there was an attempt to preserve forensic evidence, including the covering of two muddy footprints from the light rain that fell the following day during investigation, and a second post-mortem performed by Dr. Samuel Johnson (no relation) with another colleague, Dr. Pierson, after he determined there was not enough information to establish the fatal wound. There are at least two popular "murder ballads" based upon the case. The bludgeon, deliberately made by Crowninshield with beading on the handle to increase the grip, was eventually donated to the Peabody Essex Museum in Salem in 1865, where it is on display along with Crowninshield's confession, while the tale held enough resonance that it is included over 12 pages in Thomas S. Duke's famous *Celebrated Criminal Cases of America* (1910).

To the same point in reverse, the case was for a time sometimes excluded from other local histories, due to the unfavorable light it appears to show upon an already infamous town: the vicious killing by bludgeoning and stabbing of an elderly man in his own bed, a dead slave trader, a murderer and his gambling, prostitute-cavorting brother with a famous name, and abandonment of traditional legal norms that held an unpleasant familiarity. The vigilance committee—set up to patrol and investigate in the wake of the murder and false claims by the killers to have been attacked by a gang in the surrounding days to create a distraction—ended up arrogating to themselves right to enter property and imprison without a warrant. Even Webster's great oratory was not the deciding factor in the conviction

---

6. It would thus be possible that Lovecraft knew the facts of the case as two intruders having gone into the house and one standing watch.

of Frank, but rather the mistaken evidence of Dr. Pierson from the second autopsy that there had been multiple assailants, thus incorrectly placing Frank as a participant in the actual killing, and the exposure of the second jury to damning newspaper accounts resultant from the first trial.

The case held resonance with other more contemporary authors as well. Nathaniel Hawthorne was writing stories for local Massachusetts papers at the time—some have considered him the author of anonymous pieces in the *Salem Gazette* concerning the case, although proof is lacking. He did, however, discuss the case in private letters—and there are echoes of the murder and court case seen by many scholars in *The Scarlet Letter* (1850) and *The House of the Seven Gables* (1851). Likewise Poe's immortal classic "The Tell-Tale Heart" (1843) is thought to have been deeply influenced by the murder and trial by no less an authority than T. O. Mabbott. Again the minor story by Lovecraft, "The Terrible Old Man," is like Hawthorne and Poe's own tales, influenced as a foundation and drawing upon different fictional offerings. But it shows, as ever, there are always greater depths in Lovecraft than even the diligent might be aware of.

Works Cited

Derleth, August, ed. *Tales of the Cthulhu Mythos*, Sauk City, WI: Arkham House, 1969.

Lovecraft, H. P. *Letters to Robert Bloch and Others*. Ed. David E. Schultz and S. T. Joshi. New York: Hippocampus Press, 2015.

———, and August Derleth. *Essential Solitude: The Letters of H. P. Lovecraft and August Derleth*. Ed. David E. Schultz and S. T. Joshi. New York: Hippocampus Press, 2008. 2 vols.

———, and Clark Ashton Smith. *Dawnward Spire, Lonely Hill: The Letters of H. P. Lovecraft and Clark Ashton Smith*. Ed. David E. Schultz and S. T. Joshi. New York: Hippocampus Press, 2017.

How to Read Lovecraft

A Column by Steven J. Mariconda

Part 6: Is Lovecraft Amusing?; or, You've Got to Be Kidding Me

Readers who turn to H. P. Lovecraft's books arrive with a certain set of expectations. Today many are nominally familiar with the weird writer from mention of the Cthulhu Mythos on the Internet. In previous periods, readers may have come to him in the context of the pulp magazines or of horror anthologies. Readers' response will be shaped not only by their expectations but also by their past experience of reading. Those who turn to a Lovecraft story with their expectations shaped by role-playing game experiences, or slasher movies, or a Cthulhu plush toy, will naturally be confounded. The best way to read Lovecraft is just to get in his literary vehicle, go along for the ride, and then, when you step off at the end of the story, consider its emotional effects on you. Were you frightened? Anxious? Disoriented? Amused? Annoyed? Probably you were not bored.

Lovecraft meant to evoke fear in his stories—but there is something more than that. It is not just fear, but it is a sense of displacement—a sense that all is not as we thought, that something is seriously out of kilter. At the end of this column I include several excerpts from the author's stories. If you wish to play along, pause here and read them; note to what degree you shiver, or chuckle, or wince. Each will experience a different blend of responses, of course. Then, after reading this column, go back and try it again.

Readers who understand that Lovecraft intends to have a little fun with them are far more likely to have a little fun with Lovecraft.

Ha Ha—The Joke Is on Us

Humor is a form of intellectual play; that is, play with ideas. Under the *superiority theory* of humor, the latter is a manifestation of derision directed at a person or a thing, or a quality in the abstract. The *relief theory* of humor proposes that laughter is a release of pent-up energy that would ordinarily be used to contain or repress psychic activity (primarily feelings which would otherwise cause discomfort). The *incongruity theory* of humor says the latter is produced by the experience of a "felt disconnect" between what we expect and what actually occurs. We will see that most occurrences of what might be humor in Lovecraft are best interpreted as attempts to disorient the reader (i.e., relief theory) or as instances of incongruity which show that things are not what they seem.

S. T. Joshi, in an excellent overview of Lovecraft's humor and satire, notes that the author explicitly disavowed the use of humor in of the weird tale: "it is a definitely diluting element" (308). But—stop and consider that humor is a general category with two major divisions. The first is *humor of comedy* characterized by direct wit; it includes irony and parody. The second is *humor of sentiment*, the artistic investing of experience with a warmth that conveys positive appreciation (Collins 4). This latter kind of humor is characteristic of Dickens, and is the type of humor Lovecraft disliked. What the weird writer is against is not humor *per se*, but the use of narration and handling that are "jaunty," bathetic, or artificially romanticized.

One of Lovecraft's most interesting comments on humor is in the essays collected under the title "In Defense of Dagon" (1921). These were written in response to comments on the eponymous story and other items the weird writer submitted to the Atlantic Circulator, an amateur journalism organization that exchanged and commented upon one another's works through the mail. Responding to a member's comments, Lovecraft comes up with several epigrams that are real zingers:

> I observe Mr. Bullen's complaint that no humour enters into my tales; which omission he deplores, assuming that these tales

are designed to present a view of the universe. In reply, I would suggest that none of my narratives aims at scientific accuracy and inclusiveness, each being rather a mere transcript of an isolated mood or idea with its imaginative ramifications. Moreover, humour is itself but a superficial view of that which is in truth both tragic and terrible—the contrast between human pretense and cosmic mechanical reality. Humour is but the faint terrestrial echo of the hideous laughter of the blind mad gods that squat leeringly and sardonically in caverns beyond the Milky Way.[1] It is a hollow thing, sweet on the outside, but filled with the pathos of fruitless aspiration. . . . When I was younger I wrote humorous matter—satire and light verse—and was known to many as a jester and parodist . . . But I cannot help seeing beyond the tinsel of humour, and recognising the pitiful basis of jest—the world is indeed comic, but the joke is on mankind. So when I delineate an intense mood I plough down to the subsoil and do not try to trifle with the layer of levity on top. Humour is the whistling of man to keep up his courage as he travels the dark road. . . . Let it not be thought that I fail to appreciate humour—indeed, I employ it in discourse; being regarded as satirical and given to repartee. (CE 5.54)

In person and in his letters, Lovecraft was quite funny in his idiosyncratic way. But what of the tales? Joshi finds that there are three types of humor in the fiction: 1) puns, 2) in-jokes that only he and perhaps a friend or two would understand, and 3) "bitter, mirthless satire and cynicism." *Mirthless* is the key word here, because, following the incongruity theory, humor minus mirth equals anxiety.

The Incongruous

Comedy portrays situations and people at their most unstable; one example is the well-worn scenario where a person suddenly undergoes a transformation from his normal personality to an-

---

1. Note that similar imagery is used in several places in the fiction, at times in describing Ultimate Chaos at the center of the cosmos; cf. my essay "Lovecraft's Cosmic Imagery" in *H. P. Lovecraft: Art, Artifact, and Reality* (New York: Hippocampus Press, 2013), 80–91.

other personality with "superpowers." This motif can cause amusement on the screen but would evoke terror in real life. Without the humorous context, the incongruity would be a reason for questioning reality. The anxiety of unreality is a fear of sudden changes, a fear of the strange, and an uneasy sense that an unfamiliar world is encroaching upon the real. Dean Anthony Granitsas details how the incongruous can affect us.

> Consistency is one of the ways we can distinguish reality from other modes of consciousness . . . and incongruities may be seen as glitches in this reality-testing method. . . . Absurdity violates rules that we expect reality to operate by. By doing this, it forces us to reconsider what will happen next, potentially creating an anarchic sense that "anything can happen," or a panic that one is "losing control" over the situation. . . . In addition to making reality look unstable, a certain kind of incongruity can also make separate events appear connected. . . . A more improbable event will generate an even stronger response, either positive [amused] or negative [afraid]. Mirth de-signifies coincidences—for example, by severing the apparent connection between events. You might begin to feel that you have been tricked [e.g., the victim of a prank]. . . . Once an event reaches a certain degree of improbability, explanations like this actually become reasonable. Thus, mirth may also restrain us from making preemptive connections between events when coincidental or intentional juxtaposition misleadingly suggests that a connection exists. (635–36)

Mirth thus tempers the connection between incongruous events, preventing judgments that may result in anxiety.

Incongruity in fiction tends to be clearly marked as humor by rhetorical structures (e.g., an inapposite comparison or inappropriate metaphor), and thus is likely to induce a playful state of mind—unless the context offsets this influence and calls forth confusion or unease. And in the context of Lovecraft's work, as Joshi noted, mirth is generally absent.

Incongruity Minus Mirth Equals Anxiety

Most theories acknowledge that attempts at humor can generate anxiety instead of mirth. Without the benefit of amusement, incongruity is a generator of anxieties such as suspicion, self-doubt, and even panic. Research into the concept of "play" emphasizes the importance of signals, like laughter, to differentiate hostile intentions from mischievous ones in ambiguous situations.

Granitsas proposes that there are similarities between the external stimuli of mirth responses and the external stimuli of paranoid responses; both demonstrate ambiguity and uncanniness. "Mirth," he says, "deactivates a fearful reaction to incongruity, suppressing suspicion and event delusions that may be triggered when a surreal event is interpreted in a non-playful way." He continues:

> The start of an anxiety-based understanding of humor—one that sees humor and anxiety as necessarily rather than coincidentally connected—is the realization that the stimuli of mirth and the stimuli of anxiety are the same, or can be grouped into similar categories. . . . Numerous theories have observed that apparently all humorous situations are dualistic containing both a negative response potential [anxiety] and a positive response potential [mirth]. . . . The concept of "nervous laughter" is misleading since all humor is generated by initially uncomfortable circumstances. Laughter can thus be an anxiety-mitigating reaction, or, a false-front to way to mask nervousness. . . . Incongruity in humor contains two of the ingredients of a paranoia trigger: without mirthful appreciation it is *anomalous* (unexpected, unusual, uncanny) and it is often ambiguous—hence the importance of laughter to indicate playful motives. (626ff.)

How exactly do incongruities transmute from humor into horror? Noël Carroll has written extensively on the connection between humor and horror in literature. Horror fiction, he says, includes antagonists who elicit fear and disgust through their lack of "purity." Both humor and horror involve transgressions of cultural categorizations. Horror violates norms and concepts and its monsters typically evoke disgust (that is, they lack purity) (151ff.) The impurities of horror serve as incongruities that may provoke laughter in certain contexts. The Lovecraft referent here would be the clinical description of the hybrid progeny of human and Yog-Sothoth in "The Dunwich Horror":

Above the waist it was semi-anthropomorphic; though its chest, where the dog's rending paws still rested watchfully, had the leathery, reticulated hide of a crocodile or alligator. The back was piebald with yellow and black, and dimly suggested the squamous covering of certain snakes. Below the waist, though, it was the worst; for here all human resemblance left off and sheer phantasy began. The skin was thickly covered with coarse black fur, and from the abdomen a score of long greenish-grey tentacles with red sucking mouths protruded limply. Their arrangement was odd, and seemed to follow the symmetries of some cosmic geometry unknown to earth or the solar system. On each of the hips, deep set in a kind of pinkish, ciliated orbit, was what seemed to be a rudimentary eye; whilst in lieu of a tail there depended a kind of trunk or feeler with purple annular markings, and with many evidences of being an undeveloped mouth or throat. The limbs, save for their black fur, roughly resembled the hind legs of prehistoric earth's giant saurians; and terminated in ridgy-veined pads that were neither hooves nor claws. When the thing breathed, its tail and tentacles rhythmically changed colour, as if from some circulatory cause normal to the non-human side of its ancestry. In the tentacles this was observable as a deepening of the greenish tinge, whilst in the tail it was manifest as a yellowish appearance which alternated with a sickly greyish-white in the spaces between the purple rings. Of genuine blood there was none; only the foetid greenish-yellow ichor which trickled along the painted floor beyond the radius of the stickiness, and left a curious discolouration behind it. (CF 2.439-440)

Some readers will find this description terrifying; some will find it revolting. Some will find it simply laughable; nonetheless, that laughter effectively operates as a means of regulation over the reader's emotional reactions. It permits him or her to implicitly accept what they would otherwise condemn or reject. Humor, in its essence, acts as a protective mechanism, under which we can tacitly accept truths that we would otherwise deny.

The Absurd

R. G. Collins makes similar points regarding humor: he says that those things that we would otherwise have to condemn or reject, we allow ourselves tacitly to admit—*if* we interpret it as funny.

> One of the main girders on which comedy is hung is the absurdity of logic, the upsetting of form and the formal. . . . Carried one more step it can be seen as the insanity of logic—that formula which aims at accounting for the eternal and the infinitely various. . . . Humor reveals life as paradox—the simultaneous existence of mutually contradictory, fundamental truths. (5)

There is also a significant connection between humor and dreams: they share elements of unreality and disbelief. The relationship has been noted by past researchers; both Freud and Bergson, for example, explicitly connected the two. Consider the experience of an incongruous happening as a kind of cognitive "break," during which reality appears dreamlike. This situation carries with it the potential for anxiety. The encroachment of the dream world into reality contributes to the feeling of unreality. Of course, we know that dreams are the keystone of Lovecraft's work.

Granitsas notes that, when reality starts to waver, people are unsure whether to laugh or shiver. "As a confusion-generator," he says, "there are several types of anxiety-driven quandaries that incongruity may provoke." Incongruity can be the pretext for questioning others: has someone tricked us, or are we the victim of some larger deception? Incongruity can also be a reason for questioning ourselves; this is when an incompatibility is so confusing that it causes us to doubt the reliability of our own perception (Granitsas 633).

Making a similar point from a different perspective Carroll notes that, when presented out of context (for example, during an author's reading or movie highlight reel), people tend to chuckle rather than recoil at isolated passages from horror stories and films. This reminds us of Edmund Wilson's wisecracks about Lovecraft's "omniscient conical snails" (287) and "invisible whistling octopus" (288). Very funny out of context, until the revelation of our place in the Lovecraftian grand scheme of things hits home.

The Grotesque

Related to the concept of the absurd is the literary use of the grotesque. David Mikics tells us that the latter is "an artistic style that audaciously rouses disgust and astonishment in the viewer or reader. It can become a form of monstrous play, entangled in its own encumbrances" and subject the reader to a kind of "aesthetic overcrowding" (138–39).

A major locus of the grotesque is in the satirical writing of the eighteenth century. Lovecraft was a specialist in this period, not merely reading deeply in obscure works but even creating a persona for himself as an eighteenth-century gentleman. Jonathan Swift's *Gulliver's Travels* provides a variety of approaches to grotesque representation. In poetry, the works of Alexander Pope—one of Lovecraft's favorites—provide many examples of the grotesque. Geoffrey Galt Harpham sees the grotesque not as a formal property of particular works but as a feature of the *response* to those works—a time interval of partial comprehension when, confronting an incoherent object, the perceiver senses a hidden principle of unity or intelligibility that he or she does not quite comprehend (5). The description of Wilbur Whateley cites above certainly checks all the boxes for grotesquerie.

The Irrational

According to Lois Gordon, Cain and Abel are "the Old Testament's first innocent victims in a gratuitously capricious, unfathomable universe" (84). This reminds us that "The Colour out of Space" is often seen as Lovecraft's take on another gratuitously capricious, unfathomable tale: the Book of Job. Lovecraft's work sits firmly within the narrow literary heritage of works exploring the irrational. A major branch of this stream runs from Poe through Baudelaire to the Symbolists, and ultimately to the Surrealists.

Lovecraft did not have much regard for traditional fictional elements such as motivation, linear narrative arc, well-rounded characters, manners, morals, and so forth. His approach was largely focused on reader response: "What is art but a matter of impressions, of pictures, emotions, and symmetrical sensations? It must have poignancy and beauty, but nothing else counts. It may or may not have coherence" (CE 2.71). *It may or may not have coherence.* This is a very important statement to keep in mind when reading the author.

Lovecraft championed a "third way" beyond romanticism and realism, both of which, he said, "have the common quality of dealing almost wholly with the objective world, with things rather than with what things suggest" (CE 5.47). He considered himself to be an "imaginative writer": "one who not only sees objects, but follows up all the bizarre trails of associated ideas which encompass and lead away from them" (CE 5.47). The author states that he pursues "what things suggest" farther down the "bizarre trail"; in other words, he goes right past symbolism and into the realm of surrealism.

In his essay Lovecraft denigrates the schools of the romantics and of the realists, who alike sit "stolid and unmoved" when the imaginative writer tells them that the moon is "a hideous nightmare eye watching . . . ever watching" (CE 5.47). The image evokes Edgar Allan Poe. Poe is acknowledged as an innovator in psychological fiction, detective fiction, and, to a lesser extent, science fiction. Most important for our purposes are two other branches of "imaginative literature" that Poe informed: Symbolism and Surrealism. In *Literary Origins of Surrealism*, Anna Balakian succinctly lays out the literary lineage in question:

> My motive in exploring . . . pathways leading from Romanticism to Baudelaire and from Baudelaire to Lautreamont, Rimbaud, and Mallarmé down to the nihilism of Dada, is to attempt to show that these writings have contributed not so much to each other as to one general revolution in poetic mysticism; that this change, finding expression in a fusion of poetry with prose, has not only affected the form of art but has developed a new philosophy of reality which has been shaped around materialism, the mystical propensity of a considerable number of twentieth-century artists. (1)

It is evident that Lovecraft was an exponent of Balakian's "poetic mysticism": in addition to an alienation of sensation, she sees the predominance of an "anti-natural, anti-human, anti-social, anti-rational, [and] anti-emotional attitude" (20). By being "anti-" so many things, Lovecraft's work is a breeding ground for incongruity, which as we have seen involves at least two elements set in opposition. One is reminded of what is probably the most terrifying scene in all Lovecraft—the rapid collapse of Nahum Gardner from a desiccated but articulate human being into a pile of grayish dust that had "caved in." In a detail that in other contexts might pass as "homely," the neighbor who witnesses the horrible death lays "a *red checked* tablecloth over what was left"[2] (CF 2.388). Here and elsewhere, Lovecraft brought forth new techniques of representation, techniques that make the more traditional "spookiness" of E. T. A. Hoffman and Charles Robert Maturin seem quite familiar and even comfortable to certain readers. Lovecraft's strangeness is less in the manner of a typical "ghost story writer" like F. Marion Crawford and more in the manner of (for example) Louis Aragon's surreal *Paris Peasant*. Balakian notes that the *"irrationnel"* exhibits a "destruction of logical language, which proves inadequate to express alienation of sensations" (18).

The Indeterminate

Lovecraft often wrote of his wish to create atmosphere—but Lovecraftian atmosphere has a special flavor. It is not just scary, it is weird. I do not mean "weird" in the sense of the "weird tale." I mean weird in the sense of *odd*. There are many passages in the fiction (some at the end of this installment) in which readers do not know whether to laugh, cry, or simply scratch their head. Let us return to a story mentioned in a prior column: "Facts Concerning the Later Arthur Jermyn and His Family." I have been reading this story for fifty years and continue to find this passage problematic (italics mine):

---

2. My italics; note that the particular design of the tablecloth is mentioned; the quotidian design further heightens by context the alienness of the Colour's effects.

Sir Alfred Jermyn [Arthur's hybrid father] was a baronet before his fourth birthday, but his tastes never matched his title.
At twenty he had joined a band of music-hall performers, and at
thirty-six had deserted his wife and child to travel with an itin-
erant American circus. His end was very revolting. Among the
animals in the exhibition with which he travelled was a huge
bull gorilla of lighter colour than the average; a surprisingly
tractable beast of much popularity with the performers. With
this gorilla Alfred Jermyn was singularly fascinated, and on
many occasions the two would eye each other for long periods
through the intervening bars. Eventually Jermyn asked and ob-
tained permission to train the animal, astonishing audiences
and fellow-performers alike with his success. One morning in
Chicago, as the gorilla and Alfred Jermyn were rehearsing *an exceedingly clever boxing match,* the former delivered a blow of more
than usual force, hurting both the body and dignity of the amateur trainer. Of what followed, members of *"The Greatest Show
on Earth"* do not like to speak. They did not expect to hear Sir
Alfred Jermyn emit a shrill, inhuman scream, or to see him seize
his clumsy antagonist with both hands, dash it to the floor of
the cage, and bite fiendishly at its hairy throat. The gorilla was
off its guard, but not for long, and before anything could be
done by the regular trainer the body which had belonged to a
baronet was past recognition. (CF 1.176–77)

Is the narrator simply smirking when he calls the idea of a boxing match between a primate and a human "exceedingly clever"? My reaction is: the very idea is appalling on multiple
dimensions. And Lovecraft's use of the phrase "The Greatest
Show on Earth," instead of simply saying "the circus" or something more denotative, seems to me to be grotesquely inapposite.[3] My reaction is: to use a colloquial phrase, an advertising

---

3. This passage, in which a word or phrase ("The Greatest Show on Earth")
sits in for another word or phrase with which it is associated (the Ringling
Brothers' Circus) is an example of the rhetorical trope *metonymy;* cf. Bredin
48ff. Upon re-reading this "Arthur Jermyn" passage now, I do not wish Lovecraft had written it differently; it strikes me as *sardonic,* as if the narrator is
"twisting the knife" to heighten the horror.

slogan for the circus is completely unfitting in a paragraph in which one of the characters was just mutilated and mauled to death. Are these instances merely poor choices by Lovecraft, or are they intended to alarm? Yet, certain well-read friends familiar with the passage find nothing amiss with it. I find it odd. How do you, reader, respond to this passage?

In quite a number of stories Lovecraft cuts away from the serious and intellectual tone of the narrative and inserts a paragraph of colloquial dialogue. The contrast between the narrator and the character speaking could not be more pronounced (see "Excerpts" at the end of this item for examples). Not only does the dialogue itself sound unconvincing, but the speakers seem almost moronic—especially in comparison to the erudite tones of the narrator. In these instances, Lovecraft is apparently attempting to make some kind of literary point. I doubt he was mocking the characters for their stupidity, because that would not serve the story well. What this tactic accomplishes is to pull the reader up short and inject a kind of disorientation. I propose that Lovecraft did this on purpose as part of the noxious mix of his especial atmosphere; he is not simply trying to scare us, he is trying to throw us off balance. He is not trying to be funny; he is attempting to illustrate the absurdity of the human condition, which is only marginally less absurd that the horrors of an indifferent universe.

The incongruities seen in "Arthur Jermyn" are not limited to Lovecraft's minor efforts. Even his primary literary achievement, "The Colour out of Space," is full of non-sequiturs. It speaks of colors that aren't really colors, and messengers that become messages and then go back to being messengers. It says that a forest is dark, even though it glows at night. It describes elements of the meteorite that poisons the Gardner farm as large, but then later describes them as small. These contradictions are not mistakes in the writing. In letters, the author states he took extra care in this story's composition.

The opening paragraph of "Colour" sets the tone and introduces the theme of incongruity. It describes hills and valleys; things made by people and things made by nature; things that are temporary and things that are permanent. The description of the farms make them seem old and persistent at first, but they are actually falling apart. As the story goes on, the whole world starts falling apart. Everything is quiet but at the same time restless. The woods shine at night, but they are still described as dark.

The meteorite in the story, too, is described in incongruous ways. It is called a messenger, a message, and a visitor. After the aerolite landed on their farm, the Gardner family started listening carefully, even though they could not identify any specific sounds. They also began watching at night, looking in all directions for something they could not see. Lovecraft plays with the connotations and denotations of words to create a sense of incongruity. He cycles through variant meanings of the Greek word *pneuma*—wind, breath, or a bodiless being—to describe the strange movements caused by the Colour. As the Gardner family is affected by the contaminated soil and water, their neighbor Ammi Pierce feels like they are walking between two worlds, heading toward their doom.[4]

The Theatrical

The degree to which people have a sense of humor is associated with their personality style. There is a positive relationship between the joy of being laughed at and the joy of laughing at others. These traits are "significantly associated with the histrionic self-presentation style that is characterized by performing explicit As-If behaviors (e.g., irony, parodying others) in everyday interactions" (Renner and Manthey 78). Certainly, Lovecraft's self-presentation style, with its mock pompousness and eighteenth-century-gentleman pose, is nothing if not histrionic. Recall the comments of his neighbor Muriel Eddy. Lovecraft read aloud several stories to her and her husband. She notes that Lovecraft "chuckled a little when he explained that he liked to use such phrases as 'unnamable monster' and 'eldritch horror,' as it made

4. For complete details, see my essays "The Subversion of Sense in 'The Colour out of Space" in *H. P. Lovecraft: Art, Artifact, and Reality* 184–189, and "Atmosphere and the Qualitative Analysis of 'The Colour out of Space,'" *Lovecraft Annual* No. 14 (2020): 14–25.

the reader wonder what it was all about" (8). This reminds us of another author abundant in incongruity, Franz Kafka. Colleague and biographer Max Brod recalled that "when Kafka read aloud . . . [his] humor became particularly clear. . . . [He] laughed so much that there were moments when he couldn't read any further" (178). Yet few would characterize "The Judgment" or anything else by Kafka as a real knee-slapper.

Perhaps comedy and tragedy are truly opposite sides of the same coin. Eighteenth-century rhetorician Hugh Blair—one of Lovecraft's mainstays—discusses the rules that apply equally to both comedy and tragedy in terms of dramatic action. He emphasizes that for both, it is essential to maintain unity of action and of subject, to preserve the agreements of time and place, to link scenes together, and to provide logical reasons for characters entering and exiting the stage. These rules aim to make the "imitation" (i.e., realism) presented in the work seem likely, which is crucial for creating a compelling experience for the reader (Blair 542–43).

In March 1921 Lovecraft traveled to Boston for a St. Patrick's Day gathering of amateur journalists at a member's home. Apparently there were quite a number of attendees, perhaps three dozen or more. At some point they were seated in a circle in a very large parlor, and literary contributions were read. Eventually it was Lovecraft's turn: "Extracting from my pocket the fatal manuscript, I proceeded to horrify the assemblage with my spectral 'Moon-Bog', rendered with all the rhetorical effect needed to heighten the terror, though prefaced by a few impromptu comic remarks. From the amount of applause received, I judge that it was not wholly a failure, though probably only about half the company really liked it" (letter to Sarah Susan Phillips Lovecraft, 17 March 1921; *Letters to Family* 1.32).

Lovecraft's reading must have been quite something to behold. In the story, American Denys Barry has moved to Kilderry, Ireland, to reclaim his ancestral estate. He wishes to reclaim the wasted space of the bog on his land—even though it holds a small ruin of some kind—and decides to drain it. The local peasants refuse to help due to their fear of disturbing the bog's spirits. Barry hires outside workers who experience strange and troublesome dreams during the project. One night the narrator hears distant piping and witnesses the workers dancing as if hypnotized, accompanied by spectral wraiths from the haunted bog. The following night the situation escalates: the piping resumes, and the narrator sees the wispy wraiths leading the mesmerized workers into the bog. A shadowy figure is observed struggling as it ascends into a mysterious lunar radiance; and Denys Barry is never seen again.

What was the audience's reaction observing the (normally shy and awkward) author's performative rendering—with the alluded-to "rhetorical effect" heavily laid on—of the story's climax? Imagine the piping-voiced, gaunt, prognathous-jawed writer (and aspiring ham actor) emoting the following:

> Half gliding, half floating in the air, the white-clad bog-wraiths were slowly retreating toward the still waters and the island ruin[. . . .] Their waving translucent arms, guided by the detestable piping of those unseen flutes, beckoned in uncanny rhythm to a throng of lurching labourers who followed dog-like with blind, brainless, floundering steps as if dragged by a clumsy but resistless daemon-will[. . . . A] new line of stumbling stragglers zigzagged drunkenly out of the castle from some door far below my window, groped sightlessly across the courtyard and through the intervening bit of village, and joined the floundering column of labourers on the plain. Despite their distance below me I at once knew they were the servants brought from the north, for I recognised the ugly and unwieldy form of the cook, whose very absurdness had now become unutterably tragic. [. . .] Then silently and gracefully the naiads reached the water [. . .] while the line of followers, never checking their speed, splashed awkwardly after them and vanished amidst a tiny vortex of unwholesome bubbles which I could barely see in the scarlet light. And as the last pathetic straggler, the fat cook, sank heavily out of sight in that sullen pool, the flutes and the drums grew silent, and the blinding red rays from the ruins snapped instantaneously out, leaving the village of doom lone and desolate in the wan beams of a new-risen moon.

> My condition was now one of indescribable chaos. Not

knowing whether I was mad or sane, sleeping or waking, I was
saved only by a merciful numbness. I believe I did ridiculous
things such as offering prayers to Artemis, Latona, Demeter,
Persephone, and Plouton. [. . . N]ew terrors convulsed me, and
I fell to the floor; not fainting, but physically helpless. [. . .] The
stagnant waters, lately quite devoid of animal life, now teemed
with a horde of slimy enormous frogs which piped shrilly and in-
cessantly in tones strangely out of keeping with their size. They
glistened bloated and green in the moonbeams. [. . .] I followed
the gaze of one very fat and ugly frog, and saw the second of the
things which drove my senses away.

Stretching directly from the strange olden ruin on the far is-
let to the waning moon, my eyes seemed to trace a beam of faint
quivering radiance having no reflection in the waters of the bog.
And upward along that pallid path my fevered fancy pictured a
thin shadow slowly writhing; a vague contorted shadow struggling as if drawn by unseen daemons. Crazed as I was, I saw in
that awful shadow a monstrous resemblance—a nauseous, unbelievable caricature—a blasphemous effigy of him who had
been Denys Barry. (CF 1.262–64)

Even in this short, "scary" passage we see words that sometimes
denote humor: absurd, awkward, brainless, caricature, clumsy,
contorted, dog-like, drunken, fat, lurching, pathetic, ridiculous,
ugly, unwieldy. So is the passage strange or merely silly? Now
consider this: Lovecraft composed this Irish-themed item specifically for the occasion and *knew he was going to be performing this
piece for a relatively large audience of his peers.*

Have a Little Fun with Lovecraft

I hope this installment is useful to you as a reader and enriches
your enjoyment of Lovecraft when you encounter one of the per-
plexing passages discussed here—whether your read it as absurd,
grotesque, incongruous, irrational, theatrical, or otherwise. By approaching Lovecraft with a receptive mindset, perhaps we can appreciate his work as a distinct kind of comedy, or at least horror
which provides a strange sort of delight—a uniquely Lovecraftian kind of fun. But regardless, your distinct blend of reactions—

too complex to characterize—will have been provoked by something unique in literature: Lovecraftian atmosphere.

Works Cited

Balakian, Anna. *The Literary Origins of Surrealism: A New Mysticism in French Poetry.* New York: New York University Press, 1947.

Blair, Hugh. *Lectures on Rhetoric and Belle-Lettres.* 1783. Ed. Linda Ferreira-Buckley and S. Michael Halloran. Carbondale: Southern Illinois University Press, 2005. "Lecture XLVII. Comedy–Greek and Roman–French–English Comedy." 542–53.

Bredin, Hugh. "Metonymy." *Poetics Today* 5, No. 1 (1984): 45–58.

Brod, Max. *Franz Kafka: A Biography.* Tr. G. Humphrey Roberts and Richard Winston. New York: Schocken Books, 1960.

Carroll, Noël. "Horror and Humor." *Journal of Aesthetics and Art Criticism* 7, No. 2 (Spring 1999): 145–60.

Collins, R. G. "Nineteenth Century Literary Humor: The Wit and Warmth of Wiser Men?" *Mosaic* 9, No. 4 (Summer 1976): 1–42.

Cornwell, Neil. *The Absurd in Literature.* Manchester: Manchester University Press, 2006.

Critchley, Simon. *On Humour (Thinking in Action).* London: Routledge, 2002.

Eddy, Muriel. "The Gentleman From Angell Street." 3-29. In Muriel Eddy and C. M. Eddy, Jr. *The Gentleman from Angell Street: Memories of H. P. Lovecraft.* Narragansett, RI: Fenham Publishing, 2001.

Fusillo, Massimo. "Self-Reflexivity in the Ancient Novel." *Revue Internationale de Philosophe* No. 248 (2009): 165–176.

Gordon, Lois. *Reading Godot.* New Haven, CT: Yale University Press, 2013.

Granitsas, Dean Anthony. "All Laughter Is Nervous: An Anxiety Based Understanding of Incongruous Humor." *Humor* 33, No. 4 (September 2020): 625–43.

Harpham, Geoffrey Galt. *On the Grotesque: Strategies of Contradiction in Art and Literature.* Aurora, CO: Davies Group, 2006.

Joshi, S. T. "Humour and Satire in Lovecraft." In *Lovecraft and a World in Transition: Collected Essays on H. P. Lovecraft*. New York: Hippocampus Press, 2014. 308–21.

Lovecraft, H. P. *Letters to Family and Family Friends*. Ed. S. T. Joshi and David E. Schultz. New York: Hippocampus Press, 2020. 2 vols.

Mikics, David. *A New Handbook of Literary Terms*. New Haven, CT: Yale University Press, 2010.

Palmer, Jerry. *Taking Humour Seriously*. London: Routledge, 1994.

Renner, Karl-Heinz and Leonie Manthey. "Relations of Dispositions toward Ridicule and Histrionic Self Presentation with Quantitative and Qualitative Humor Creation Abilities." *Frontiers in Psychology* 9 (2018): 78–88.

Wilson, Edmund. "Tales of the Marvellous and the Ridiculous." In *Classics and Commercials: A Literary Chronicle of the Forties*. New York: Farrar, Straus, 1950. 286–90.

––––––

EXCERPTS: *Play Along with Lovecraft: or, HPL sure was "funnee"*

As an exercise in reader-response, some excerpts from Lovecraft's tales are presented here for your consideration. As you read, observe your reactions. (If you are feeling bold, take a tip from Lovecraft and read them aloud using "rhetorical effect.") Did you shudder? Laugh? Cringe? All of the above? Something unnamable? In each excerpt, I have tipped the game by italicizing phrases that seem to me to be especially problematic.

BEYOND THE WALL OF SLEEP (1919)
One day near noon, after a profound sleep begun in a whiskey debauch at about five of the previous afternoon, the man had roused himself most suddenly; with ululations so horrible and unearthly that they brought several neighbours to his cabin—*a filthy sty where he dwelt with a family as indescribable as himself.* Rushing out into the snow, he had flung his arms aloft and commenced a series of leaps directly upward in the air; the while shouting his determination to reach some *"big, big cabin with*

brightness in the roof and walls and floor, and the loud queer music far away". As two men of moderate size sought to restrain him, he had struggled with maniacal force and fury, screaming of his desire and need to find and kill a certain "thing that shines and shakes and laughs". At length, after temporarily felling one of his detainers with a sudden blow, he had flung himself upon the other in a daemoniac ecstasy of bloodthirstiness, shrieking fiendishly that he would "jump high in the air and burn his way through anything that stopped him". Family and neighbours had now fled in a panic, and when the more courageous of them returned, Slater was gone, leaving behind an unrecognisable pulp-like thing that had been a living man but an hour before. (CF 1.73–74)

NYARLATHOTEP (1920)
And I saw the world battling against blackness; against the waves of destruction from ultimate space; whirling, churning; struggling around the dimming, cooling sun. Then the sparks played amazingly around the heads of the spectators, and hair stood up on end whilst shadows more grotesque than I can tell came out *and squatted on the heads.* And when I, who was colder and more scientific than the rest, mumbled a trembling protest about "imposture" and "static electricity", Nyarlathotep drave us all out, down the dizzy stairs into the damp, hot, deserted midnight streets. I screamed aloud that I was not afraid; that I never could be afraid; and others screamed with me for solace. We sware to one another that the city was exactly the same, and still alive; and when the electric lights began to fade *we cursed the company over and over again, and laughed at the queer faces we made.* (CF 1.204)

COOL AIR (1926)
Looking about, I saw that the ceiling was wet and dripping; the soaking apparently proceeding from a corner on the side toward the street. Anxious to stop the matter at its source, I hastened to the basement to tell the landlady; and was assured by her that the trouble would quickly be set right.

"Doctair Muñoz," she cried as she rushed upstairs ahead of me, "he have speel hees chemicals. He ees too seeck for doctair heemself—seecker and seecker all the time—but he weel not have no othair for help. He ees vairy queer in hees seeckness—all day *he take funnee-smelling baths*, and he cannot get excite or warm. All hees own housework he do—hees leetle room are full of bottles and machines, and he do not work as doctair. But he was great once—my fathair in Barcelona have hear of heem—and only joost now he feex a arm of the plumber that get hurt of sudden. He nevair go out, only on roof, and my boy Esteban he breeng heem hees food and laundry and mediceens and chemicals. *My Gawd, the sal-ammoniac that man use for keep heem cool!*"

Mrs. Herrero disappeared up the staircase to the fourth floor, and I returned to my room. (CF 2.12–13)

MEDUSA'S COIL (with Zealia Bishop, 1930)
It was wrinkled Sophonisba, the ancient Zulu witch-woman who had fawned on Marceline, keening from her cabin in a way which crowned the horrors of this nightmare tragedy. We could both hear some of the things she howled, and knew that secret and primordial bonds linked this savage sorceress with that other inheritor of elder secrets who had just been extirpated. Some of the words she used betrayed her closeness to daemonic and palaeogean traditions.

"'*Iä! Iä! Shub-Niggurath! Ya-R'lyeh! N'gagi n'bulu bwana n'lolo!* Ya, yo, pore Missy Tanit, pore Missy Isis! Marse Clooloo, come up outen de water an' git yo chile—she done daid! She done daid! De hair ain' got no missus no mo', *Marse Clooloo.* Ol' Sophy, she know! Ol' Sophy, she done got de black stone outen Big Zimbabwe in ol' Affriky! Ol' Sophy, she done dance in de moonshine roun' de crocodile-stone befo' de N'bangus cotch her and sell her to de ship folks! No mo' Tanit! No mo' Isis! No mo' witch-woman to keep de fire a-goin' in de big stone place! Ya, yo! *N'gagi n'bulu bwana n'lolo! Iä! Shub-Niggurath!* She daid! Ol' Sophy know!'

"That wasn't the end of the wailing, but it was all I could pay attention to." (CF 4.329–30)

Reviews

EDWARD GUIMONT and HORACE A. SMITH. *When the Stars Are Right: H. P. Lovecraft and Astronomy*. New York: Hippocampus Press, 2023. 411 pp. $25.00 tpb. Reviewed by Bobby Derie.

"*There* are the stars, and they who can may read them," wrote Henry David Thoreau in *Walden* (1854)—and therein lies the rub. Even a casual reader of H. P. Lovecraft will pick up on the phrase "when the stars are right," the references to visible stars and the phases of the moon, the cosmic hints of black stars and black planets that abound in his fiction and letters. Very few readers are familiar enough with the science of astronomy to appreciate that these works reveal how deep Lovecraft's astronomical knowledge went, and fewer still are qualified to dig a little deeper and talk about the historical context of that knowledge and both popular and scientific understandings of astronomy during Lovecraft's lifetime.

When the Stars Are Right: H. P. Lovecraft and Astronomy is an almost exhaustive treatise on the subject, and while it is a substantial tome of a book it can hardly be claimed the length isn't justified. Astronomy was, after all, one of Lovecraft's earliest and most enduring scientific interests, the one that he published the most on as a boy and an adult. Volume 3 of Lovecraft's *Collected Essays* by Hippocampus Press is nominally devoted to his scientific essays in general, but in practice that work is a collection of his writings on astronomy with few exceptions. Lovecraft was not ignorant of chemistry, geology, physics, anthropology, or other sciences, and would touch on these subjects in his fiction and voluminous letters, but he wasn't publishing series of newspaper articles on these subjects.

Not to romanticize the subject too much, but it seems clear from his fiction, nonfiction, and letters that astronomy was important to Lovecraft. If for no other reason than that, astronomy should be important to scholars and critics of Lovecraft's life and works.

Guimont and Smith's book begins with what Lovecraft knew about astronomy and how he learned it, beginning with his grandmother's astronomy textbooks and working forward throughout his life. This is the kind of solid research that should establish *When the Stars Are Right* as the default work on Lovecraft and astronomy for the foreseeable future. This segues naturally into Lovecraft's first writings on astronomy, tracing a pre-amateur journalism, pre–*Weird Tales* career that normally forms a gap in most readers' understanding of Lovecraft's writing life. A critical take-home point not often emphasized is that understanding of the movement of stars and planets was changing during Lovecraft's lifetime, most notably with Einstein's theory of relativity and the discovery of Pluto. The astronomical biographical approach to Lovecraft's life helps to highlight why and how he would later use astronomy in his fiction.

As the book delves into the nuts and bolts of Lovecraft's alien planets and the sometimes fantastic astronomy that appears in his weird fiction, Guimont and Smith touch on the issue of how Lovecraft's work relates with the prevailing depiction of stars and planets in pulp fiction of the era—the 1930s being the heyday of space opera, the playground of worlds of writers such as Edmond Hamilton and E. E. "Doc" Smith. This is relatively brief, as the focus is on Lovecraft and his work, but it easy to forget that Lovecraft in writing about the planet Yekub in the round-robin "The Challenge from Beyond," Yuggoth in "The Whisperer in Darkness," and Venus in "In the Walls of Eryx" (with Kenneth Sterling) was working within a weird astronomical tradition. Whereas astronomy had weird false starts such as Percival Lowell's canals on Mars and William Henry Pickering's lunar vegetation, weird fiction had its fair share of evocative if astronomically unlikely inspirations as well, from the twin suns and black stars of Robert W. Chambers's *The King in Yellow* (1895) to the fantastic (if implausible) worlds of Edgar Rice Burroughs and Leigh Brackett.

There is an intriguing point along this line of thought, where Guimont and Smith note the "evil toad-things" associated with the cats from Saturn in Lovecraft's *The Dream-Quest of Unknown Kadath*, and suggest a possible connection with Clark Ashton Smith's toadlike Tsathoggua, whose arrival from Saturn was a key part of the plot of "The Door to Saturn" (*Strange Tales of Mystery and Terror*, January 1932). However, I'm not sure if the math quite works out for that influence to be plausible: Lovecraft wrote the *Dream-Quest* in late 1926 and early 1927, and the first mention of the eldritch entity in *Dawnward Spire, Lonely Hill: The Letters of H. P. Lovecraft and Clark Ashton Smith* is in 1929.

If a quibble must be made, there is also a slight blind spot in the matter of E. Hoffmann Price. Guimont and Smith are aware of Price's correspondence with Lovecraft and cite pages from the relevant volume of Lovecraft's letters to Price published by Hippocampus Press, but they seem to have either overlooked or chosen not to address Price's work as an astrologer (at first amateur, and later professional), or Price's later comments on Lovecraft and astrology:

> In a letter to the *Providence Sunday Journal*, commenting on astrological predictions in that newspaper, he refers to what he terms a "striking inaccuracy," in that the writer mentions a transit of Mars over the Sun. He goes on to state that since Mars is a superior planet, one outside the earth's orbit, it can not transit over the Sun. *Astronomically*, Lovecraft is correct: only Venus and Mercury can apparently cross over the disc of the Sun. However, Lovecraft was so wholly ignorant even of basic *astrological* terminology that he did not know that by the definitions assigned to actual planetary motions (as determined by the U.S. Naval and many other observatories) any planet, from Mars to Pluto, can cross any of the 360 degrees of the Zodiac, and that every planet in the course of one revolution about the Sun does cross each degree. [. . .] In a letter to me, HPL stated that although he knew nothing of astrology, he had "proved" that it was a fraud, nonsense. Ignorance, I submit, is not a good foundation for rebuttal. (Price, *Book of the Dead* [Sauk City, WI: Arkham House, 2001], 61–62.)

To their credit, Guimont and Smith specifically address the issue of a different definition of transit in astronomy and astrology in discussing this specific letter by Lovecraft in the *Providence Sunday Journal*. So they capture the substance of Price's complaint, but rather miss the broader context of how this matter touched on Lovecraft's relationship with Price. Again, this is a bit of a quibble, as the book is focused on Lovecraft's life and work, not so much the posthumous reception of both.

Like all biographical treatments, *When the Stars Are Right* finishes with a look at astronomy in Lovecraft's waning years. Even to the last, Lovecraft never lost his interest in the study of the stars. His letters describe comets and lunar rainbows, he took fastidious care to make sure the moon was in the right phase for the date of his stories, he sought in his own limited way to instill some interest or knowledge of astronomy to his friends and correspondents by the gift of cheap planispheres and the like, and practically to the end he never stopped learning about astronomy, attending lectures, reading up on the subject . . . and, perhaps most important, looking up from the dull Earth to gaze at the sky.

It is not too much to say that *When the Stars are Right* fills a gap in Lovecraft studies, pulling together various disparate threads and combining them with a solid basis of astronomical historiography and biographical research. While works such as Joshi's *I Am Providence* fulfill the need for a general biography, specialist works like Guimont and Smith's volume complement it by providing an in-depth look at Lovecraft's life in relation to a single subject, going into detail that would be out of place in even the most comprehensive general biography.

In what might have been a rather dry accounting of facts and figures, *When the Stars Are Right* is careful never to dismiss the romance of astronomy, the deep sweep of vast distances and depths of time and space involved. Astronomy helped give Lovecraft a sense of scale, but as much as the untapped potentialities of deep space were the spawning place for various horrors such as Cthulhu and Tsathoggua, the Colour out of Space and the Mi-Go, the stars and planets themselves had wonder and fascination for Lovecraft, not terror. To miss out on that humanistic element—Lovecraft the stargazer—is to miss out on an essential element of his character and a critical influence on his body of work.

Lovecraft could read the stars—not for mystic portents of the future, but to catch a glimpse of the invisible machinery of the universe of which he was the smallest, most fleeting part. And that gave birth to black planets that roll without name, and strange regions of space where life might take different forms, and a legacy that has not yet ended.

H. P. LOVECRAFT et al. *Letters to Hyman Bradofsky and Others*. New York: Hippocampus Press, 2023. 595 pp. $30.00 tpb. Reviewed by Sean Donnelly.

Amateur journalism (ajay) figures prominently in *Letters to Hyman Bradofsky and Others*, the latest collection of H. P. Lovecraft's letters edited by David E. Schultz and S. T. Joshi. But what is it? The subject is unavoidable because the hobby was part of Lovecraft's social life, correspondence, and writing career for half of his life, from 1914 until 1937. In his day there were several amateur associations (such as the National and United) of writers, editors, and printers who issued journals, corresponded, and socialized. The journals were the heart of the hobby, offering a forum where fiction, poetry, essays, and editorials by the members was shared and critiqued. Lovecraft was drawn to ajay for the opportunity to see his work in print and for the sense of community it offered those with literary ambitions.

Schultz and Joshi prepare the reader with an introduction that opens with a concise summary of ajay during Lovecraft's time. Equally important are the biographical sketches of each correspondent in this collection: Richard Ely Morse, Helm C. Spink, Ralph W. Babcock, Hyman Bradofsky, Jennie K. Plaisier, Margaret Sylvester, Frank Utpatel, Virgil Finlay, and John J. Weir. Even those who have read Lovecraft's biographies may not be familiar with all these names, and it is exciting to discover new aspects to his life. The editors also gathered together more than a hundred pages of relevant supporting material in the appendix. Much of it is related to amateur journalism and provides additional background and perspectives on issues brought up by Lovecraft and his correspondents.

Each new collection like this, and each letter, is a treat, because Lovecraft is never predictable as a letter writer. He does not write about exactly the same subjects, or in the same style, to any two of his correspondents. The letters are conversations in print—the give and take delayed only by the speed of the mail—as Lovecraft responds to the intellect, sympathies, interests, and concerns of his correspondents. He can be serious and fatherly, funny and charming, poetic and expansive, personal and confidential—all depending on his correspondent.

Opening this collection with the letters to Richard Ely Morse is a perfect choice, for they show Lovecraft at his best. Morse was a fellow poet—examples of his poems are printed in the appendix so readers can sample his work—but as a writer he apparently didn't have commercial ambitions. As such, Lovecraft could write to him about the challenge of trying to produce good work for a medium (the pulps) that didn't generally reward quality. The fact that the pulps paid by the word reduced writing to an industrial enterprise, and yet Lovecraft persevered. In a frank assessment of his own work he opined that he wasn't good enough for the slicks but better than the average pulp writer. He also turned his critical judgment on friends who wrote for the pulps. He is regretful in noting, about Robert E. Howard, that "financial necessity defeats his real personality," but is more blunt when he remarks that E. Hoffmann Price "is turning out pulp junk." When he laments the negative effect that writing for the pulps has on his friends one understands he is also talking about himself.

Lovecraft can talk to Morse about weird fiction because he is a fellow enthusiast and book collector. He was part of a group—including W. Paul Cook, H. Warner Munn, Clark Ashton Smith, Donald Wandrei, and Herman C. Koenig—that lent, bought, and traded books. For example, the group borrowed Koenig's William Hope Hodgson books and passed them around. The letters to Morse give us insights on Lovecraft's personal opinions and domestic life as well. We learn that he spent his forty-second birthday alone on the cliffs of Newport but had Thanksgiving with his aunt and put up a tree for Christmas. He employs his keen perceptivity as a writer when appraising his friends' personalities: Samuel Loveman's hypersensitivity (Lovecraft had to console Morse during a feud he had with Loveman), Donald Wandrei's worldliness (compared to Frank Belknap Long, who was older), and the "wide human sympathies" of August Derleth. In another letter he praises Salvador Dali and the value of modern art, which may surprise anyone familiar with his antiquarian tastes. But even readers who know that Lovecraft hated the cold might be surprised to learn how much it debilitated him: he wrote to Morse on 9 February 1936 that he had not been out of his house since January 13.

There is a fluency in Lovecraft's letters to Morse, as their intellectual and aesthetic sympathies elicit passages that are as fine as anything he ever wrote. For example, as someone who lived through the Great War and knew the world before and after it, Lovecraft was able to write poetically on the changes it wrought: "No one born since 1905 or so can ever have known the full smugness & naive optimism prevailing in that idyllic fools' paradise—that world whose securities were all anchored in conditions forever vanished. The rude suddenness of the awakening has created a sharp cleavage seldom met with in history . . ." After reading the letters to Morse it is intriguing to recall from the introduction to this book that Lovecraft described him as "dandified" and "sissified" to other correspondents. He could dislike aspects of Morse's personality and not care to socialize with him, yet carry on a rich epistolary friendship.

The next group of letters, to and from Helm C. Spink, reveals Lovecraft's abiding interest in ajay. After first contacting Lovecraft about joining the United in 1925, Spink ultimately decided to join the National. He would be a mainstay of the association for the next several decades. They began corresponding regularly in 1929 after Spink agreed to be Official Editor, which made him responsible for producing the *National Amateur*. Lovecraft is quick to offer helpful advice—"I would advocate the development of the critical department as the central feature of each issue"—and shares his belief that "mutual literary aid & encouragement ought to form the prime function of amateurdom."

As with other younger correspondents, Lovecraft assumes an avuncular tone with Spink, though he quickly drops the "Mr." and addresses him more familiarly as "Spink." Spink, perhaps a little in awe of Lovecraft, always addresses him as "Mr. Lovecraft." Spink wasn't Lovecraft's intellectual equal, like Morse was, but Lovecraft recognized that he was dedicated to ajay and eager to learn. Though they did not know each other well, that did not keep Lovecraft from being warm and friendly. A shared enthusiasm for ajay nourished their correspondence.

The names of well-known amateurs of the day recur in their letters. Lovecraft recounts a visit to C. W. Smith, famous for his typo-prone journal, the *Tryout*. Smith was hard of hearing and they had to communicate by writing with a pencil. Lovecraft would lead an effort to raise funds so that Smith could purchase new fonts of type to replace his worn-out type. Spink made social calls, too. He visited Edna Hyde McDonald and enjoyed her "charming conversation." Spink and "Vondy" would correspond for years, and she also exchanged letters with Lovecraft. (The nickname Vondy comes from her maiden name—von der Heide—which was Anglicized to Hyde because of anti-German sentiment during the Great War.)

Spink and Lovecraft also discuss Burton Crane, a financial writer for the *New York Times* based in Tokyo at the time, who produced a journal called *Masaka*. When he was back in New York in the 1940s, a young man named Sheldon Wesson was working at the *Times*. One day Wesson passed Crane's desk and something caught his eye. "What is that?" he asked Crane. "That's an amateur journal," Crane replied. "What's an amateur journal?" Wesson asked. Crane's answer to that question changed Wesson's life. He became active in ajay for years, along with his wife Helen, and they shared an enthusiasm for Lovecraft. It should be remembered that Wesson was responsible for getting Spencer's *History of Amateur Journalism* printed, in Japan, after multiple delays.

In the early letters, Spink's side of the correspondence is cool and a bit stilted, but Lovecraft shares news and opinions with him as freely as he does with his longtime correspondents. In one instance he is surprisingly candid, admitting that "poverty" is his reason for moving in 1933. Touching details come out, such as the fact that he and his aunts had carefully stored family possessions since 1904 that were only brought out again after twenty-nine years when they moved to 66 College Street.

The common bond of ajay brings out much in the letters about Lovecraft's social activities with fellow amateurs as he visits and travels with them. Most of them he had known well for years, such as W. Paul Cook, Charles A. A. Parker, J. Bernard Lynch, and Edward H. Cole. There were a number of others he did not meet often but they kept in touch: Paul J. Campbell, Maurice W. Moe, Alfred Galpin, Rheinhart Kleiner, and Sam Loveman. New friendships were made too, as when Ernest Edkins returned to ajay in 1932. Edkins's fine essays and literary criticism seem to have given Lovecraft added enthusiasm for the hobby.

Edkins won praise for the first issue of his journal *Causerie* (1936), designed and printed by Spink. In a letter to Lovecraft, Spink says, "if it looks to the average reader just like it fell together in the only possible way (without any thought or effort on my part) I'll be delighted." He was echoing theories of good typography espoused at the time by Beatrice Warde in a 1930 lecture titled "Printing Should Be Invisible." Spink finally warms up in this letter and seems less self-conscious, perhaps because he is talking about something close to his heart. In another letter he says he is considering Kennerley in lieu of Caslon for a second issue of *Causerie*. Kennerley was one of Frederic Goudy's most famous type designs, and Spink's concern with type shows he had a serious interest in printing as an art. He printed books later in his career for clients such as the Rowfant Club, who hired the best typographers and printers for their publications.

The more mundane letters to Spink show Lovecraft's readiness to lend a hand with amateur affairs. This includes arbitrating disputes between members. A discussion of one in particular, between Hyman Bradofsky and Ralph W. Babcock, runs through the last forty pages of their letters. Bradofsky attracted a lot of attention with his handsome "de luxe" journal, the *Californian*. Babcock's publications were less ostentatious but produced with meticulous care. It was said he would rewrite "in the stick" as he was setting type to avoid hyphenations. Lovecraft and Spink go back and forth about them. Spink observes that Bradofsky "cannot stand critics of any kind" and goes further in saying that "Bradofsky is hopelessly mediocre and cannot help it." Lovecraft's opinions are along the same lines, but he defends Bradofsky as "better-intentioned" than Babcock. They may express negative opinions of Bradofsky privately, but Lovecraft is disgusted by Babcock's public abuse of him: "the poor cuss means well—& nothing makes me see red quicker than the baiting & tormenting of a well-meaning plodder."

These later letters between Lovecraft and Spink provide useful background for Lovecraft's correspondence with Babcock and Bradofsky themselves. There are just a few to Babcock, but they show that Lovecraft was not two-faced when it came to his true feelings. The criticisms he made in his letters to Spink are made directly to Babcock. He rebukes Babcock with his belief that the "purpose of the hobby is to furnish mutual encouragement, criticism, and avenues of expression in writing; and it seems to me that the element of personal attack ought to be restricted to the fighting of influences hostile to these objects."

The correspondence between Lovecraft and Bradofsky is narrowly focused on ajay, as Bradofsky does not engage much with his colleague on other subjects. Lovecraft was genuinely grateful for the *Californian* because it had room for "good amateur prose" that most journals could not accommodate. This seems to have motivated him to spend time writing to Bradofsky to encourage his efforts. Lovecraft also steered numerous contributions to him, from Samuel Loveman, R. H. Barlow, the late Edith Miniter, and himself.

In several letters we see Lovecraft in the role of counselor, advising Bradofsky on how best to respond to Babcock's attacks. He recommends that he go head-to-head in the public arena and give as good as he got. He specifies points on which Bradofsky can attack Babcock. He sounds like a modern Machiavelli when he advises that "you can literally rip him to pieces—but do it suavely & ironically, keeping an appearance of amused tranquility & avoiding the display of excitement or of a sense of injury."

In a later letter Lovecraft's advice is more blunt: "make the bastards prove that they have a right to criticise you . . . I've been through the mill myself—in 1916, and again in 1921–22—& in each case I may say without undue boasting that I made the enemy damn sorry they ever started after me . . . And I really had quite a good time lambasting 'em back . . . ridiculing and exposing the sons-of-bitches in both prose & satirical verse." Lovecraft seems to have nursed a lingering bitterness over his treatment all those years earlier. He does not sound regretful when he reports that "poor old Mrs. Houghton, my arch-foe of 1921–22, was burned to death a year or two ago when her clothing ignited at a fireplace."

There is only one letter to Jennie K. Plaisier, but a fascinating one because of Lovecraft's discussion of political and economic ideas. The Great Depression made him realize how "capitalism works—always piling up concentrated wealth and impoverishing the bulk of the population until the strain becomes so intolerable as to force artificial reforms." He is a bona fide New Dealer and believes "it is time that the state adopted general public welfare, rather than the protection of heavy individual profits, as its guiding policy and aim."

The collection is rounded out with several shorter selections of letters. Among the best are the wonderfully chatty ones to Margaret Sylvester. Years later she would edit (as Margaret Ronan) a collection of Lovecraft's stories for Scholastic Books that introduced many young readers to his work. Lovecraft's first letter to her is a detailed reply to her question about Walpurgis Night. He makes it clear that his fiction may have supernatural themes but he is not a believer. Supposed witches and wizards are "largely morbid, hysterical, & degenerate types." And he ridicules Montague Summers's "childish belief in the supernatural background of witchcraft."

One part of a long letter includes a beautifully poetic description, worthy of Dunsany, of a walk he took around Neutaconkanut Hill:

> I secured truly marvellous glimpses of the remote urban skyline—a dream of enchanted pinnacles & domes half-floating in air, & with an obscure aura of mystery around them. The upper windows of some of the taller towers held the fire of the sun after I had lost it, affording a spectacle of cryptic & curious glamour. Then I saw the great round disc of the Hunter's Moon (2 days before full) floating above the belfries & minarets, while in the orange-glowing west Venus & Jupiter commenced to twinkle.

Lovecraft may have been a self-avowed materialist, but he seems to have spiritual or transcendent experiences in the natural world. Though grateful for such beautiful prose, one laments that he put so much fine writing into work not for publication, like Oscar Wilde in his letters and Nathaniel Hawthorne in his notebooks.

Lovecraft changes tack easily in his letters with Sylvester and can be charmingly playful. There is an endearing description of his adventures with two cats; a funny quip about his horoscope—"Worried about my children's inheritance? Yeh—I wonder who they'll get it from!"; and he says of his dark rooms at 10 Barnes, "I was perfectly satisfied with my dark ground-floor cave (ogres always did take to caves!)". One wonders how their correspondence may have developed if he had lived longer.

In the last year of his life Lovecraft was introduced to two fine artists who would be associated with his work for decades to come. August Derleth's friend Frank Utpatel illustrated the only substantial book published in Lovecraft's lifetime, *The Shadow over Innsmouth* (1936). Lovecraft was encouraging and complimentary, admiring the results Utpatel achieved with linoleum cuts. The book disappointed him, owing to numerous typos and cheap production values, but he told Utpatel that "your illustrations form its sole redeeming feature."

The other artist, Virgil Finlay, elicits a series of excellent letters from Lovecraft. Again, we see that he is never the same with any two correspondents. By the second letter the exchange is revealing and personal in tone. Lovecraft makes a fascinating admission: "I am probably the least sensuous of all living beings . . . tending to view and enjoy all things as a passive, detached, & sometimes remote spectator." That feeling of being a spectator to life might be admitted by any number of writers. Despite his obvious talents, Lovecraft had a sense of failure about his own work: "I never really say what I want to say, & am discouraged by the clumsy mechanisms I employ in suggesting this or that impression." Though he dismissed the numerous failed attempts to place a collection of stories with a major publisher, they do seem to have diminished his confidence. Yet it didn't alter his determination to aim at a higher standard. Rather than write junk, he believed a writer should earn one's living in some other way and "refuse to write with any other aim than sheer excellence in mind." Thankfully, he had one good outlet for his work: *Weird Tales*. Though Lovecraft had his differences with editor Farnsworth Wright, he is magnanimous when he declares "it is of all pulps the least rigid in its exclusion of originality."

The collection closes with Lovecraft's brief correspondence with John J. Weir. One isn't surprised to learn that Weir is a fifteen-year-old boy. He sounds like one as he pesters Lovecraft for contributions to his fanzine, *Fantasmagoria*. Lovecraft came in contact with a number of young fans in his final years, just as science fiction fandom was on the verge of a boom. One wonders how deeply he would have let himself be drawn into fandom in the late 1930s. Might he have attended the first World Con in 1939? These are just melancholy speculations, though, as his final letters hint at the health issues that would cut his life short at age forty-six. Fortunately, we are all inheritors of this rich legacy of letters that will delight and enlighten readers for generations to come.

Contributors

Francesco Borri lives and works in Venice, where he teaches medieval history at the Ca' Foscari University. He researches on the Age of Migration, focusing on issues of aristocratic identity, navigation, and paganism, having published articles and monographs on these topics. He is also the author of "A Placid Island: H. P. Lovecraft's 'Ibid'" (*Lovecraft Annual*, 2018).

Bobby Derie is the author of *Sex and the Cthulhu Mythos* (2014) and *Weird Talers: Essays on Robert E. Howard and Others* (2019). His essays have been published in the *Lovecraft Annual*, *The Dark Man: Journal of Robert E. Howard and Pulp Studies*, *Occult Detective Quarterly*, and *Skelos*, as well as *The Unique Legacy of Weird Tales: The Evolution of Modern Fantasy and Horror* (2015).

Sean Donnelly worked for twenty years at the University of Tampa Press, editing and designing books and journals. While there he helped establish a letterpress studio and a special collections. For eleven years he also co-owned a used bookstore. He now works for the Pinellas County library system. Sean has written or edited books and articles about the Peter Pauper Press, A. Merritt, Henry S. Whitehead, W. Paul Cook, and Edith Miniter (with Ken Faig, Jr.).

Ken Faig, Jr. has been writing about H. P. Lovecraft, his family, and his associates for more than fifty years. He is a graduate of Northwestern University (B.A., 1970) and a retired actuary. He has published books with Hippocampus Press, Sarnath Press, Necronomicon Press, and his own imprint, Moshassuck Press. He is the father of two grown children and lives in Glenview, Illinois, with his wife Carol.

James Goho is a researcher and writer with many publications on dark fiction. In 2014, Rowman & Littlefield published his *Journeys into Darkness: Critical Essays on Gothic Horror*. McFarland published his *Caitlín R. Kiernan: A Critical Study of Her Dark Fiction* in 2020. His higher education research is found in academic journals, and his infrequent short stories appear in literary magazines. He lives in Winnipeg, Canada.

Edward Guimont received his Ph.D. in history from the University of Connecticut and is assistant professor of world history at Bristol Community College in Fall River, Massachusetts. With Horace A. Smith, he coauthored *When the Stars are Right: H. P. Lovecraft and Astronomy*, published in 2023 by Hippocampus Press. He is currently writing a political history of the Flat Earth movement.

Dylan Henderson was born in Green Country, the northeastern corner of Oklahoma. Despite dropping out of school, which he loathed, at sixteen, he would eventually earn degrees in history, literature, and library science. He is now a doctoral student at Purdue University in Indiana, where he is studying H. P. Lovecraft, the British ghost story, pulp magazines, and weird fiction in general.

Ron L. Johnson II graduated from Webster University with a Bachelor of Photography. Since digitalization has put film on the endangered list, he writes now with words instead of light. Ron has received Honorable Mention from *Photographer Forum* and has been published in *Best of College Photography Annual*. He has also been published in numerous issues of *Spectral Realms*.

Steven J. Mariconda's first essay, "H. P. Lovecraft: Consummate Prose Stylist," was published in *Lovecraft Studies* No. 9 (Fall 1984). His articles and reviews are collected in *H. P. Lovecraft: Art, Artifact, and Reality* (Hippocampus Press, 2013). He is co-editor, with S. T. Joshi, of *Dreams of Fear: Poetry of Terror and the Supernatural* (Hippocampus Press, 2013). Mariconda was Scholar Guest of Honor at the NecronomiCon Providence 2017.

In accordance with the standard paradigm, **Duncan Norris** was a nerdy kid who sought out Lovecraft as a teenager and had his life changed thereby. As a resident of Australia, he has sought endlessly to recover the statue from the *Alert* donated to the Sydney Museum, which the authorities continue to deny possessing. His expedition to Western Australia is forthcoming.

Andrew Paul Wood is an independent cultural historian, critic, translator, and occasional poet, based in the South Island of New Zealand and very much in love with the high weird. His most recent book is *Shadow Worlds: A History of the Occult and Esoteric in New Zealand* (Massey University Press, 2023).

Milton Keynes UK
Ingram Content Group UK Ltd.
UKHW020910220424
441551UK00017B/1108